MOZILLA®

Firefox™

Introductory Concepts and Techniques

Gary B. Shelly
Thomas J. Cashman
Steven G. Forsythe
Steven M. Freund

THOMSON COURSE TECHNOLOGY

25 THOMSON PLACE

BOSTON MA 02210

SHELLY CASHMAN SERIES®

Australia • Canada • Denmark • Japan • Mexico • New Zealand • Philippines • Puerto Rico • Singapore
South Africa • Spain • United Kingdom • United States

THOMSON

COURSE TECHNOLOGY

Mozilla Firefox
Introductory Concepts and Techniques

Gary B. Shelly
Thomas J. Cashman
Steven G. Forsythe
Steven M. Freund

Managing Editor:
Alexandra Arnold

Senior Product Manager:
Karen Stevens

Product Manager:
Reed Cotter

Associate Product Manager:
Selena Coppock

Editorial Assistant:
Patrick Frank

Series Consulting Editor:
Jim Quasney

Production Editor:
Kelly Robinson

Copyeditor:
Mary Kemper

Proofreader:
Nancy Lamm

Indexer:
Liz Cunningham

Quality Assurance:
Burt LaFountain, John Freitas,
Ken Ryan, Alex White

Senior Manufacturing Coordinator:
Justin Palmeiro

Cover Image:
John Still

Compositor:
GEX Publishing Services

MOZILLA

Introductory Concepts and Techniques

Contents

Project Three

Communicating Over the Internet Using Mozilla Thunderbird

Special Feature

Open Source Concepts and Firefox Customization

Appendix A

Installing Mozilla Firefox

Appendix B

Installing Mozilla Thunderbird

Appendix C

Mozilla Firefox Options

Quick Reference Summary

Mozilla Firefox Quick Reference Summary

Preface

The Shelly Cashman Series® offers the finest textbooks in computer education. We are proud of the fact that the previous editions of this textbook have been so well received by computer educators. With each new edition, we have made significant improvements based on the software and comments made by the instructors and students. This new text on *Mozilla Firefox: Introductory Concepts and Techniques* continues with the innovation, quality, and reliability that you have come to expect from the Shelly Cashman Series.

In the few short years since its birth, the World Wide Web, or Web, has grown beyond all expectations. During this time, Web usage has increased from a limited number of users to more than 600 million users worldwide, accessing Web pages on any topic you can imagine. Individuals, schools, businesses, and governmental agencies all are taking advantage of this innovative way of accessing the Internet to provide information, products, services, and education electronically. Mozilla Firefox provides the novice as well as the experienced user a window with which to look into the Web and tap an abundance of resources.

Objectives of this Textbook

Mozilla Firefox: Introductory Concepts and Techniques is intended for use in a one-credit, three- to-five week course or in combination with other books in an introductory computer concepts or applications course. Specific objectives of this book are as follows:

- To teach students how to use Firefox, an open-source browser from Mozilla
- To expose students to various World Wide Web resources
- To acquaint students with the more popular search engines
- To show students how to evaluate Web pages and do research using the World Wide Web
- To teach students how to communicate across the Internet, using Mozilla Thunderbird for e-mail and Yahoo Chat for instant messaging
- To introduce students to the concept of open-source software development

The Shelly Cashman Approach

Features of the Shelly Cashman Series *Mozilla Firefox: Introductory Concepts and Techniques* book include:

- **Step-by-Step, Screen-by-Screen Instructions:** Each of the steps required to complete a task is presented in an easy-to-understand manner. Full-color screens with call outs accompany the steps.
- **Thoroughly Tested Projects:** Unparalleled quality is assured because every screen in the book is produced by the author only after performing a step, and then each project must pass Course Technology's award-winning Quality Assurance program.
- **Other Ways Boxes:** The Other Ways boxes displayed at the end of most of the step-by-step sequences specify the other ways to do the task completed in the steps. Thus, the steps and the Other Ways box make a comprehensive reference unit.
- **More About and Q&A Features:** These marginal annotations provide background information, tips, and answers to common questions that complement the topics covered, adding depth and perspective to the learning process.

Other Ways

1. Click Start button on Windows taskbar, click Mozilla Firefox icon on Start menu
2. Double-click Mozilla Firefox icon on desktop

More About

HTML

More than 50 HTML editing programs make it easy to create Web pages without learning HTML syntax. These programs include Mozilla Composer, Microsoft FrontPage, Adobe GoLive, Hot Dog, HomeSite, Coffee Cup, Power Web, Web Express, Cool Page, Sothink, and Macromedia Dreamweaver.

• Integration of the World Wide Web: The World Wide Web is integrated into the Firefox learning experience by (1) More About annotations that send students to Web sites for up-to-date information and alternative approaches to tasks; and (2) the Learn It Online page at the end of each project, which has project reinforcement exercises, learning games, and other types of student activities.

Organization of this Textbook

Mozilla Firefox: Introductory Concepts and Techniques consists of three projects, one special feature, and two appendices. Each project ends with a large number of exercises to reinforce what students learn in the project. The projects and appendices are organized as follows:

Project 1 – Introduction to Firefox In Project 1, students are introduced to the Internet, World Wide Web, and Firefox. Topics include starting Firefox; browsing the World Wide Web; refreshing a Web page; using the History sidebar and Bookmarks sidebar to display Web pages; adding Web pages to and removing Web pages from the Bookmarks menu; saving and printing a picture, text, or Web page; copying and pasting text or pictures from a Web page into WordPad; and using Firefox Help.

Project 2 – Web Research Techniques and Search Engines In Project 2, students are introduced to nine general Web page categories, techniques for searching the Web, and criteria for evaluating a Web page. Topics include searching the Web using keywords or a directory; using tabbed browsing to view multiple Web pages; performing an advanced search; evaluating and recording relevant information about a Web source; creating a working bibliography; searching for addresses, maps, definitions, or pictures; and using the Location bar to search for a Web page or view folders.

Project 3 – Communicating Over the Internet Using Mozilla Thunderbird In Project 3, students use Mozilla Thunderbird to access existing e-mail accounts, view and send e-mail messages, work with Address Book, read and post an article to a newsgroup, and send and receive instant messages using Yahoo! Messenger. Topics include reading, replying to, printing, and deleting an e-mail message; viewing an attachment; adding and deleting Address Book cards; reading and posting a newsgroup article; subscribing and unsubscribing to a newsgroup; starting, signing in, and sending an instant message.

Special Feature – Open Source and Firefox Customization In the Special Feature, students learn about open source software and various methods of customizing the Firefox browser. Topics include describing and listing advantages of open source software; learning the Open Source Definition; and installing and uninstalling an extension, a theme, and a plug-in.

Appendix A – Installing Mozilla Firefox Appendix A explains how to install Firefox from the accompanying software CD.

Appendix B – Installing Mozilla Thunderbird Appendix B explains how to install Thunderbird from the accompanying software CD.

Appendix C – Mozilla Firefox Options Appendix C explains how to view and modify Firefox's default settings using the Options Dialog Box. Topics include changing the default home page; deleting cookies and temporary Internet files stored in the cache; specifying how Firefox handles downloads; and controlling advanced settings such as software updates, security, and certificates.

End-of-Project Student Activities

A notable strength of the Shelly Cashman Series Web browser books is the extensive student activities at the end of each project. Well-structured student activities can make the difference between students merely participating in a class and students retaining the information they learn. The following activities are included in this book.

- **What You Should Know** A listing of the tasks completed within a project together with the pages on which the step-by-step, screen-by-screen explanations appear. This section provides a perfect study review for students.
- **Learn It Online** Every project features a Learn It Online page consisting of twelve exercises. These exercises utilize the Web to offer project-related reinforcement activities that will help students gain confidence in their browser abilities. They include Project Reinforcement (True/False, Multiple Choice, and Short Answer questions), Flash Cards, Practice Test, Learning Games, Tips and Tricks, Newsgroups, Expanding Your Horizons, Search Sleuth, Firefox How-To Articles, and Getting More From the Web.
- **In the Lab** Several assignments per project require students to apply the knowledge gained in the project to solve problems on the Web.
- **Cases and Places** Up to seven unique case studies including one small-group activity require students to apply their knowledge to real-world situations.

Instructor Resources

The Shelly Cashman Series is dedicated to providing you with all of the tools you need to make your class a success. Information on all supplementary materials is available through your Course Technology representative or by calling one of the following telephone numbers: Colleges and Universities, 1-800-648-7450; High Schools, 1-800-824-5179; Private Career Colleges, 1-800-648-7450; Canada, 1-800-268-2222; Corporations with IT Training Centers, 1-800-648-7450; and Government Agencies, Health-Care Organizations, and Correctional Facilities, 1-800-477-3692.

Instructor Resources CD-ROM

The Instructor Resources for this textbook include both teaching and testing aids. The contents of each item on the Instructor Resources CD-ROM (ISBN 1-4188-5962-1) are described below.

INSTRUCTOR'S MANUAL The Instructor's Manual is made up of Microsoft Word files, which include detailed lesson plans with page number references, lecture notes, teaching tips, classroom activities, discussion topics, projects to assign, and transparency references. The transparencies are available through the Figure Files described below.

SYLLABUS Sample syllabi, which can be customized easily to a course, are included. The syllabi cover policies, class and lab assignments and exams, and procedural information.

FIGURE FILES Illustrations for every figure in the textbook are available in electronic form. Use this ancillary to present a slide show in lecture or to print transparencies for use in lecture with an overhead projector. If you have a personal computer and LCD device, this ancillary can be an effective tool for presenting lectures.

POWERPOINT PRESENTATIONS PowerPoint Presentations is a multimedia lecture presentation system that provides PowerPoint slides for each project. Presentations are based on project objectives. Use this presentation system to present well-organized lectures that are both interesting and knowledge based. PowerPoint Presentations provides consistent coverage at schools that use multiple lecturers.

SOLUTIONS TO EXERCISES Solutions are included for the end-of-project exercises, as well as the Project Reinforcement exercises.

TEST BANK & TEST ENGINE The ExamView test bank includes 110 questions for every project (25 multiple-choice, 50 true/false, and 35 completion) with page number references, and when appropriate, figure references. A version of the test bank you can print also is included. The test bank comes with a copy of the test engine, ExamView, the ultimate tool for your objective-based testing needs. ExamView is a state-of-the-art test builder that is easy to use. ExamView enables you to create paper-, LAN-, or Web-based tests from test banks designed specifically for your Course Technology textbook. Utilize the ultra-efficient QuickTest Wizard to create tests in less than five minutes by taking advantage of Course Technology's question banks, or customize your own exams from scratch.

ADDITIONAL ACTIVITIES FOR STUDENTS These additional activities consist of Project Reinforcement Exercises, which are true/false, multiple choice, and short answer questions that help students gain confidence in the material learned.

Online Content

Course Technology offers textbook-based content for Blackboard, WebCT, and MyCourse 2.1

BLACKBOARD AND WEBCT As the leading provider of IT content for the Blackboard and WebCT platforms, Course Technology delivers rich content that enhances your textbook to give your students a unique learning experience. Course Technology has partnered with WebCT and Blackboard to deliver our market-leading content through these state-of-the-art online learning platforms. Course Technology offers customizable content in every subject area, from computer concepts to PC repair.

MYCOURSE 2.1 MyCourse 2.1 is Course Technology's powerful online course management and content delivery system. Completely maintained and hosted by Thomson, MyCourse 2.1 delivers an online learning environment that is completely secure and provides superior performance. MyCourse 2.1 allows non-technical users to create, customize, and deliver World Wide Web-based courses; post content and assignments; manage student enrollment; administer exams; track results in the online gradebook; and more. With MyCourse 2.1, you easily can create a customized course that will enhance every learning experience.

MOZILLA

Introduction to Firefox

CASE PERSPECTIVE

As an art history major in a local community college, you have found that you can enhance your experience if you learn more about using the Internet. In fact, your art history instructor recommends you take a short college course to help you understand how to search for articles and pictures on the Internet.

You browse through your school's class schedule for the upcoming semester and sign up for an Introduction to the Internet class offered by the Computer Information Science Department for those with little or no experience using the Internet. The topics listed in the course description include accessing the Internet using Mozilla Firefox, searching the Internet for information, and saving information you find on a Web page. After completing the course, you decide to earn money by using your knowledge of Firefox to perform Internet research for college instructors and local businesses. Instead of the usual resume/cover letter approach to obtaining a job, you decide to take out an advertisement in the local newspaper that advertises your Internet search skills.

Among the responses you receive from the advertisement is one from the manager of the Livingston Gallery. She hires you to identify the origin and authenticity of a piece of Asian art, titled *Three Leaves*, that the gallery wants to purchase. You agree to search for information about the Asian art and supply the gallery with pictures and text associated with the art.

As you read through this project, you will learn how to use Firefox to access the Internet, search the Web, and save and organize information you find on Web pages.

Introduction to Firefox

Objectives

You will have mastered the material in this project when you can:

- Describe the Internet and the World Wide Web
- Define link, Uniform Resource Locator, and Hypertext Markup Language
- Describe key Firefox features and the Firefox window
- Enter a Uniform Resource Locator (URL)
- Browse the World Wide Web using the History sidebar, Bookmarks sidebar, and URLs
- Display Web pages using the Back list and the Back, Forward, and Home buttons
- Display recently displayed Web pages using the History sidebar
- Add and remove a Web page from the Bookmarks menu
- Save Web page text, a Web page picture, and an entire Web page on a floppy disk
- Copy and paste text and a picture from a Web page into WordPad
- Print a WordPad document and a Web page
- Use Firefox Help

Introduction

The Internet is the most popular and fastest growing area in computing today. Using the Internet, you can do research, participate in online auctions, shop for services and merchandise, post a resume and search for a job, buy and sell stocks, check weather and traffic conditions, obtain medical advice, purchase movie and concert tickets, play online video games, listen to online radio stations, and converse with people worldwide.

Once considered mysterious, the Internet is now accessible to the general public because personal computers with user-friendly tools have reduced its complexity. The Internet, with its billions of connected computers, continues to grow, with thousands of new users coming online every day. Schools, businesses, newspapers, television and radio stations, and government services all can be found on the Internet. Service providers all around the country provide inexpensive access to the Internet from home. But, exactly what is the Internet?

The Internet

The **Internet** is a worldwide collection of networks (Figure 1-1), each of which is composed of a collection of smaller networks. A **network** is composed of several computers connected together to share resources and data. For example, on a college campus, the network in the student computer lab can connect to the faculty computer network, which is connected to the administration computer network, and they all can connect to the Internet.

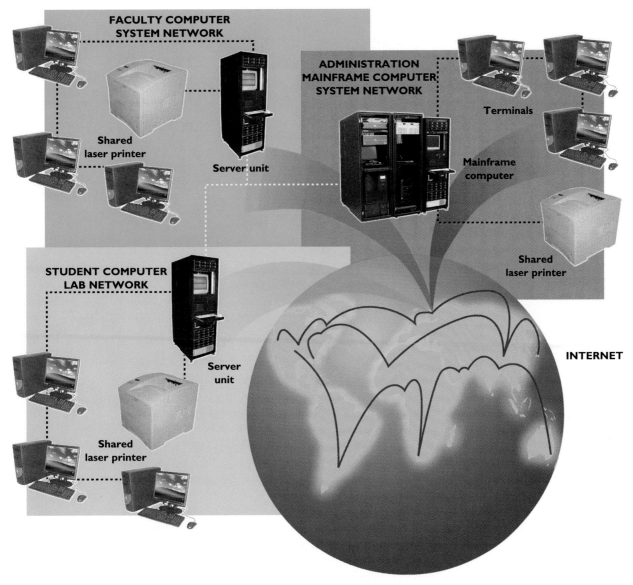

FIGURE 1-1

Networks are connected with high-, medium-, and low-speed data lines that allow data to move from one computer to another (Figure 1-2 on the next page). The Internet has high-speed data lines that connect major computers located around the world, which form the **Internet backbone**. Other, less powerful computers, such as those used by local ISPs (Internet service providers) often connect to the Internet backbone using medium-speed data lines. Finally, the connection between your computer at home and your local ISP, often called **the last mile**, employs low-speed data lines such as telephone lines. In many cases today, cable is replacing telephone lines over the last mile, which significantly speeds up access to the Internet.

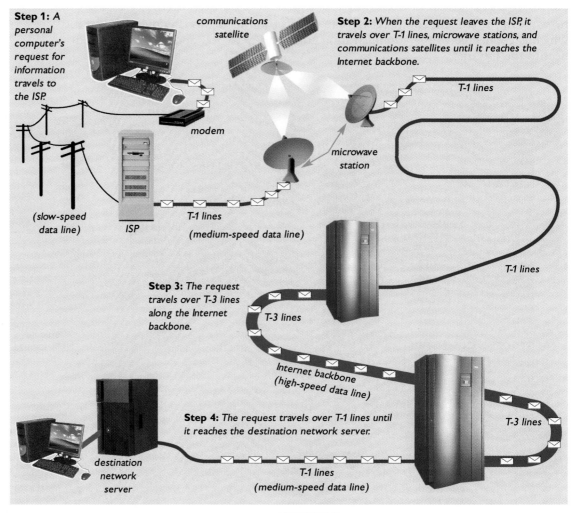

Step 1: A personal computer's request for information travels to the ISP.

communications satellite

Step 2: When the request leaves the ISP, it travels over T-1 lines, microwave stations, and communications satellites until it reaches the Internet backbone.

T-1 lines

modem

microwave station

T-1 lines

(slow-speed data line)

ISP

T-1 lines

(medium-speed data line)

Step 3: The request travels over T-3 lines along the Internet backbone.

T-3 lines

T-3 lines

Internet backbone (high-speed data line)

Step 4: The request travels over T-1 lines until it reaches the destination network server.

destination network server

T-1 lines (medium-speed data line)

FIGURE 1-2

The World Wide Web

Modern computers have the capability of delivering information in a variety of ways, such as graphics, sound, video clips, animation, and, of course, regular text. On the Internet, this multimedia capability is available in a form called **hypermedia**, which is any variety of computer media, including text, graphics, video, sound, and virtual reality.

You access hypermedia using a **hyperlink**, or simply **link**, which is a special software pointer that directs your computer to the computer on which the hypermedia is stored and to the hypermedia itself. A link can point to hypermedia on any computer connected to the Internet that is running the proper software. Thus, clicking a link on a computer in Los Angeles could display text and graphics located on a computer in New York.

The collection of links throughout the Internet creates an interconnected network called the **World Wide Web**, which also is referred to as the **Web**, or **WWW**. Each computer within the Web containing hypermedia that you can reference with a link is called a **Web site**. Millions of Web sites around the world are accessible through the Internet.

Graphics, text, and other hypermedia available at a Web site are stored in a file called a **Web page**. Therefore, when you click a link to display a picture, read text, view a video, or listen to music, you actually are viewing a Web page.

More About

Web Sites

An organization can have more than one Web site. Separate departments may have their own Web servers, allowing faster response to requests for Web pages and local control over the Web pages stored at that Web site.

Figure 1-3 illustrates a Web page at the Disney Online Web site. This Web page contains numerous links. For example, the seven graphics on the Web page are links. Clicking a link, such as Disney Destinations, could display a Web page from a travel agency located on the other side of the world.

FIGURE 1-3

Uniform Resource Locators (URLs)

Each Web page has a unique address, called a **Uniform Resource Locator (URL)**, which distinguishes it from all other pages on the Internet. The URL in Figure 1-3 is http://disney.go.com/home/today/index.html.

A URL often is composed of four parts (Figure 1-4). The first part is the protocol. A **protocol** is a set of rules. Most Web pages use the Hypertext Transfer Protocol. **Hypertext Transfer Protocol (HTTP)** describes the rules used to transmit Web pages electronically over the Internet. You enter the protocol in lowercase as "http" followed by a colon and two forward slashes (http://). If you do not begin a URL with a protocol, Firefox will assume it is http, and automatically will append http:// to the front of the URL.

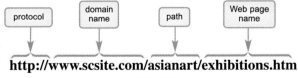

FIGURE 1-4

The second part of a URL is the domain name. The **domain name** is the Internet address of the computer on the Internet where the Web page is located. Each computer on the Internet has a unique address, called an **Internet Protocol address**, or **IP address**.

The domain name identifies where to forward a request for the Web page referenced by the URL. The domain name in the URL in Figure 1-4 on the previous page is www.scsite.com.

The last part of the domain name ("com" in Figure 1-4) indicates the type of organization that owns the Web site. For example, "com" indicates a commercial organization, usually a business or corporation. Educational institutions have "edu" at the end of their domain names. Government entities use "gov" at the end of their domain names. Table 1-1 shows some types of organizations and their extensions.

Table 1-1 Organizations and Their Domain Name Extensions	
TYPES OF ORGANIZATIONS	ORIGINAL DOMAIN NAMES
Commercial organizations, businesses, and companies	.com
Educational institutions	.edu
Government agencies	.gov
Military organizations	.mil
Network providers	.net
Nonprofit organizations	.org
TYPES OF ORGANIZATIONS	NEWER DOMAIN NAMES
Accredited museums	.museum
Businesses of all sizes	.biz
Businesses, organizations, or individuals providing general information	.info
Individuals or families	.name
Certified professionals such as doctors, lawyers, and accountants	.pro
Aviation community members	.aero
Business cooperatives such as credit unions and rural electric co-ops	.coop

The optional third part of a URL is the file specification of the Web page. The **file specification** includes a directory or folder name. This information is called the **path**. The fourth part of a URL is the **Web page name**. The Web page name identifies the currently displayed Web page.

You can find URLs that identify interesting Web sites in magazines or newspapers, on television, from friends, or even from just browsing the Web.

URLs of well-known companies and organizations usually contain the company's name and institution's name. For example, ibm.com is IBM Corporation, and ucf.edu is the University of Central Florida.

Hypertext Markup Language

To create Web pages, Web page authors use a special formatting language called **Hypertext Markup Language (HTML)**. Behind all the formatted text and eye-catching graphics you see on a Web page is plain text in a simple text file. Special HTML codes, written in plain text, control attributes such as font size, colors, and alignment.

More About

HTML

More than 50 HTML editing programs make it easy to create Web pages without learning HTML syntax. These programs include Mozilla Composer, Microsoft FrontPage, Adobe GoLive, Hot Dog, HomeSite, Coffee Cup, Power Web, Web Express, Cool Page, Sothink, and Macromedia Dreamweaver.

These codes are placed on each side of the text and picture references in the text file. Figure 1-5 shows part of the hypertext markup language used to create the Web page shown in Figure 1-3 on page FX 5.

Though it looks somewhat cryptic, HTML is similar to a computer programming language. Using HTML, you can create your own Web pages and place them on the Web for others to see. Easier-to-use Web page development software, such as Microsoft's FrontPage, is one of the many HTML authoring tools available.

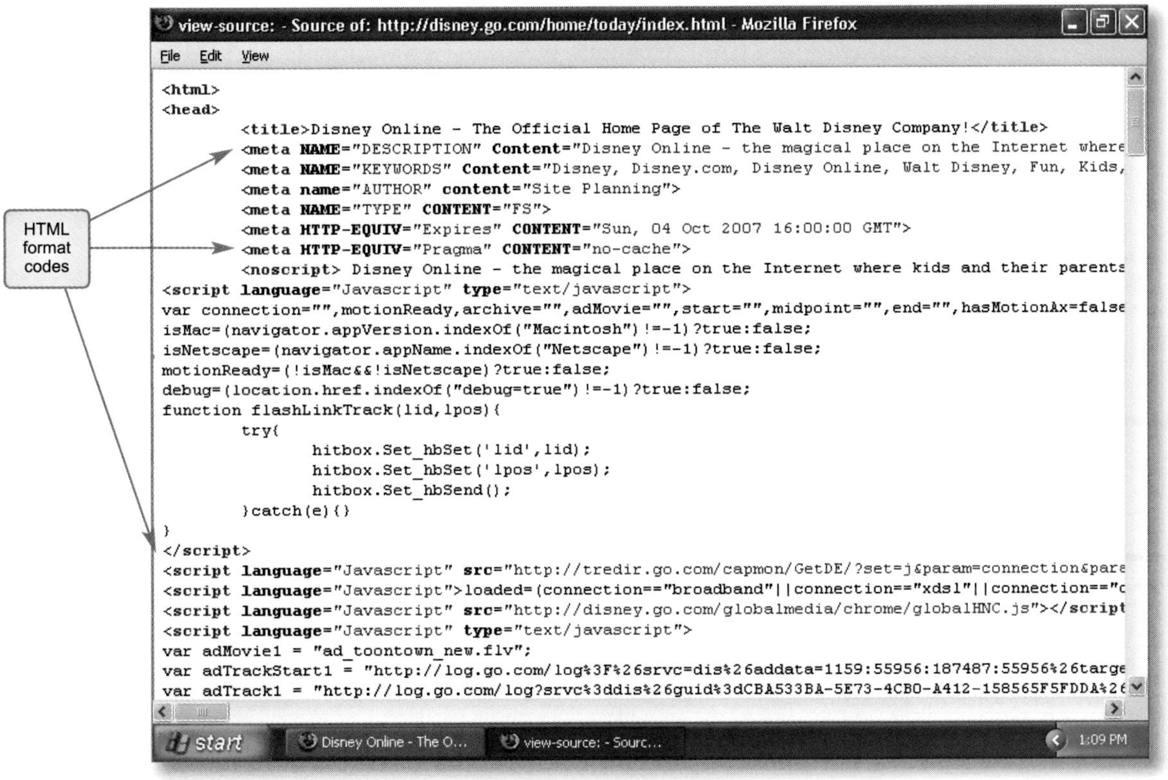

FIGURE 1-5

Home Pages

No main menus or any particular starting points exist in the World Wide Web. Although you can reference any page on the Web when you begin, most people start with specially designated Web pages called home pages. A **home page** is the introductory page for a Web site. All other Web pages for that site usually are accessible from the home page via links. In addition, the home page is the page that is displayed when you enter a domain name with no file specification, such as disney.com or nbc.com.

Because it is the starting point for most Web sites, designers try to give the home page a good first impression by displaying attractive eye-catching graphics, specially formatted text, and a variety of links to other pages at the Web site, as well as to other interesting and useful Web sites.

> *More About*
>
> **Home Pages**
>
> A Web site can consist of a single home page. A computer used by faculty members or students for their hypertext documents would have many Web sites: one for each person. Each faculty or student Web site would have its own home page.

Internet Browsers

Just as graphical user interfaces (GUIs), such as Microsoft Windows, simplify working with a computer by using a point-and-click method, a browser, such as Firefox, makes using the World Wide Web easier by removing the complexity of having to remember the syntax, or rules, of commands used to reference Web pages at Web sites. A **browser** is a program that takes the URL associated with a link or the URL entered by a user, locates the computer containing the associated Web page, and then reads the HTML codes returned to display a Web page.

What Is Firefox?

Firefox is a Web browser that you use to search for and view Web pages, save pages for use in the future, and maintain a list of the pages you visit. The Firefox program can be downloaded free from Mozilla's Web site (www.mozilla.org). Mozilla Firefox is an example of open source software. **Open source** is a philosophy for software licensing and distribution designed to encourage the use and improvement of the software by allowing anyone to use and modify the software code. For more information about open source, see the Special Feature. For more information about installing Firefox, see Appendix A. The projects in this book illustrate the use of the Firefox browser.

Starting Firefox

If you are stepping through this project on a computer and you want your screen to match the figures in this book, then you should change your computer's resolution to 800 × 600. For more information on how to change the resolution on your computer, see your instructor. The following steps show how to start Firefox.

More About

Open Source

Mozilla Firefox is an example of open source software, allowing people and companies to modify the program as necessary to meet their needs, redistribute the original or modified program free-of-charge, and use the program for any purpose. For more information on open source, visit the Firefox More About Web page (scsite.com/ firefox/more), and then click one of the Open Source links.

To Start Firefox

1

• **Click the Start button on the Windows taskbar, point to All Programs on the Start menu, point to Mozilla Firefox on the All Programs submenu, and then point to Mozilla Firefox on the Mozilla Firefox submenu.**

Windows displays the Start menu, the All Programs submenu, Mozilla Firefox submenu, and Mozilla Firefox command (Figure 1-6).

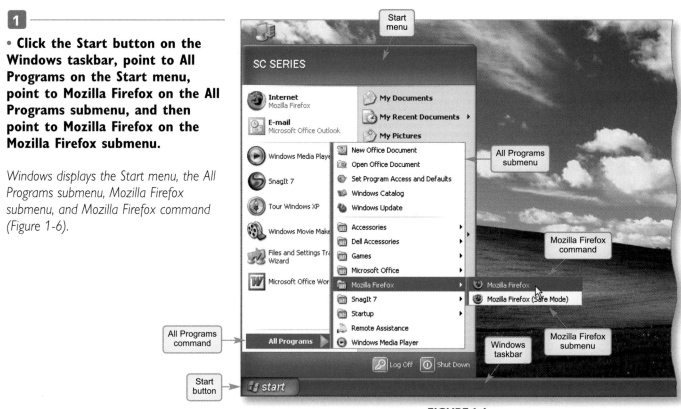

FIGURE 1-6

2

- **Click Mozilla Firefox.**

- **If the Default Browser dialog box is displayed, click the No button.**

Firefox starts. After several seconds, Firefox displays the Mozilla Firefox Start Page - Mozilla Firefox window, adds the Mozilla Firefox Start Page - Mozilla Firefox button to the taskbar, displays the Mozilla Firefox Start Page Web page title in the window title, and displays the Firefox Start Page in the display area (Figure 1-7). The home page may display differently on your computer.

- **If the Mozilla Firefox window is not maximized, double-click its title bar to maximize it.**

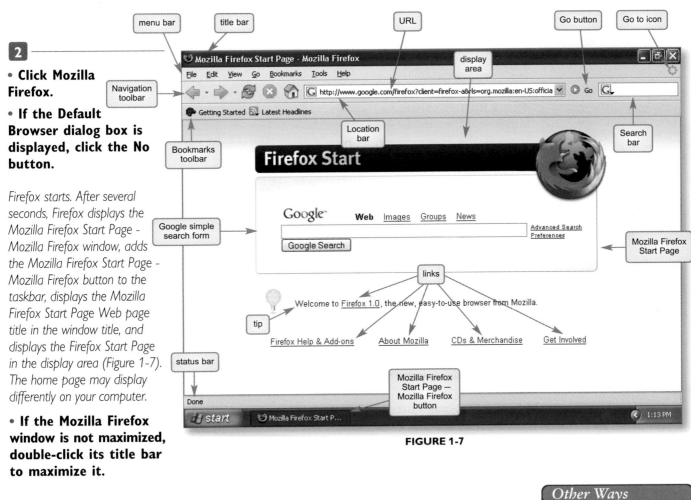

FIGURE 1-7

Normally, when Firefox starts, the Mozilla Firefox Start Page is displayed. Because users can change the **Home Page**, or the page that is displayed when you first start Firefox, the page shown in Figure 1-7 may be different on your computer. For example, some schools and businesses have their own Web site display when starting Firefox. For more information about how to customize the Home Page in Firefox, see Appendix C.

The Mozilla Firefox Window

The **Mozilla Firefox window** (Figure 1-7) consists of innovative features that make browsing the Internet easy. It contains a title bar, menu bar, Navigation toolbar, Bookmarks toolbar, status bar, and a display area where pages from the World Wide Web display. The menu bar, Navigation toolbar, and Bookmarks toolbar are displayed at the top of the screen just below the title bar. The status bar is displayed at the bottom of the screen.

DISPLAY AREA You view the portion of the page displayed on the screen in the **display area** (Figure 1-7). By default, Firefox displays the Mozilla Firefox Start Page. The Mozilla Firefox Start Page contains a Google simple search form. **Google** is one of many widely used search engines available for searching the Internet. The Google simple search form shown in Figure 1-7 contains links you can use to search for images, groups, and news. You also can perform advanced searches and change search preferences. The Google Search button is displayed in the search form and a tip is displayed below the Google simple search form. You use the five links below the Google simple search form to update Firefox, access Firefox Help and Add-ons, find information about Mozilla, access the official Mozilla store, and get involved with improving Firefox. The mouse

Q&A

Q: Can I change the Home Page in the Mozilla Firefox window?

A: Yes. You can change the Home Page by clicking Tools on the menu bar, clicking Options on the Tools menu, clicking General in the left pane, and clicking the Use Current Page, Use Bookmark, or Use Blank Page button. You also can change the Home Page by dragging the icon on the Location bar to the Home button on the Navigation toolbar. The Web page in the display area becomes the Home Page.

More About

The Display Area

You can increase the size of the display area shown in Figure 1-7 by customizing or removing the Navigation toolbar or Bookmarks toolbar.

pointer changes to a pointing hand when you position the mouse pointer on a link. This change in the shape of the mouse pointer identifies these elements as links. Clicking a link retrieves the Web page associated with the link and displays it in the display area.

TITLE BAR The title bar is displayed at the top of the Mozilla Firefox Start Page window. As shown at the top of Figure 1-7 on the previous page, the **title bar** includes the System menu icon on the left, the title of the window, and the Minimize, Restore Down (or Maximize), and Close buttons on the right. Clicking the **System menu icon** on the title bar displays the System menu, which contains commands to carry out the actions associated with the Mozilla Firefox window. Double-click the System menu icon or click the Close button to close the Mozilla Firefox window and quit Firefox.

Click the **Minimize button** to minimize the Mozilla Firefox window. When you minimize the Mozilla Firefox window, the window no longer is displayed on the desktop, though the program is still running. The Mozilla Firefox taskbar button becomes inactive (a lighter color) to indicate this. When you click the taskbar button, the Mozilla Firefox window returns to the previous position it occupied on the desktop and changes the button to an active state (a darker color).

Click the **Maximize button** to maximize the Mozilla Firefox window so it expands to fill the entire desktop. When the window is maximized, the Restore Down button replaces the Maximize button on the title bar. Click the **Restore Down button** to return the Mozilla Firefox window to the size and position it occupied before being maximized. The Restore Down button changes to the Maximize button when the Mozilla Firefox window is in a restored state.

You also can restore and maximize the Mozilla Firefox window by double-clicking the title bar. If the window is in a restored state, you can drag the title bar to move the window on the desktop.

MENU BAR The **menu bar**, which is located below the title bar, displays menu names (Figure 1-7). Each **menu name** represents a set of commands you can use to perform actions, such as saving Web pages, copying and pasting, customizing toolbars, reading and composing e-mail, setting Firefox options, quitting Firefox, and so on. To display a menu, click the menu name on the menu bar. To select a command on a menu, click the command name or press the **shortcut keys** shown to the right of some commands on the menu.

The **Go to icon** at the right end of the menu bar goes into motion (animates) when Firefox transfers a Web page to the Mozilla Firefox window and stops moving when the transfer is complete. You also can click the Go to icon to go to the Firefox home page, where you can get help on Firefox, learn how to customize the program, and more.

More About

Navigation Toolbar Buttons

If the text label is not displayed on the buttons on the Navigation toolbar, right-click the toolbar, click Customize on the shortcut menu, click the Show box arrow, click Icons and Text, and then click the Done button. You also can change the size of the icons on the toolbar buttons using the Use Small Icons check box.

NAVIGATION TOOLBAR The **Navigation toolbar** (Figure 1-7) contains buttons that allow you to perform frequently-used tasks more quickly than using the menu bar. For example, to display the Home Page in the Mozilla Firefox window, click the Home button on the Navigation toolbar.

Each of the six buttons on the Navigation toolbar contains an icon. One button, the Go button, contains a text label, describing the function of the button. Table 1-2 illustrates the buttons on the Navigation toolbar. The table also briefly describes the functions of the buttons. Each of the buttons will be explained in detail as it is used. The buttons on the Navigation toolbar may be different on your computer.

By right-clicking the Navigation toolbar, you can customize its buttons. For example, you can show or remove the text label on each button.

Table 1-2 Navigation Toolbar Buttons and Functions

BUTTON	FUNCTION
⬅	Retrieves the previous page, (provided it was previously just viewed). To go more than one page back, click the Back button arrow, and then click a Web page title in the list.
➡	Retrieves the next page. To go more than one page forward, click the Forward button arrow, and then click a Web page title in the list.
🔄	Requests the Web page in the display area to be retrieved from the Web site again.
❌	Stops the transfer of a Web page.
🏠	Requests the default Home Page to be displayed.
▶ Go	Displays the page associated with the URL on the Location bar.

The **Location bar** (Figure 1-7 on page FX 9) contains the Uniform Resource Locator (URL) for the page currently shown in the display area. The URL updates automatically as you browse from page to page. If you know the URL of a Web page you want to visit, click the URL on the Location bar to highlight the URL, type the new URL, and then click the Go button (or press the ENTER key) to display the corresponding page.

You also can type the location and name of a folder located on your computer and click the Go button to view the contents of that folder, and type a keyword or phrase (search inquiry) and click the Go button to display Web pages containing the keyword or phrase. In addition, you can click the **Location bar arrow** at the right end of the Location bar to display a list of previously displayed Web pages. Clicking a URL in the Address list displays the corresponding Web page.

The **Search bar,** located at the far right on the Navigation toolbar, allows you to search for a topic on the Internet and search for words on a Web page. The Search bar uses one of six search engines and allows you to add additional search engines. You can remove the entire toolbar by clicking View on the menu bar, pointing to Toolbars, and then clicking the appropriate toolbar name on the shortcut menu.

BOOKMARKS TOOLBAR The Bookmarks toolbar allows quick access to Web sites you frequently visit. In Figure 1-7, the Getting Started and Latest Headlines buttons display on the Bookmarks toolbar.

Each button on the Bookmarks toolbar contains an icon and text label. Table 1-3 illustrates the Bookmarks toolbar buttons and briefly describes the functions of the buttons. Additional buttons or different buttons may display on the Bookmarks toolbar on your computer.

Table 1-3 Bookmarks Toolbar Buttons and Functions

BUTTON	FUNCTION
Getting Started	Displays the Firefox Central Web page
Latest Headlines	Displays a list of over twenty of the latest headlines

More About

The Location Bar

To highlight the contents of the Location bar when the contents are not highlighted, press CTRL+L or ALT+D.

Q: Can I store links to Web pages on the Bookmarks toolbar?

A: Yes. The Bookmarks toolbar is a good place to store links to the Web pages you use frequently. You can add a Web page to the Bookmarks toolbar by dragging the icon from the Location bar or dragging a link from a Web page to the Bookmarks toolbar. Clicking the button on the Bookmarks toolbar displays the associated Web page.

Q: Can I add more buttons to the Navigation toolbar?

A: Yes. Simply right-click the Navigation toolbar and click Customize on the shortcut menu. When the Customize Toolbar dialog box is displayed, drag the buttons you wish to add from the Customize Toolbar dialog box to a location of your choice on the Navigation toolbar.

More About

The Asian Arts Web Site

Notice that the URL you enter for the Asian Arts page contains a domain name (scsite.com) of the company that publishes this book. The entire Asian Arts site has been stored on the publishing company's computer server to guarantee that the content of the Asian Arts Web site remains the same for all students. Type `asianart.com` on the Location bar to view the real Asian Arts site. See if you notice any differences.

Browsing the World Wide Web

The most common way to browse the World Wide Web is to obtain the URL of a Web page you want to visit and then enter it into the Location bar on the Navigation toolbar. It is by visiting various Web sites that you can begin to understand the enormous appeal of the World Wide Web. The following steps show how to view a Web site titled Asian Arts, which contains information and pictures of artwork from various countries in Asia. The URL for the Asian Art page is:

www.scsite.com/asianart

You are not required to provide the leading http:// protocol when initially typing the URL on the Location bar. Firefox will insert http:// and assume the www automatically, if you do not supply it. The following steps show how to browse the Web by entering a URL.

To Browse the Web by Entering a URL

1

• **Click the Location bar.**

The mouse pointer changes to an I-beam and Firefox highlights the URL on the Location bar (Figure 1-8).

FIGURE 1-8

2

• **Type** scsite.com/asianart **on the Location bar.**

The new URL is displayed on the Location bar (Figure 1-9).

FIGURE 1-9

3

• **Click the Go button.**

The Go to icon on the menu bar goes into motion (animates) while the Asian Arts Web page is displayed and then stops moving when the Asian Arts Web page is displayed. The Asian Arts Web page title is displayed on the title bar and on the active button on the taskbar, and the URL of the Web page is displayed on the Location bar (Figure 1-10).

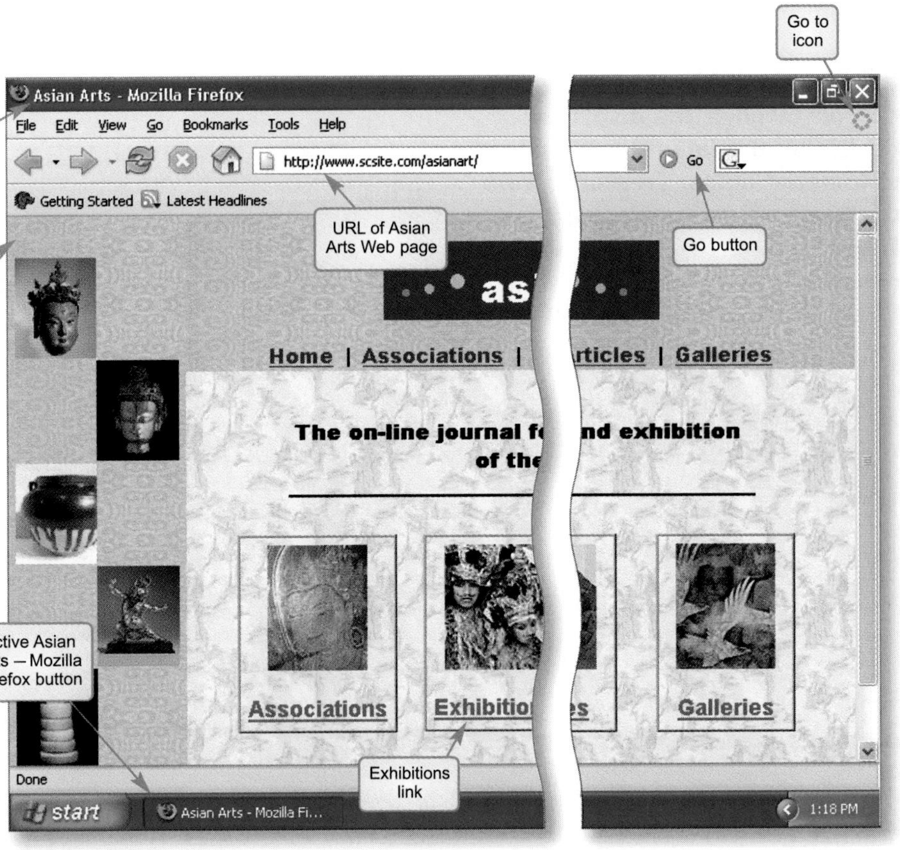

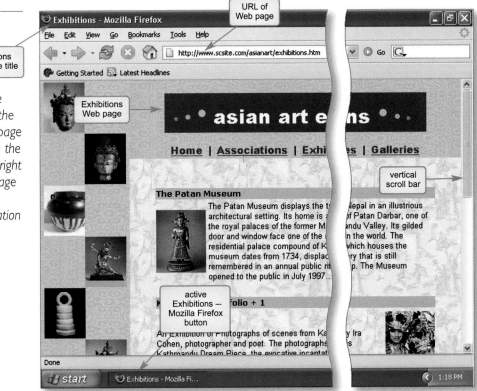

FIGURE 1-10

4

• **Click the Exhibitions link.**

After a brief interval, Mozilla Firefox displays the Exhibitions page (Figure 1-11). The URL of the Web page is displayed on the Location bar and the Exhibitions Web page title is displayed on the title bar and on the taskbar button. A vertical scroll bar on the right side of the display area indicates the page is larger than the display area. You will have to scroll to view additional information and pictures on the page.

FIGURE 1-11

5

• **Scroll through the display area to display the link, The Splendors of Imperial China: Treasures from the National Palace Museum, Taipei.**

The display area scrolls and The Splendors of Imperial China: Treasures from the National Palace Museum, Taipei link is displayed (Figure 1-12). The picture at the right of the display area also is a link to the same page.

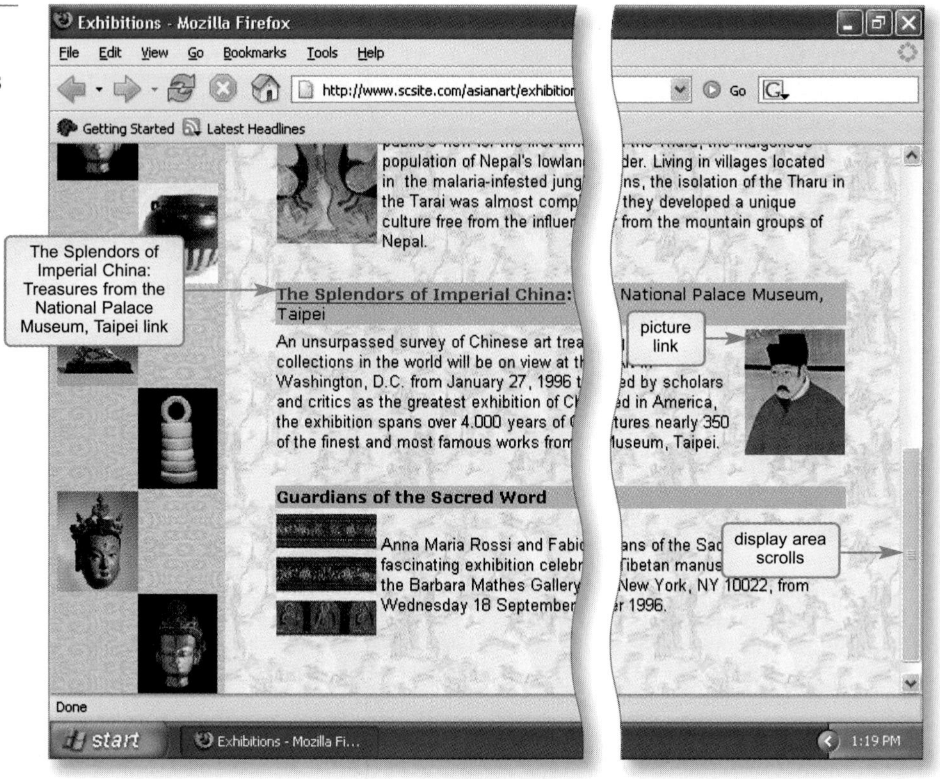

FIGURE 1-12

6

• **Click The Splendors of Imperial China: Treasures from the National Palace Museum, Taipei link.**

After a brief interval, The Splendors of Imperial China Web page is displayed (Figure 1-13). The URL of the Web page is displayed on the Location bar and the Web page title is displayed on the title bar and on the taskbar button. The Web page contains pictures and descriptions of the Chinese art located in the National Palace Museum in Taipei, China.

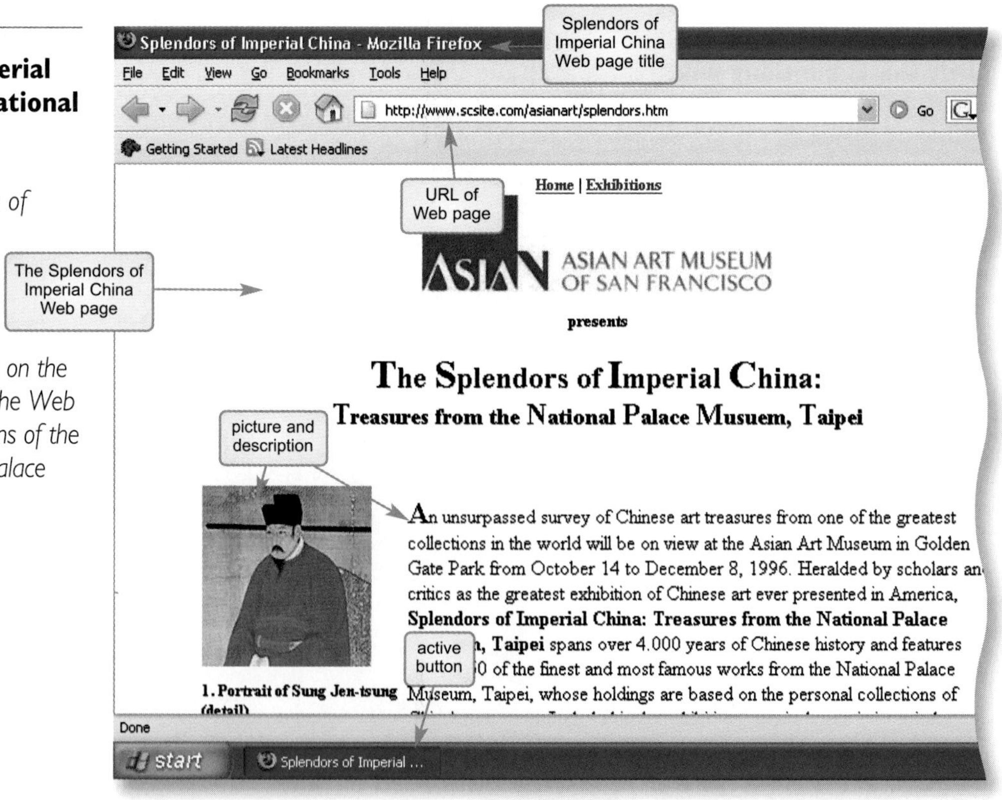

FIGURE 1-13

7

• **Scroll through the display area to view the three pictures numbered 8, 9, and 10.**

The display area scrolls to display the pictures of a stem cup, various leaves and flowers, and a globe vase (Figure 1-14). The title, Three leaves from Landscapes and Flowers, is displayed below the center picture.

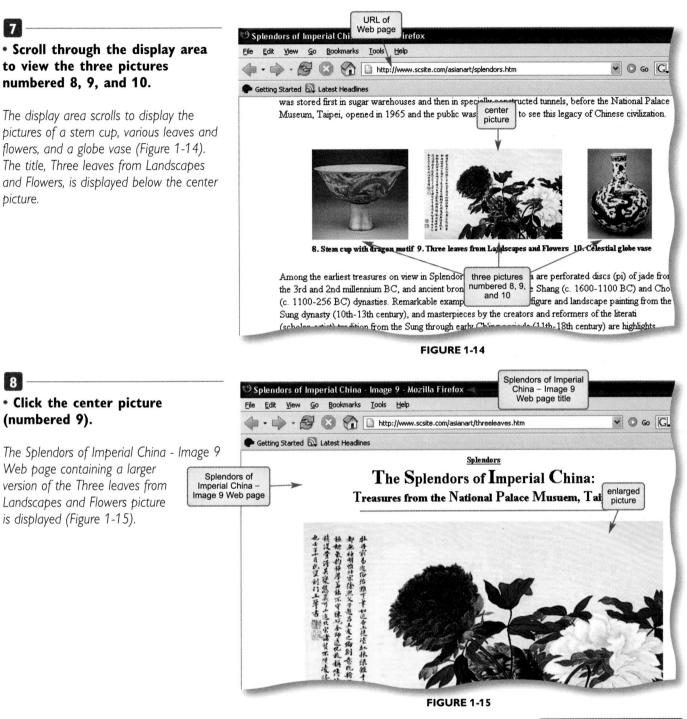

FIGURE 1-14

8

• **Click the center picture (numbered 9).**

The Splendors of Imperial China - Image 9 Web page containing a larger version of the Three leaves from Landscapes and Flowers picture is displayed (Figure 1-15).

FIGURE 1-15

The preceding steps illustrate how simple it is to browse the World Wide Web. Displaying a Web page associated with a link is as easy as clicking a text or picture link.

Step 2 on page FX 12 involved typing a URL. If you type the wrong letter and notice the error before clicking the Go button, use the BACKSPACE key to erase all the characters back to and including the one that is wrong. If the error is easier to retype than correct, click the URL and retype the entire text.

Other Ways

1. On File menu, click Open Location, type URL on Location bar, click Go button
2. Press CTRL+L, type a URL on Location bar, press ENTER
3. Press ALT+D, type a URL on Location bar, press ENTER
4. Press ALT+F, press L, type a URL on Location bar, press ENTER

More About

Stopping the Transfer of a Page

In addition to clicking the Stop button on the Navigation toolbar to stop the transfer of a page, you also can click the Stop command on the View menu, press the ESC key, or press ALT+V and then press the S key.

Stopping the Transfer of a Page

If a Web page you are trying to view is taking too long to transfer or if you clicked the wrong link, you may decide not to wait for the page to finish transferring. The Stop button on the Navigation toolbar (Figure 1-16) allows you to stop the transfer of a page while the transfer is in progress. You will know the transfer is still in progress if the Go to icon on the menu bar remains animated. Stopping the transfer of a Web page will leave a partially transferred Web page in the display area. Pictures or text that display before the Stop button is clicked remain visible in the display area and links that display can be clicked to display the associated Web pages.

Reloading a Web Page

If you decide you want to reload the Web page, use the **Reload button** on the Navigation toolbar (Figure 1-16). This is particularly useful with Web pages that are updated every few minutes, such as stock quotes, weather, and the news. You don't see the updates until you click the Reload button. The following step shows how to refresh the Splendors of Imperial China - Image 9 Web page.

To Reload a Web Page

1

• **Click the Reload button on the Navigation toolbar.**

Firefox initiates a new transfer of the Web page from the computer where it is located to your computer. The Go to icon goes into motion while the transfer progresses and a message is displayed on the status bar providing information about the progress of the transfer. The Splendors of China - Image 9 Web page displays in the display area (Figure 1-16).

FIGURE 1-16

Other Ways

1. On View menu click Reload
2. Click URL on Location bar, click Go button
3. Press ALT+V, press R
4. Press CTRL+R
5. Press F5

In the event that the connection to the Web site where the page is located malfunctions and the page transfer does not finish, you can use the Reload button to request the page again.

Finding a Previously Displayed Web Page

As you display different Web pages, Firefox keeps track of the pages you visit so you can quickly find those pages in the future. When you display a previously displayed Web page, the page is displayed quickly because Firefox is able to retrieve the page from your computer's hard disk instead of from a Web site on the Internet.

One method to find a previously displayed Web page is to use the Back button and Forward button on the Navigation toolbar (Figure 1-17a). Each time a Web page is displayed in the display area, the title of the previously displayed page is added to the Back button list. Right-clicking the Back button displays the **Back button list** that allows you to display a previously displayed page from the list (Figure 1-17a). Although not shown in Figure 1-17a, right-clicking the Forward button when the Forward button is active displays the **Forward button list** that also allows you to display a previously displayed page from the list. The Back button list and Forward button list can hold up to 15 previously displayed Web pages. Each time you end an Internet session by quitting Firefox, the Back button and Forward button lists are cleared. A session begins when Firefox starts and ends when Firefox closes.

You also can click the **Go menu** on the menu bar to see a list of up to the last 10 Web pages you visited (Figure 1-17b). Clicking a Web site name on the Go menu displays the associated Web page in the display area.

A third method to display a previously displayed Web page is to use the History sidebar (Figure 1-17c on the next page). The **History sidebar** contains links for Web sites and pages visited in the last nine days. Each time you display a Web page, Firefox saves the URL for that Web page and adds a link for it to the History sidebar. Clicking History on the Go menu displays the History sidebar. Clicking a Web site name on the History sidebar displays the associated Web page on the display area.

A fourth method uses the Location bar arrow to display a list of previously displayed Web pages you viewed by typing the URL on the Location bar. Clicking the Location bar arrow displays the **Location bar list** containing a list of previously visited Web pages (Figure 1-17d on the next page).

FIGURE 1-17a

FIGURE 1-17b

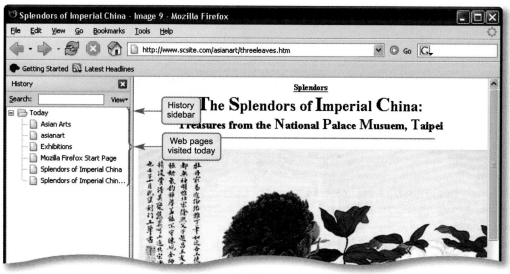

FIGURE 1-17c

FIGURE 1-17d

Finding a Recently Displayed Web Page Using the Back and Forward Buttons

When you start Firefox, the Back and Forward buttons and their arrows appear dimmed and are unavailable (see Figure 1-7 on page FX 9). When you visit the first Web page after starting Firefox, the Back button is no longer dimmed and is available for use. Pointing to the button changes the button to a three-dimensional button, indicating the button is active.

The following steps illustrate how to use the Back and Forward buttons to find previously displayed Web pages.

To Use the Back and Forward Buttons to Find Recently Displayed Web Pages

1

• **Click the Back button on the Navigation toolbar.**

A ScreenTip is displayed while you point to the Back button. Once you click the Back button, the Splendors of Imperial China Web page is displayed (Figure 1-18). The Back button is three-dimensional, the Forward button is active, and The Splendors of Imperial China Web page is not the last Web page visited in this session.

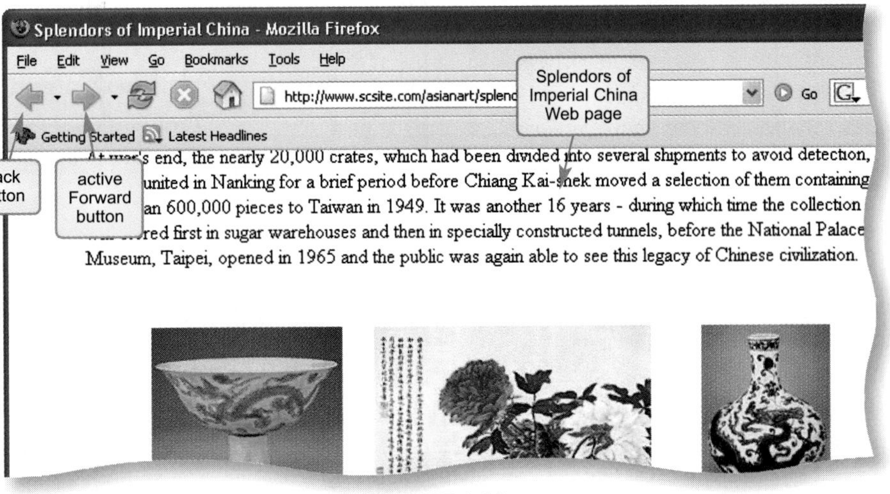

FIGURE 1-18

2

• **Click the Back button again.**

The Exhibitions Web page is displayed (Figure 1-19).

FIGURE 1-19

3

• **Click the Forward button on the Navigation toolbar.**

The Splendors of Imperial China Web page is displayed again (Figure 1-20).

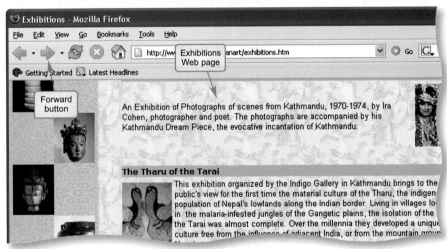

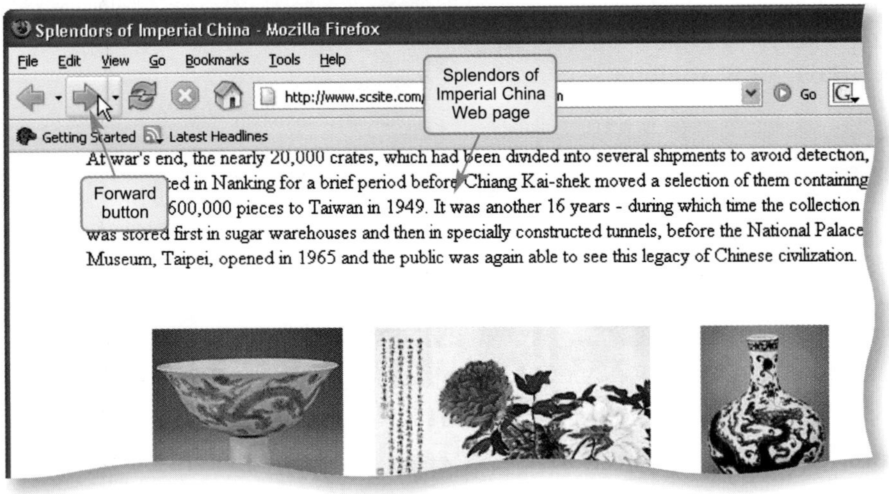

FIGURE 1-20

4

• **Click the Forward button again.**

The Splendors of Imperial China - Image 9 Web page is displayed (Figure 1-21). The Forward button is now inactive, which indicates there are no additional pages to which you can move forward.

inactive Forward button

Splendors of Imperial China – Image 9 Web page

FIGURE 1-21

You can continue to page backward until you reach the beginning of the Back button list. At that time, the Back button becomes inactive, which indicates that no additional pages to which you can move back are contained in the list. You can, however, move forward by clicking the Forward button.

You can see that traversing the list of pages is easy using the Back and Forward buttons. Because many pages may be displayed before the one you want to view, this method can be time-consuming.

Displaying a Web Page Using the Back Button List

It is possible to skip to any previously visited page by clicking its title in the Back button list. Thus, you can find a recently visited page without displaying an intermediate page, as shown in the following steps.

To Display a Web Page Using the Back Button List

1

• **Right-click the Back button on the Navigation toolbar.**

The Back button list displays a list of titles of Web pages you visited during this session beginning with the most recent (Figure 1-22). The list may be different on your computer.

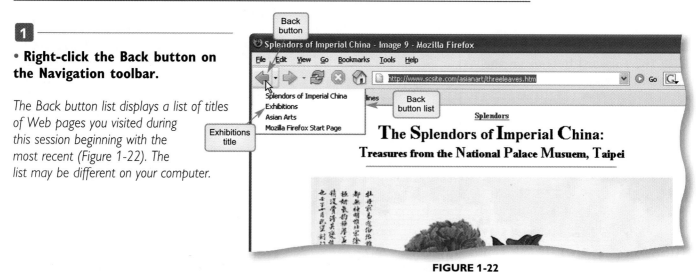

Back button

Back button list

Exhibitions title

FIGURE 1-22

2

- **Click Exhibitions on the Back button list.**

Firefox displays the Exhibitions Web page (Figure 1-23). Both the Back and Forward buttons are active, indicating there are Web pages to which you can move backward or forward.

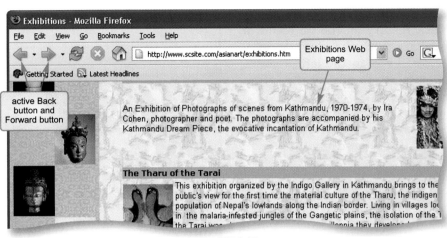

FIGURE 1-23

If you have a small list of pages you have visited, or the Web page you wish to view is only one or two pages away, using the Back and Forward buttons to traverse the lists probably is faster than displaying the Back button list and selecting the correct title. If you have visited a large number of pages, however, the list will be long, and it may be easier to use the Back button list to select the exact page.

Using the History Sidebar to Display Web Pages

Firefox maintains another list of Web pages visited on the History sidebar. The **History sidebar** contains an alphabetical list of Web pages visited over the last nine days (over many sessions). You can use this list to display Web pages you may have accessed during that time. Clicking History on the Go menu displays the History sidebar.

To find a recently visited Web page using the History sidebar, first display the History sidebar, and then click the desired Web page title, as shown in the following steps.

To Display a Web Page Using the History Sidebar

1

- **Click Go on the menu bar.**

Firefox displays the Go menu (Figure 1-24).

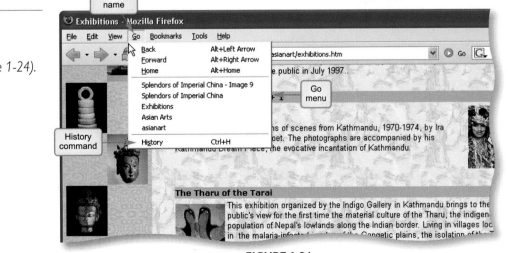

FIGURE 1-24

2

• **Click History on the Go menu. If necessary, click the plus sign in the small box to the left of the Today folder to display the contents of the Today folder.**

The History sidebar is displayed (Figure 1-25). Indented below the Today folder on the History sidebar are the names of the Web pages you viewed in the Asian Arts Web site.

FIGURE 1-25

3

• **Click Asian Arts in the Today folder.**

The Asian Arts Web page is displayed (Figure 1-26). The mouse pointer points to the highlighted Asian Arts title in the Today folder and the Web page title on the title bar and URL on the Location bar change.

4

• **Click the Close button on the History sidebar.**

The History sidebar closes.

FIGURE 1-26

Other Ways

1. On View menu point to Sidebar, click History on Sidebar submenu
2. Press CTRL+H
3. Press ALT+G, press S
4. Press ALT+V, press E, S

If you have a small History list or the page you want is only one or two pages away, you can display a Web page more quickly using the Back and Forward buttons than displaying the History sidebar and then selecting individual pages. If you have visited a large number of Web pages, however, the Back and Forward lists will be long, and you may find it easier to use the History sidebar to find the precise page to display.

The History sidebar is useful for returning to a Web page you have visited recently. You can set the number of days Firefox keeps the URLs on the History sidebar by using the Options command on the Tools menu (see Appendix C). Because the History sidebar is occasionally cleared, you should not use the History sidebar to permanently store the URLs of favorite or frequently visited pages.

You can see from the previous figures that URLs can be long and cryptic. It is easy to make a mistake while entering such URLs. Fortunately, you can use Firefox to keep track of favorite Web pages. You can store the URLs of favorite Web pages permanently on the Bookmarks sidebar.

Keeping Track of Favorite Web Pages

The Bookmarks feature of Firefox allows you to save the URLs of favorite Web pages. A **bookmark** consists of the title of the Web page and the URL of that page. The title of the Web page is added to the Bookmarks list, which you can access from the Bookmarks menu and from the Bookmarks sidebar. The following steps show how to add the Asian Arts Web page to the Bookmarks sidebar.

More About

Bookmarks

You can change the name that identifies a bookmark. Click Bookmarks on the menu bar, click Manage Bookmarks, right-click the bookmark you want to change in the Bookmarks Manager dialog box and then click Properties. When the Properties for dialog box displays, type the new bookmark name in the Name text box and click the OK button. You also can rearrange the order of your bookmarks by dragging a bookmark to another location in the Bookmarks Manager dialog box.

To Add a Web Page to the Bookmarks Sidebar

1

• **Click View on the menu bar, point to Sidebar on the View menu, and then point to Bookmarks on the Sidebar submenu.**

The View menu is displayed, the Sidebar command is selected, and the Bookmarks command is selected on the Sidebar submenu (Figure 1-27).

FIGURE 1-27

2

• **Click Bookmarks on the Sidebar submenu.**

Firefox displays the Bookmarks sidebar (Figure 1-28). The Bookmarks sidebar on your computer may contain a different list of Web sites.

FIGURE 1-28

3

• **Click Bookmarks on the menu bar and then point to Bookmark This Page.**

The Bookmarks menu is displayed and the Bookmark This Page command is selected (Figure 1-29). The Bookmarks menu may look different on your computer.

FIGURE 1-29

4

• **Click Bookmark This Page on the Bookmarks menu.**

Firefox displays the Add Bookmark dialog box (Figure 1-30). The Name text box contains the title of the Asian Arts Web page and the Create in box contains the Bookmarks folder, where the Asian Arts bookmark will be stored.

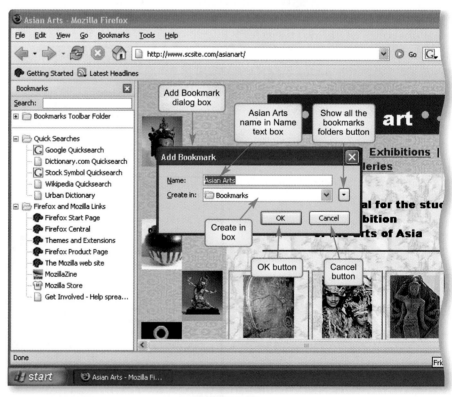

FIGURE 1-30

5

• **Click the OK button in the Add Bookmark dialog box.**

The Add Bookmark dialog box closes and the Asian Arts bookmark is added to the Bookmarks sidebar (Figure 1-31).

6

• **Click the Close button on the Bookmarks sidebar.**

The Bookmarks sidebar closes.

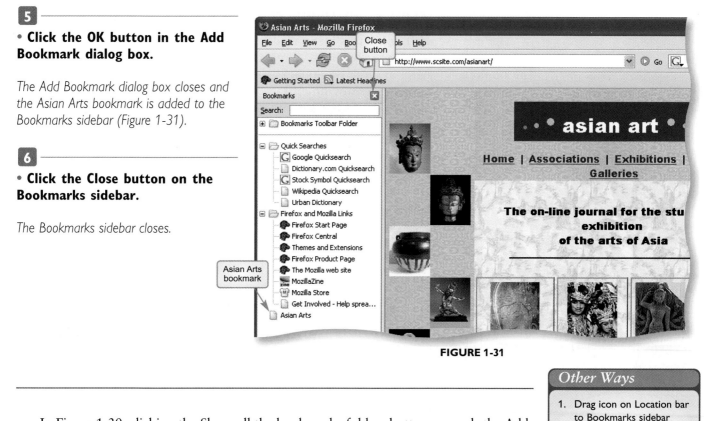

FIGURE 1-31

In Figure 1-30, clicking the Show all the bookmarks folders button expands the Add Bookmark dialog box, displays a hierarchy of the Bookmarks, and allows you to select a folder in which to store a bookmark. You also can change the name of the bookmark being added by highlighting the name in the Name text box and typing the new name.

> **Other Ways**
> 1. Drag icon on Location bar to Bookmarks sidebar
> 2. Press ALT+B, press B, press ENTER
> 3. Press CTRL+D, press ENTER

Using the Home Button to Display a Web Page

At anytime, you can display the Home Page in the display area using the Home button on the Navigation toolbar. The following step shows how to display the Firefox Home Page (Firefox Start Page).

To Display the Home Page Using the Home Button

1

• **Click the Home button on the Navigation toolbar.**

The Firefox Start Page is displayed in the Mozilla Firefox Start Page - Mozilla Firefox window and the URL for the Home Page is displayed on the Location bar (Figure 1-32).

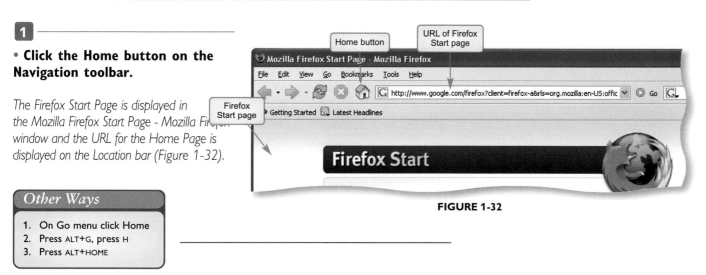

FIGURE 1-32

> **Other Ways**
> 1. On Go menu click Home
> 2. Press ALT+G, press H
> 3. Press ALT+HOME

Displaying a Web Page Using the Bookmarks Menu

You can use the Bookmarks menu to display favorite or frequently accessed Web pages quickly, without having to navigate through several unwanted pages. The Bookmarks menu and the Bookmarks sidebar contain the same list of bookmarks. The following steps show how to use the Bookmarks menu to display the Asian Arts Web page.

To Display a Web Page Using the Bookmarks Menu

1

• **Click Bookmarks on the menu bar and then point to Asian Arts.**

The Bookmarks menu is displayed and the Asian Arts command is selected (Figure 1-33). Other folders and bookmarks may display in the Bookmarks menu on your computer.

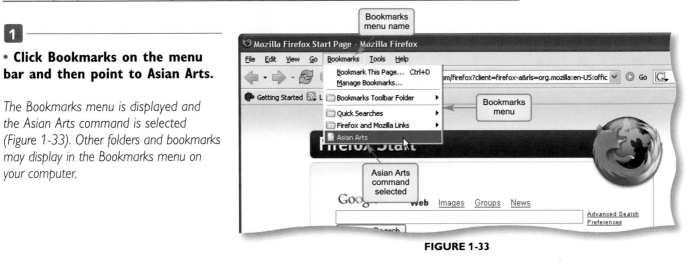

FIGURE 1-33

2

• **Click Asian Arts in the Bookmarks menu.**

The Asian Arts Web page again is visible in the display area and the Asian Arts URL is displayed on the Location bar (Figure 1-34).

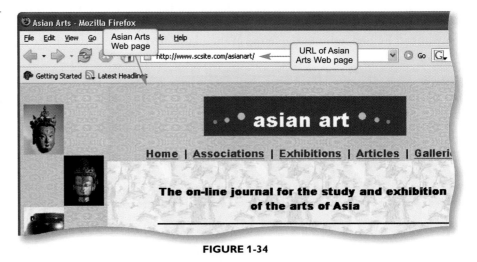

FIGURE 1-34

Other Ways

1. Press ALT+B, click bookmark
2. Press CTRL+B, click bookmark

Additional bookmarks and folders are displayed in the Bookmarks menu in Figure 1-33. Among the folders is the Bookmarks Toolbar Folder that contains entries corresponding to the buttons on the Bookmarks toolbar and the Quick Searches folder that contains a list of various search tools. The Firefox and Mozilla Links folder provides links to various Firefox and Mozilla resources. Below the three folders is the Asian Arts bookmark.

You have learned how to add a URL to the Bookmarks list and how to retrieve a Web page using the Bookmarks menu. As you gain experience and continue to browse the World Wide Web and add bookmarks, it is likely that in time you will want to remove unwanted bookmarks from the list.

Removing Bookmarks

There are several reasons for removing a bookmark. With the World Wide Web changing everyday, the URL that worked today may not work tomorrow. Or perhaps you just do not want a particular bookmark in the list anymore, or maybe the list is getting too big to be meaningful. The following steps show how to remove a bookmark from the Bookmarks menu.

To Remove a Web Page from the Bookmarks Menu

1

• **Click Bookmarks on the menu bar and then point to Asian Arts.**

The Bookmarks menu is displayed and the Asian Arts bookmark is selected (Figure 1-35).

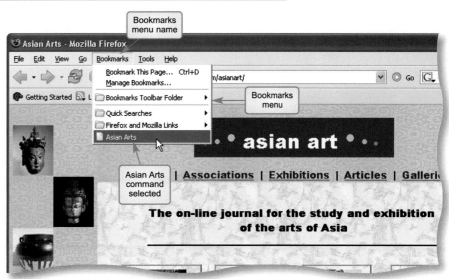

FIGURE 1-35

2

• **Right-click Asian Arts in the Bookmarks menu.**

A shortcut menu containing the Delete command is displayed (Figure 1-36).

3

• **Click Delete on the shortcut menu.**

The Asian Arts bookmark is removed and the Bookmarks menu is closed.

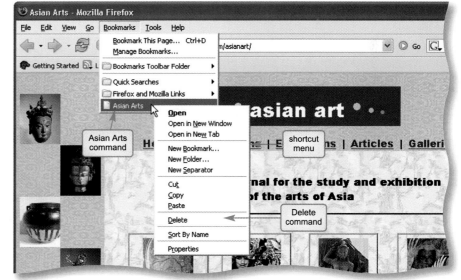

FIGURE 1-36

Other Ways

1. On Bookmarks menu click Manage Bookmarks, click bookmark, click Delete button, click Close button
2. Press CTRL+B, right-click bookmark, click Delete

More About

RSS Feeds

If you navigate to a site that provides an RSS feed, the orange Add Live Bookmark for this page's feed will display on the right side of the status bar in the Mozilla Firefox window. Clicking this icon will allow you to subscribe to the RSS feed and add a Live Bookmark.

Using the commands on the shortcut menu can help you manage bookmarks. Firefox also provides advanced features for handling bookmarks. For example, you can create folders that allow you to organize the list of bookmarks into categories. In Figure 1-33 on page FX 26, you can see three folders (Bookmarks Toolbar Folder, Quick Searches, and Firefox and Mozilla Links) that help you organize bookmarks. You can create additional folders using the Manage Bookmarks command on the Bookmarks menu. In addition to organizing bookmarks, Firefox also allows you to add Live Bookmarks. **Live Bookmarks** allow you to view the latest news headlines from your favorite sites using an RSS feed. **RSS**, or Rich Site Summary, is a format used when a Web site wishes to allow other sites or programs to utilize a portion of its content.

You have learned to create, use, and remove bookmarks. Saving URLs as bookmarks is not the only way to save information you obta in using Firefox. Some of the more interesting text and pictures you locate while displaying Web pages also are worth saving.

Saving Information Obtained with Firefox

Many different types of Web pages are accessible on the World Wide Web. Because these pages can help accumulate information about areas of interest, you may wish to save the information you discover for future reference. The different types of Web pages and the different ways you may want to use them require different methods of saving. Firefox allows you to save an entire Web page, individual pictures, or selected pieces of text. The following pages illustrate how to save an entire Web page, how to save a single picture, and how to save text.

Saving a Web Page

One method of saving information on a Web page is to save the entire Web page. The following steps show how to save the Asian Arts Web page on a floppy disk in drive A.

To Save a Web Page

1

• **With a formatted floppy disk in drive A, click File on the menu bar.**

The File menu is displayed (Figure 1-37). The Save Page As command is displayed on the File menu.

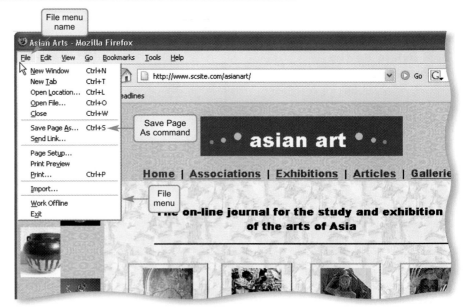

FIGURE 1-37

2

• **Click Save Page As on the File menu.**

Firefox displays the Save As dialog box. The Save in box contains the Desktop entry and the File name text box contains the name of the new file, Asian Arts (Figure 1-38). The Save As dialog box also may display file extensions on your computer. You can type a new file name in the File name box. The Desktop entry in the Save in box may be different on your computer.

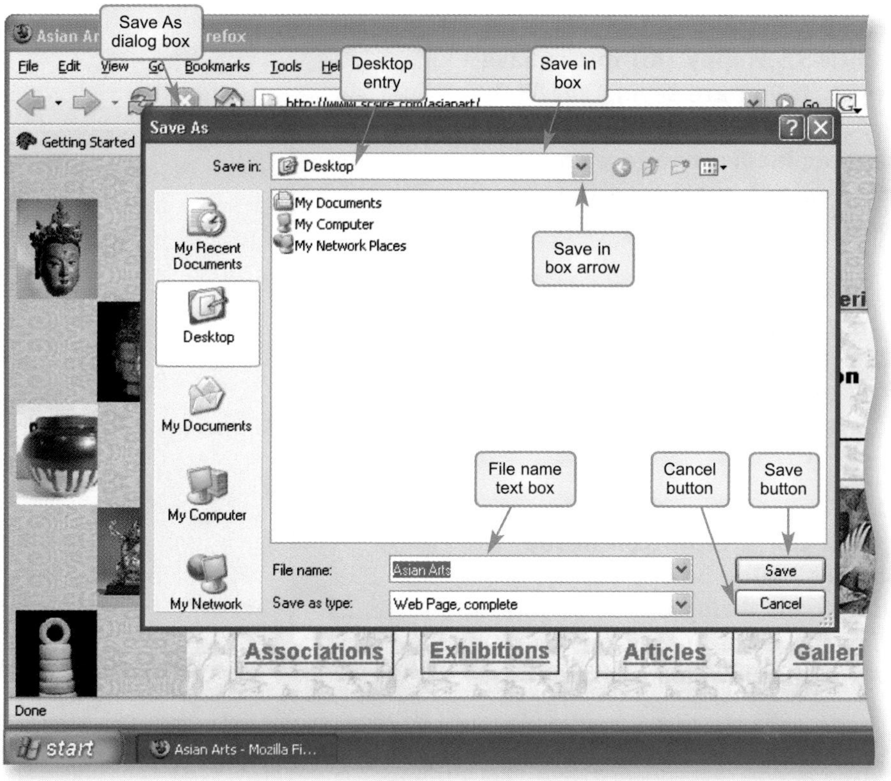

FIGURE 1-38

3

• **Click the Save in box arrow in the Save As dialog box.**

The Save in list contains various components of the computer with the Desktop entry highlighted (Figure 1-39).

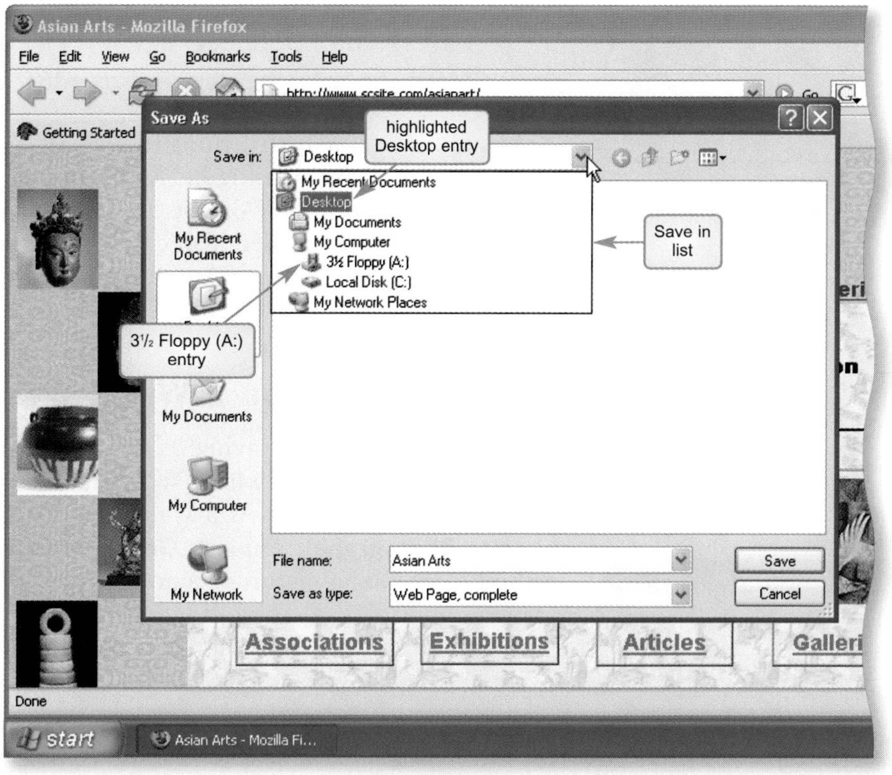

FIGURE 1-39

4

• **Click 3½ Floppy (A:) in the Save in list. If you are saving the Web page to another location or onto another media, navigate to that location and substitute the location for 3½ Floppy (A:).**

The highlighted 3½ Floppy (A:) drive name is displayed in the Save in box (Figure 1-40). The entry in the Save as type box, Web Page, complete, determines how the Web page is saved.

5

• **Click the Save button in the Save As dialog box. If the Downloads dialog box is displayed, click the Close button on the title bar of the Downloads dialog box.**

The Save As dialog box closes and the Asian Arts Web page is saved using the file name Asian Arts.htm on the floppy disk in drive A.

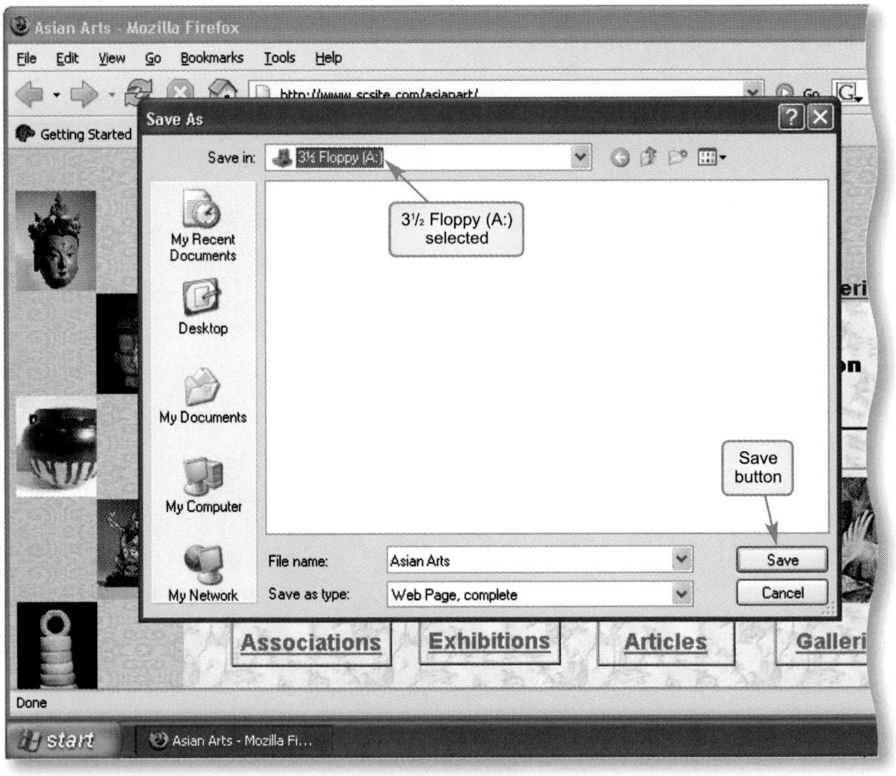

FIGURE 1-40

Other Ways

1. Press ALT+F, press A
2. Press CTRL+S

Firefox saves the instructions to display the saved Web page in the Asian Arts.htm file in drive A using HTML codes (see Figure 1-5 on page FX 7), creates the Asian Arts_files folder on the 3½ Floppy (A:) disk, and saves the pictures from the Web page in that folder. You can view the saved Web page in the Firefox window by double-clicking the Asian Arts.htm file and view a list of saved pictures by double-clicking the Asian Arts_files folder.

Saving a Picture on a Web Page

A second method of saving information is to save a picture located on a Web page, without saving the whole Web page. In the following steps, the Galleries picture located on the Asian Arts Web page is saved on the floppy disk in drive A using the **Joint Photographic Experts Group (JPEG)** format. The JPEG file format is a method of encoding pictures on a computer. When you save a picture as a JPEG file, Firefox can display it. The following steps show how to save the Galleries picture on a floppy disk in drive A in the JPEG format using the file name galleries.jpg.

More About

Setting a Picture as a Background

In addition to saving a picture, you also can set a picture as a background on your desktop by right-clicking the image and clicking Set as Wallpaper. The image is displayed on the desktop.

To Save a Picture on a Web Page

1

• **Right-click the Galleries picture on the Asian Arts Web site.**

A shortcut menu, containing the Save Image As command, is displayed (Figure 1-41).

FIGURE 1-41

2

• **Click Save Image As on the shortcut menu.**

The Save Image dialog box is displayed (Figure 1-42). The Save in box contains the 3½ Floppy (A:) drive name, the File name text box contains the image06 file name, and the Save as type box contains the JPEG Image file type. The Asian Arts_files folder contains the saved Asian Arts Web page from the last set of steps.

3

• **Click the Save button in the Save Image dialog box. If you are saving the Web page to another location or onto another media, navigate to that location and substitute the location for 3¹⁄₂ Floppy (A:).**

The picture is saved using the image06.jpg file name on the floppy disk in drive A and the Save Image dialog box closes.

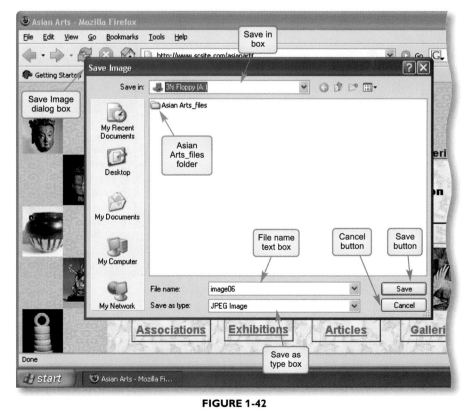

FIGURE 1-42

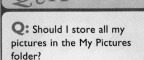

Mozilla
Firefox

Q: Should I store all my pictures in the My Pictures folder?

A: Yes. You can use folders within the My Pictures folder to organize your pictures and you easily can back up the folders to another storage device for safekeeping. Three other folders (My Documents, My Videos, and My Music) are available to store documents, videos, and music files, respectively.

Copying and Pasting Using the Clipboard

A third method of saving information, called the **copy and paste method**, allows you to copy an entire Web page, or portions thereof, and insert the information in any Windows document. The **Clipboard**, which is a temporary storage area in a computer's main memory, temporarily holds the information being copied. The portion of the Web page you select is **copied** from the Web page to the Clipboard and then **pasted** from the Clipboard into the document. Information you copy to the Clipboard remains there until you add more information or clear it.

The following pages demonstrate how to copy text and pictures from the Exhibitions Web page into a WordPad document using the Clipboard. **WordPad** is a word processing program that comes with Microsoft Windows.

Starting WordPad

Before copying information from the Web page in Firefox to the Clipboard, it's helpful to start WordPad. The following steps illustrate how to start WordPad.

To Start WordPad

1

• **Click the Start button on the Windows taskbar, point to All Programs on the Start menu, point to Accessories on the All Programs submenu, and then point to WordPad on the Accessories submenu.**

The Start menu, All Programs submenu, and Accessories submenu are displayed (Figure 1-43).

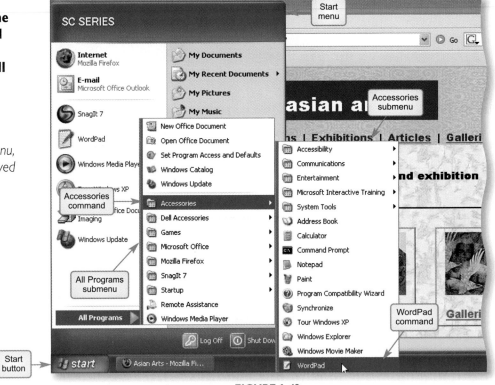

FIGURE 1-43

2

• **Click WordPad.**

Windows starts WordPad, opens the active Document - WordPad window on top of the inactive Asian Arts - Mozilla Firefox window, and displays the Document - WordPad button on the taskbar (Figure 1-44). An empty WordPad document, into which the text can be pasted, is displayed in the Document - WordPad window. An insertion point is displayed in the empty document.

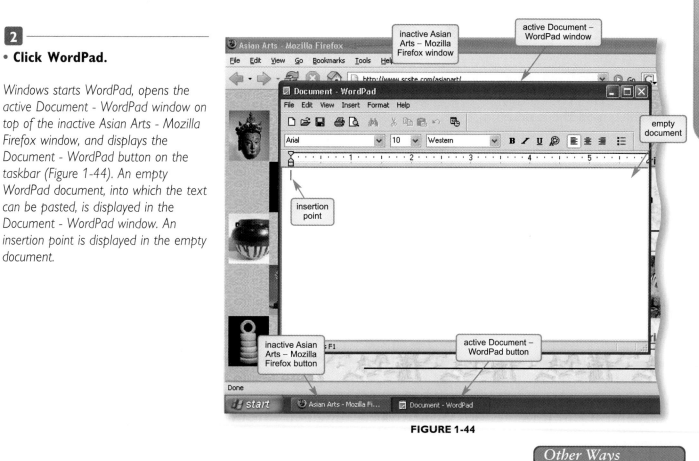

FIGURE 1-44

The Document - WordPad window is displayed on top of the Asian Arts - Mozilla Firefox window. The Document - WordPad window is the active window. The **active window** is the window currently being used. A dark blue title bar and a dark blue taskbar button identify the active window. The Asian Arts - Mozilla Firefox window is the inactive window. A light blue title bar and a light blue taskbar button identify the **inactive window**.

Using a Taskbar Button to Display an Inactive Window

Currently, the active Document - WordPad window is displayed on top of the inactive Asian Arts - Mozilla Firefox window. After starting WordPad and before copying text from a Web page to the Clipboard, display the Asian Arts - Mozilla Firefox window and then display the Exhibitions Web page. The steps on the next page show how to display the Exhibitions Web page.

Other Ways

1. Click Start button, click Run, type wordpad, click OK button

Mozilla Firefox

To Display the Exhibitions Web Page

1

• **Click the Asian Arts - Mozilla Firefox button on the taskbar.**

The active Asian Arts - Mozilla Firefox window is displayed on top of the inactive Document - WordPad window (Figure 1-45). Although not visible, the inactive window is still open, as evidenced by the taskbar button. The display area contains the Asian Arts Web page.

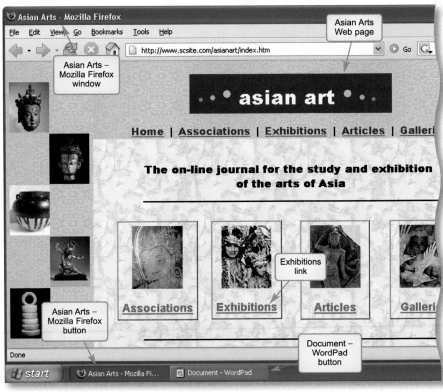

FIGURE 1-45

2

• **Click the Exhibitions link on the Asian Arts Web page.**

The Exhibitions Web page is displayed (Figure 1-46). The window title and taskbar button name change.

FIGURE 1-46

Other Ways

1. Press ALT+TAB
2. If visible, click window title bar

With the Document - WordPad window open and the text you wish to copy contained on the Exhibitions Web page, the next steps are to scroll the display area to display the text to be copied, copy the text from the Exhibitions Web page to the Clipboard, and then paste the text into the WordPad document.

Copying Text from a Web Page and Pasting It into a WordPad Document

The following steps show how to copy the text about The Splendors of Imperial China to the Clipboard, switch to WordPad, and paste the text from the Clipboard into the WordPad document.

To Copy and Paste Text from a Web Page into a WordPad Document

1

• **Scroll the Exhibitions Web page to display The Splendors of Imperial China: Treasures from the National Palace Museum, Taipei link.**

• **Position the mouse pointer (I-beam) at the beginning of the text that follows the link text.**

The Splendors of Imperial China: Treasures from the National Palace Museum, Taipei link is displayed (Figure 1-47).

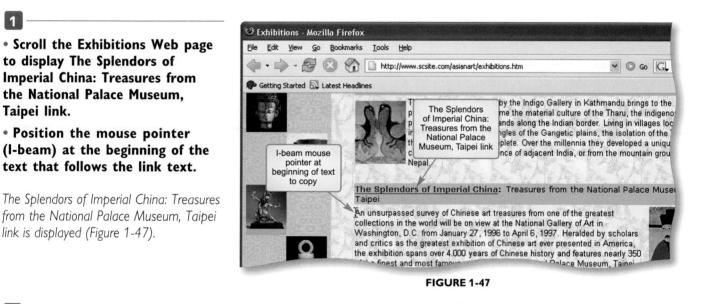

FIGURE 1-47

2

• **Drag to select the text that follows the link text.**

• **Right-click the highlighted text.**

Firefox highlights the selected text and displays a shortcut menu (Figure 1-48).

FIGURE 1-48

3

• **Click Copy on the shortcut menu.**

Firefox closes the shortcut menu and copies the selected text to the Clipboard.

• **Click the Document - WordPad button on the Windows taskbar and then right-click the empty text area in the Document - WordPad window.**

Firefox displays the Document - WordPad window and a shortcut menu (Figure 1-49).

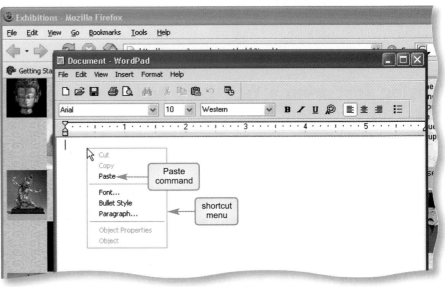

FIGURE 1-49

4

• **Click Paste on the shortcut menu.**

WordPad closes the shortcut menu and pastes the contents of the Clipboard into the Document - WordPad window (Figure 1-50).

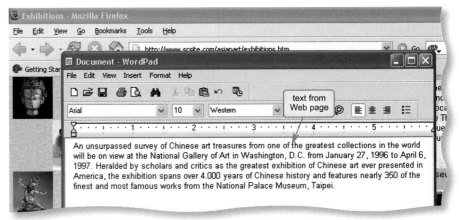

FIGURE 1-50

The text portion of the copy and paste operation is complete. The WordPad document contains a paragraph of text retrieved from a Web page.

Copying a Picture from a Web Page and Pasting It into WordPad

The steps to copy a picture from a Web page are similar to those used to copy and paste text. The following steps show how to copy and then paste a picture from a Web page into a WordPad document.

To Copy and Paste a Picture from a Web Page into a WordPad Document

1

- **Click the Exhibitions - Mozilla Firefox button on the Windows taskbar.**

- **Click outside the selected text to deselect the text.**

- **Right-click the picture to the right of the text.**

The Exhibitions - Mozilla Firefox window is displayed, the selected text in the window is deselected, and a shortcut menu is displayed (Figure 1-51).

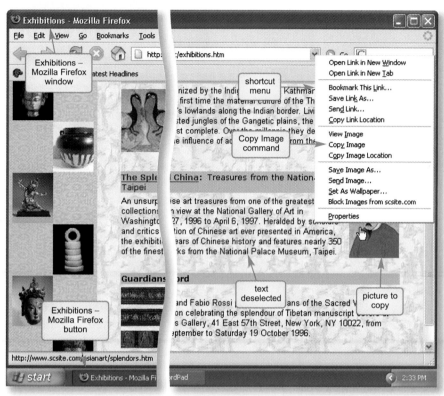

FIGURE 1-51

2

- **Click Copy Image on the shortcut menu.**

Firefox closes the shortcut menu and copies the picture to the Clipboard.

- **Click the Document - WordPad button on the taskbar.**

- **Press the ENTER key twice.**

- **Right-click the insertion point in the Document - WordPad window.**

The Document - WordPad window and a shortcut menu is displayed (Figure 1-52). The Paste command is displayed on the shortcut menu.

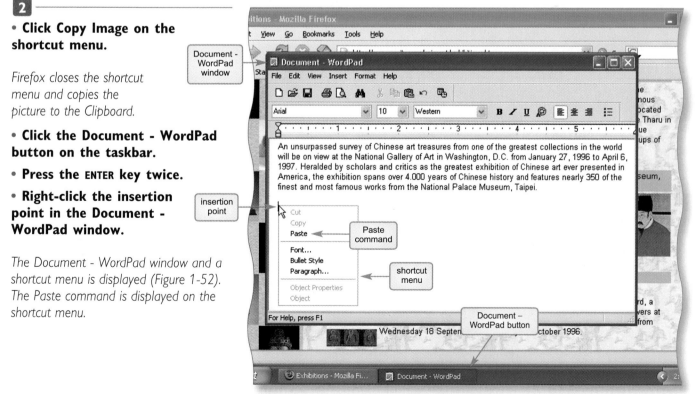

FIGURE 1-52

3

• **Click Paste on the shortcut menu.**

WordPad pastes the contents of the Clipboard in the Document - WordPad window at the location of the insertion point (Figure 1-53). After pasting the picture, you can resize the picture by dragging the corners or borders of the picture in toward the center of the picture to make it smaller or outward from the center to make it larger.

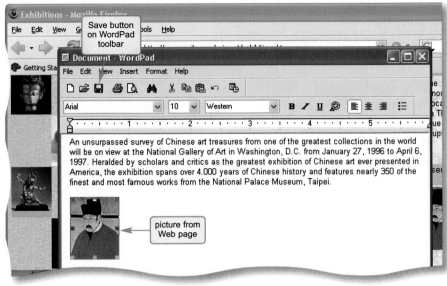

FIGURE 1-53

The copy and paste operations are complete. The WordPad window contains text and a picture retrieved from the Exhibitions Web page. You can use the tools provided with WordPad to manipulate the picture and text.

Saving the WordPad Document and Quitting WordPad

When you are finished with the WordPad document, you can save it on a floppy disk for later use and then quit WordPad. The following steps illustrate how to save the WordPad document using the Splendors of Imperial China file name and quit WordPad.

To Save the WordPad Document and Quit WordPad

1

• **Click the Save button on the WordPad toolbar in the Document - WordPad window.**

WordPad displays the Save As dialog box (Figure 1-54). The Save in box contains the 3½ Floppy (A:) entry and the File name box contains the highlighted Document file name.

FIGURE 1-54

2

• **Type** Splendors of Imperial China **in the File name text box.**

The 3½ Floppy (A:) drive name is displayed in the Save in box, the Splendors of Imperial China file name is displayed in the File name box, and the Rich Text Format (RTF) file type in the Save as type box determines how the document is saved (Figure 1-55).

3

• **Click the Save button in the Save As dialog box.**

The Save As dialog box closes and WordPad saves the Splendors of Imperial China document on the floppy disk in drive A.

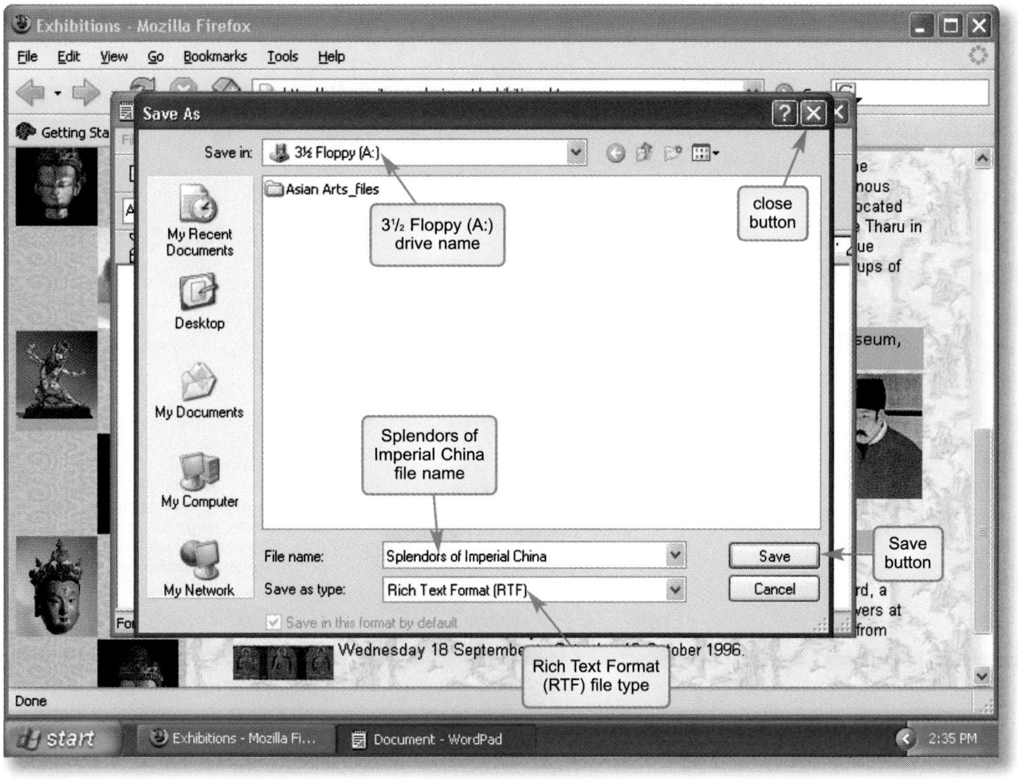

• **Click the Close button on the Splendors of Imperial China - WordPad title bar to quit WordPad.**

The WordPad window closes and the Exhibitions window is visible on the desktop.

FIGURE 1-55

Computer users commonly search for and save text and pictures found on the World Wide Web to a disk for use in the future.

Other Ways

1. Press ALT+F, press A, type file name, press ENTER
2. Press CTRL+S, type file name, press ENTER

Printing a Web Page in Firefox

As you visit Web sites, you may want to print some of the pages you view. A printed version of a Web page is called a **hard copy** or **printout**. You might want a printout for several reasons. First, to present the Web page to someone who does not have access to a computer, it must be in printed form. Second, persons other than those who prepare them often keep Web pages for reference. In some cases, Web pages are printed and kept in binders for use by others.

You can use Firefox to print both the text and pictures of a Web page. In the following steps, you will print the Exhibitions Web Page and two pieces of paper will print on the printer (Figure 1-58 on page FX 41). The following steps show how to print the Exhibitions Web page.

More About

Printing

You can suppress the title and URL of a Web page that are displayed on a printout using the Page Setup command on the File menu. The Headers & Footers dropdown lists contain options that indicate what items are displayed.

To Print a Web Page

1

• **Ready the printer according to the printer instructions.**

• **Click File on the menu bar and then point to Print.**

The File menu is displayed and the Print command is selected (Figure 1-56).

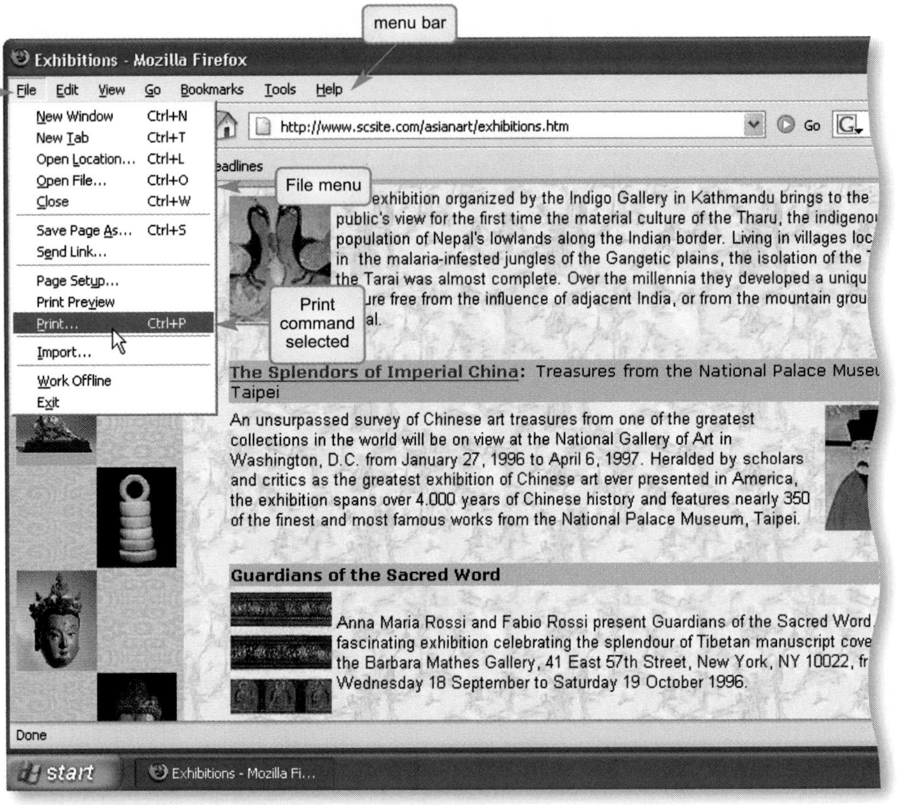

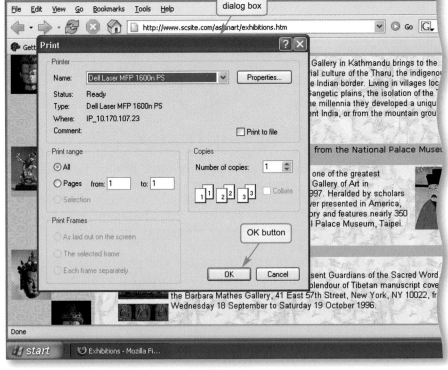

FIGURE 1-56

2

• **Click Print on the File menu.**

The Print dialog box is displayed (Figure 1-57).

FIGURE 1-57

3

• **Click the OK button in the Print dialog box.**

• **When the printer stops printing the document, retrieve the printouts.**

The Web page title is displayed in the upper-left corner of each page, the URL is displayed in the upper-right corner of each page, the page number and total number of pages in the Web site are displayed in the lower-left corner of each page, and the date and time are displayed in the lower-right corner (Figure 1-58).

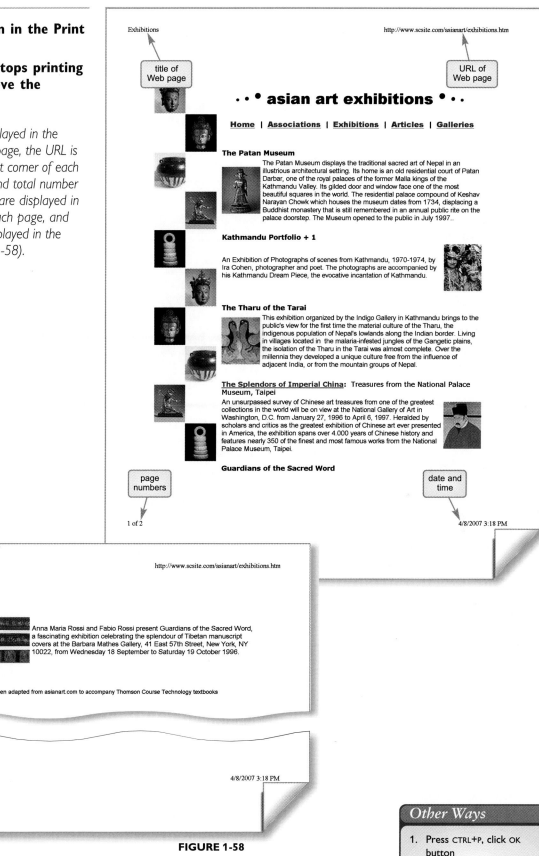

FIGURE 1-58

Firefox Help

Firefox is a program with many features and options. Although you will master some of these quickly, it is not necessary for you to remember everything about each one of them. Reference materials and other forms of assistance are available within Firefox Help. You can display these materials and learn how to use the multitude of features available with Firefox. The following steps illustrate how to use Firefox Help to find more information about using Mozilla Firefox.

To Access Firefox Help

1

• **Click Help on the menu bar.**

The Help menu is displayed (Figure 1-59). Several commands provide helpful information about Firefox.

2

• **Click Help Contents on the Help menu. If necessary, maximize the Mozilla Firefox Help dialog box.**

The Mozilla Firefox Help window contains the Help toolbar, Help sidebar, and display area (Figure 1-60). The Help sidebar contains four tabs (Glossary, Index, Search, and Contents) and the display area contains Help information. The Glossary sheet defines key terms, Index sheet contains an index of Help topics, Search sheet allows you to search for specific Help topics, and Contents sheet contains main topics and subtopics.

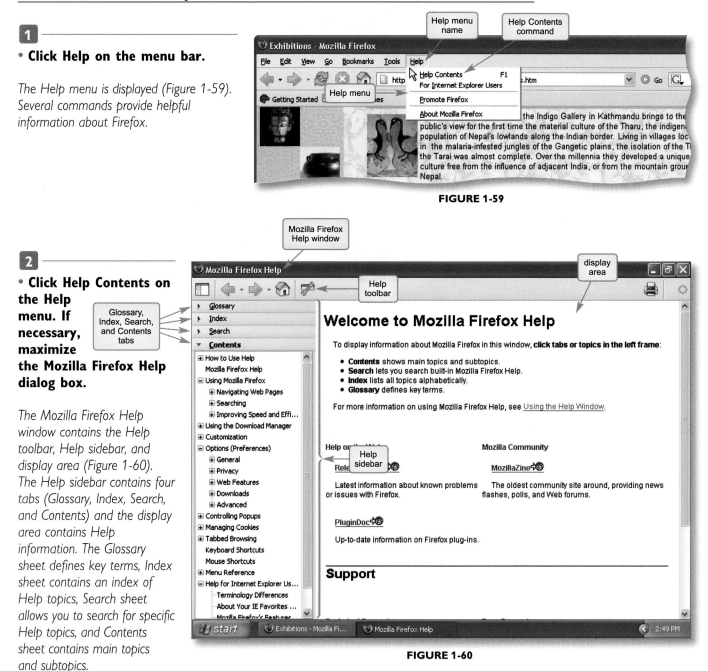

FIGURE 1-59

FIGURE 1-60

3

• **Click the Index tab in the Help sidebar.**

The Index sheet is displayed in the Help sidebar (Figure 1-61). The Index sheet contains a list of Help topics.

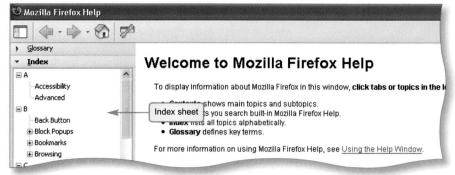

FIGURE 1-61

4

• **Scroll through the Index sheet to display the entry, Using Firefox.**

The Using Firefox entry is displayed on the Index sheet (Figure 1-62). To see additional entries in the Index sheet, use the scroll bar at the right of the Index sheet.

FIGURE 1-62

5

• **Click Using Firefox in the Index sheet.**

The Using Mozilla Firefox screen is displayed in the display area (Figure 1-63).

6

• **When you are finished viewing the information, click the Close button on the right side of the title bar to close the Mozilla Firefox Help window.**

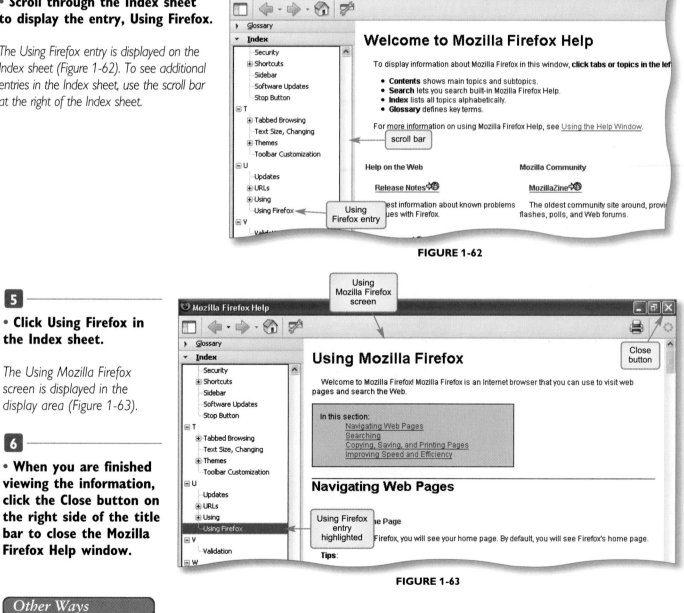

FIGURE 1-63

In Figure 1-60 on page FX 42, buttons on the Help toolbar in the Mozilla Firefox Help window allow you to perform activities such as hiding the Help sidebar, navigating among previously displayed Help topics, going to the Help Start Page, and customizing the Help toolbar.

The Help menu shown in Figure 1-59 on page FX 42 contains several other commands, which are summarized in Table 1-4.

Table 1-4 Commands on the Help Menu	
MENU COMMAND	FUNCTION
Help Contents	Displays Glossary, Index, Search, and Contents tabs.
For Internet Explorer Users	Displays tips for Internet Explorer users.
Promote Firefox	Displays the Spread Firefox Web page.
About Mozilla Firefox	Displays version, copyright, and credits.

Quitting Firefox

After browsing the World Wide Web and learning how to manage Web pages, Project 1 is complete. The following steps illustrate how to quit Firefox.

To Quit Firefox

1

• **Click the Close button in the upper-right corner of the Mozilla Firefox window.**

The Mozilla Firefox window closes and the Windows desktop is displayed (Figure 1-64).

2

• **If necessary, remove the floppy disk from drive A.**

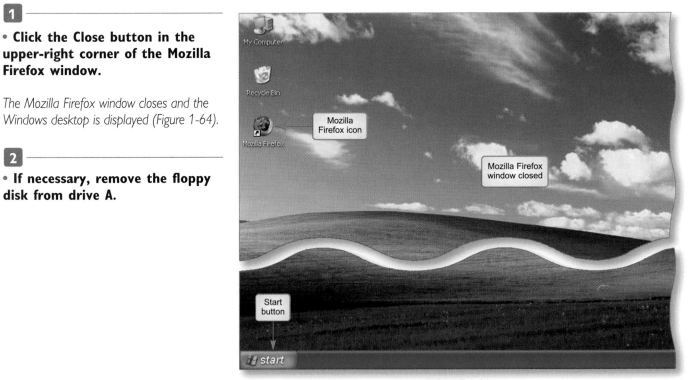

FIGURE 1-64

Other Ways

1. Double-click System menu icon at left end of title bar

Project Summary

Project 1 introduced you to the Internet and World Wide Web. You learned how to start Firefox and use the buttons on the Navigation toolbar, the Location bar, a URL, the History sidebar, and the Bookmarks sidebar to browse the World Wide Web. The project illustrated how to add and remove bookmarks; copy and paste text from a Web page into a WordPad document; save and print the document; and save text, a picture, and an entire Web page on disk. In addition, you learned how to use the Index sheet in Mozilla Firefox Help to obtain help about Firefox.

What You Should Know

Having completed the project, you now should be able to perform the tasks listed below. The tasks are listed in the same order they were presented in this project. For a list of the buttons, menus, toolbars, and commands introduced in this project, see the Quick Reference Summary at the back of this book and refer to the page number references that follow each of these tasks.

1. Start Firefox (FX 8)
2. Browse the Web by Entering a URL (FX 12)
3. Reload a Web Page (FX 16)
4. Use the Back and Forward Buttons to Find Recently Displayed Web Pages (FX 19)
5. Display a Web Page Using the Back Button List (FX 20)
6. Display a Web Page Using the History Sidebar (FX 21)
7. Add a Web Page to the Bookmarks Sidebar (FX 23)
8. Display the Home Page Using the Home Button (FX 25)
9. Display a Web Page Using the Bookmarks Menu (FX 26)
10. Remove a Web Page from the Bookmarks Menu (FX 27)
11. Save a Web Page (FX 28)
12. Save a Picture on a Web Page (FX 31)
13. Start WordPad (FX 32)
14. Display the Exhibitions Web Page (FX 34)
15. Copy and Paste Text from a Web Page into a WordPad Document (FX 35)
16. Copy and Paste a Picture from a Web Page into a WordPad Document (FX 37)
17. Save the WordPad Document and Quit WordPad (FX 38)
18. Print a Web Page (FX 40)
19. Access Firefox Help (FX 42)
20. Quit Firefox (FX 44)

Learn It Online

Instructions: To complete the Learn It Online exercises, start your browser, click the Location bar, enter scsite.com/firefox/learn, and then click the Go button. When the Firefox Learn It Online page is displayed, follow the instructions in the exercises below. Each exercise has instructions for printing your results, either for your own records or for submission to your instructor.

1 Project Reinforcement TF, MC, and SA

Below Firefox Project 1, click the Project Reinforcement link. Print the quiz by clicking Print on the File menu for each page. Answer each question.

2 Flash Cards

Below Firefox Project 1, click the Flash Cards link and read the instructions. Type 20 (or a number specified by your instructor) in the Number of Playing Cards text box, type your name in the Enter your name text box, and then click the Flip Card button. When the flash card is displayed, read the question and then click the answer box arrow to select an answer. Flip through Flash Cards. If your score is 15 (75%) correct or greater, click Print on the File menu to print your results. If your score is less than 15 (75%) correct, then redo this exercise by clicking the Replay button.

3 Practice Test

Below Firefox Project 1, click the Practice Test link. Answer each question, enter your first and last name at the bottom of the page, and then click the Grade Test button. When the graded practice test is displayed on your screen, click Print on the File menu to print a hard copy. Continue to take practice tests until you score 80% or better.

4 Who Wants To Be a Computer Genius?

Below Firefox Project 1, click the Who Wants to be a Computer Genius link. Read the instructions, enter your first and last name at the bottom of the page, and then click the PLAY button. When your score is displayed, click the Print Results link to print a hard copy.

5 Wheel of Terms

Below Firefox Project 1, click the Wheel of Terms link. Read the instructions and then enter your first and last name and your school name. Click the PLAY button. When your score is displayed, right-click the scores and then click Print on the shortcut menu to print a hard copy.

6 Crossword Puzzle Challenge

Below Firefox Project 1, click the Crossword Puzzle Challenge link. Read the instructions and then enter your first and last name. Click the SUBMIT button. Work the crossword puzzle. When you are finished, click the Submit button. When the crossword puzzle is displayed, click the Print Puzzle button to print a hard copy.

7 Tips and Tricks

Below Firefox Project 1, click the Tips and Tricks link. Click a topic that pertains to Project 1. Right-click the information and then click Print on the shortcut menu. Construct a brief example of what the information relates to in Firefox to confirm you understand how to use the tip or trick.

8 Newsgroups

Below Firefox Project 1, click the Newsgroups link. Click a topic that pertains to Project 1. Print three comments.

9 Expanding Your Horizons

Below Firefox Project 1, click the Expanding Your Horizons link. Click a topic that pertains to Project 1. Print the information. Construct a brief example of what the information relates to in Firefox to confirm you understand the contents of the article.

10 Search Sleuth

Below Firefox Project 1, click the Search Sleuth link. To search for a term that pertains to this project, select a term below the Project 1 title and then use the Google search engine at google.com (or any major search engine) to display and print two Web pages that present information on the term.

11 Firefox How-To Articles

Below Firefox Project 1, click the Firefox How-To Articles link. When your browser displays the Firefox How-To Articles Web page, scroll down and click one of the links that covers one or more of the objectives listed at the beginning of the project on page FX 2. Print the first page of the How-To article before stepping through it.

12 Getting More From the Web

Below Firefox Project 1, click the Getting More From the Web link. When your browser displays the Getting More from the Web with Firefox Web page, click one of the Top Stories or Featured Contents links. Print the first page.

In the Lab

1 Browsing the World Wide Web Using URLs and Links

Problem: You work part-time for *The Orlando Sentinel*, one of Florida's largest newspapers. Your editor has asked you to search for information on several informational Web sites and print the first page of each Web site.

Instructions: Perform the following tasks.

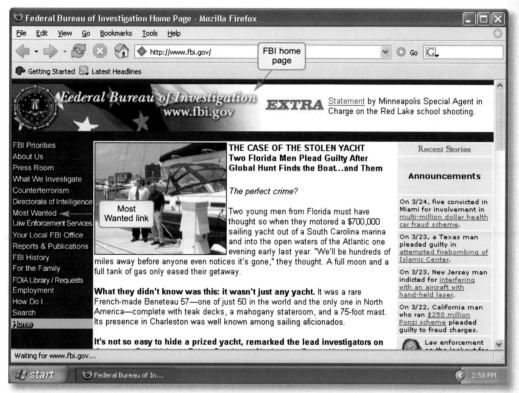

FIGURE 1-65

Part 1: *Using the Location Bar to Find a Web Page*

1. If necessary, connect to the Internet and start Firefox.
2. Click the Location bar, type www.fbi.gov, and then click the Go button to display the Federal Bureau of Investigation's home page (Figure 1-65).
3. Using links in the FBI Web site, find the Web page that contains the list of the ten most wanted fugitives.
4. Click Print on the File menu to print the Web page.
5. Use the Back button on the Navigation toolbar to display the FBI home page.
6. Click Print on the File menu to print the Web page.
7. Click the Location bar, type www.nbc.com, and then click the Go button to display the NBC home page.
8. Using links in the NBC Web site, find the Web page that lists the guest stars on the Tonight Show.
9. Click Print on the File menu to print the Web page.
10. Click the Location bar, type www.usatoday.com, and then click the Go button to display the USA TODAY home page.
11. Using links in the USA TODAY Web site, find the Web page that contains the United States weather map.

(continued)

In the Lab

Browsing the World Wide Web Using URLs and Links *(continued)*

12. Click Print on the File menu to print the Web page.
13. Click the Location bar, type `www.cbs.com`, and then click the Go button to display the CBS home page.
14. Using links in the CBS Web site, find the Web page that contains David Letterman's Top Ten List.
15. Click Print on the File menu to print the Web page.

Part 2: *Using the History Button to Find a Web Page*

1. Click the Home button on the Navigation toolbar to display your default Home Page.
2. Click the View menu on the menu bar, point to Sidebar on the View menu, and then click History on the Sidebar submenu.
3. If the contents of the Today folder are not displayed, click the Today folder in the History sidebar to show the contents of the Today folder.
4. Click NBC.com on the History sidebar to display the NBC home page.
5. Click Print on the File menu to print the Web page.
6. Click the Close button on the History sidebar.

Part 3: *Using the Back Button Arrow to Find a Web Page*

1. Right-click the Back button and then click the CBS.com entry on the menu to display the CBS home page.
2. Click Print on the File menu to print the Web page.

Part 4: *Using the Location Bar Arrow to Find a Web Page*

1. Click the Location bar arrow and then click http://www.usatoday.com in the Location bar list to display the USA TODAY home page.
2. Click Print on the File menu to print the Web page.
3. Click the Close button in the Mozilla Firefox window.
4. Discard the second page and subsequent pages of each Web site you printed. Organize the printed Web pages so the home page is first and the Web page associated with the home page is second. Hand in the eight printed pages to your instructor.

2 Working with the History Sidebar

Instructions: Perform the following tasks.

Problem: Your instructor would like you to practice browsing the Internet for Web sites and adding them to the History sidebar. As proof of completing this assignment, you should print the first page of each Web site you visit.

Part 1: *Clearing the History List*

1. If necessary, connect to the Internet and start Firefox to display the Mozila Firefox Start Page - Mozilla Firefox window (Figure 1-66).
2. Click Tools on the menu bar and then click Options to display the Options dialog box (Figure 1-66).

In the Lab

Tools menu name

FIGURE 1-66

3. Click Privacy in the left pane.
4. Click the Clear button in the History area in the Options dialog box.
5. Click the OK button in the Options dialog box.

Part 2: *Browsing the World Wide Web*

1. Click the Location bar, type `www.mtv.com` and then click the Go button to display the MTV.com home page.
2. Click the Location bar, type `www.ucf.edu` on the Location bar, and then click the Go button to display the University of Central Florida home page.
3. Click the Location bar, type `www.geocaching.com`, and then click the Go button to display the Geocaching home page.
4. Click the Location bar, type `www.espn.com`, and then click the Go button to display the ESPN home page.

Part 3: *Using the History Sidebar to Print a Web Page*

1. If the History sidebar is not displayed, click View on the menu bar, point to Sidebar on the View menu, and then click History on the Sidebar submenu (Figure 1-67 on the next page).

(continued)

In the Lab

Working with the History Sidebar *(continued)*

FIGURE 1-67

2. If the contents of the Today folder are not displayed, click the Today folder on the History sidebar to show the contents of the Today folder.
3. Click the University of Central Florida on the History sidebar. Print the Web page.
4. Click MTV.com - Home on the History sidebar. Print the Web page.
5. Click ESPN.com on the History sidebar. Print the Web page.
6. Delete Geocaching - The Official Global GPS Cache Hunt Site by right-clicking the item and clicking Delete on the shortcut menu.
7. Click the Close button on the History sidebar.

Part 4: *Clearing the History Sidebar*

1. Click Tools on the menu bar and then click Options to display the Options dialog box.
2. Click Privacy in the left pane.
3. Click the Clear button in the History area.
4. Click the OK button in the Options dialog box.
5. Click the Close button in the ESPN.com - Mozilla Firefox window.
6. Hand in the printed Web pages to your instructor.

3 Working with the Bookmarks Menu

Problem: Your instructor would like you to practice browsing the Internet for Web sites and adding them to the Bookmarks menu. As proof of completing this assignment, print out the first page of each Web site you visit.

Instructions: Perform the following tasks.

Part 1: *Creating a Folder in the Bookmarks Menu*

1. If necessary, connect to the Internet and start Firefox.
2. Click Bookmarks on the menu bar and then click Manage Bookmarks on the Bookmarks menu to display the Bookmarks Manager dialog box (Figure 1-68).

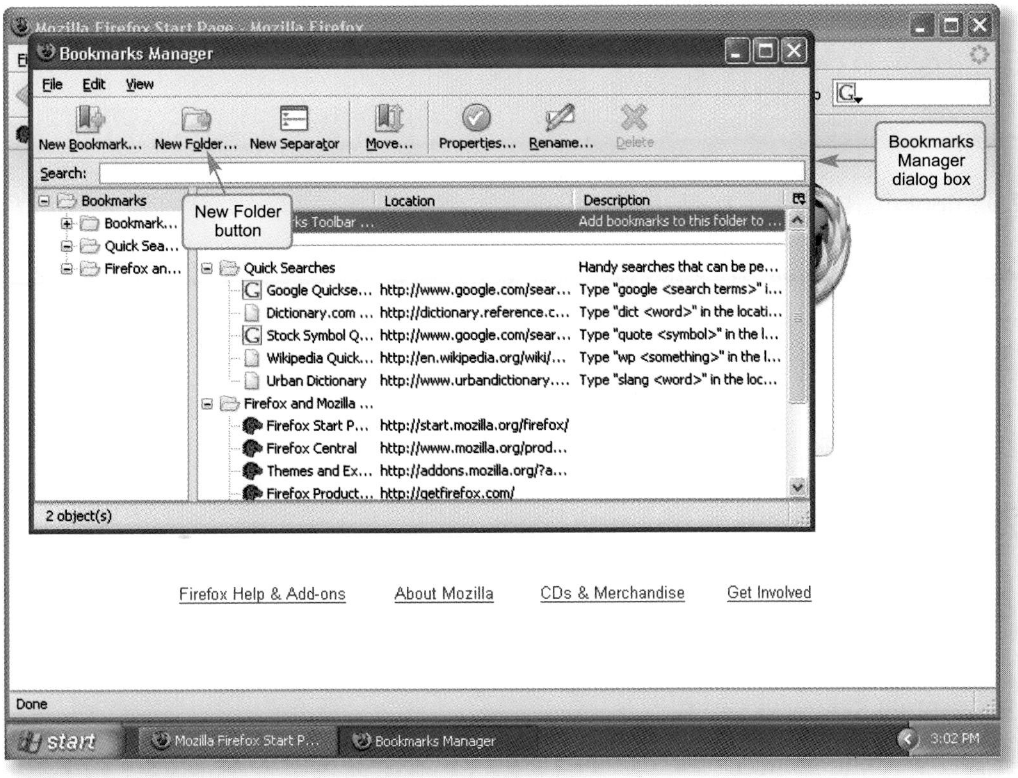

FIGURE 1-68

3. Click the New Folder button in the Bookmarks Manager dialog box to create a folder titled New Folder. When the Properties for "New Folder" dialog box is displayed, type your first and last name as the name, and then press the ENTER key.
4. Click the Close button to close the Bookmarks Manager dialog box.

Part 2: *Adding Bookmarks to Your Folder*

1. Click the Location bar, type www.hemingwayhome.com on the Location bar, and then click the Go button to display The Ernest Hemingway Home and Museum home page.
2. Add the Ernest Hemingway Home and Museum bookmark to your folder by clicking the Bookmark This Page command on the Bookmarks menu.

(continued)

In the Lab

Working with the Bookmarks Menu *(continued)*

3. Click your folder in the Create in list and then click the OK button.
4. Click the Location bar, type `www.priceline.com` on the Location bar, and then click the Go button to display the priceline.com home page.
5. Add this Web page to your folder.
6. Click the Home button on the Navigation toolbar to display your default Home Page.

Part 3: *Displaying and Printing a Bookmark from Your Folder*

1. Click Bookmarks on the menu bar.
2. Point to your folder in the Bookmarks menu and then click ERNEST HEMINGWAY HOME & MUSEUM in the submenu that is displayed.
3. Print the Web page.
4. Repeat Steps 1 and 2 to display the priceline.com Web page.
5. Print the Web page.

Part 4: *Deleting a Folder on the Bookmarks Menu*

1. Click Manage Bookmarks on the Bookmarks menu.
2. Click your folder name and then click the Delete button.
3. Click the Close button in the Bookmarks Manager dialog box.
4. Verify that you have deleted your folder.
5. Click the Close button in the Mozilla Firefox window.
6. Hand in the two printed pages to your instructor.

4 Saving a Web Page on a Floppy Disk

Problem: You work part-time at E*TRADE, one of the nation's largest online stockbrokers. Your supervisor asks you to research the current stock prices of several stocks. In the process, you are expected to find the stock prices, print Web pages containing the stock prices, and save the Web pages on a floppy disk.

Instructions: Perform the following tasks.

1. If necessary, connect to the Internet and start Firefox.
2. Click the Location bar, type `http://finance.yahoo.com` on the Location bar, and then click the Go button to display the Yahoo! Finance Web page (Figure 1-69).

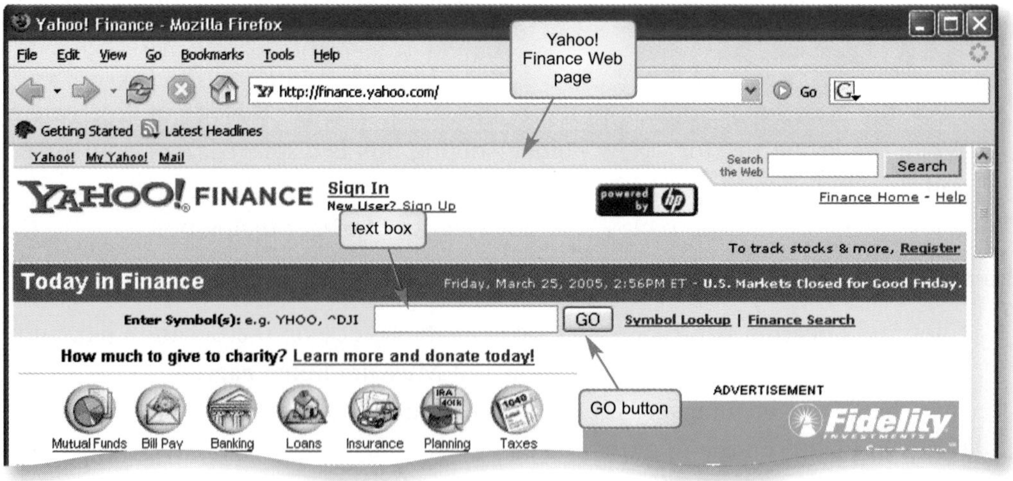

FIGURE 1-69

3. Enter the IBM stock symbol in the text box on the Web page and then click the GO button to retrieve the current IBM stock price. If the Security Warning dialog box displays, click the Continue button. Print the Web page that is displayed and then save the Web page on a floppy disk. Click the Back button to display the Yahoo! Finance Web page.

4. Enter intc, msft, te, toy, wen, wy in the text box on the Web page and then click the Go button to retrieve the stock prices of the six stocks. Print the Web page that is displayed and then save the Web page on a floppy disk.

5. Click the Close button in the Mozilla Firefox window.

6. Hand in the printed Web pages to your instructor.

5 Saving the Current U.S. Weather Map

Problem: You are interested in finding a current United States weather map to use on a road trip starting in Orlando, Florida, and ending in Santa Barbara, California. You want to save the map on a floppy disk so you can print it later.

Instructions: Perform the following tasks.

1. If necessary, connect to the Internet and start Firefox.

2. Type www.weather.com on the Location bar and then click the Go button to display the weather.com home page.

3. Scroll the home page to display the U.S. weather map. Click the Click to Enlarge link on the weather.com home page to display an enlarged weather map for the United States (Figure 1-70).

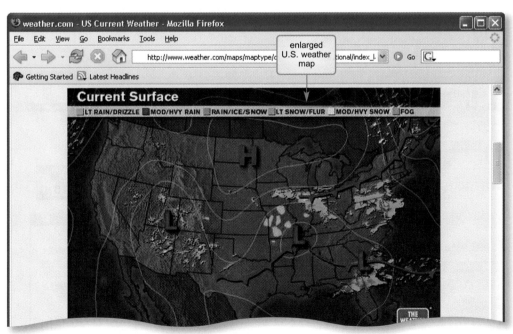

FIGURE 1-70

(continued)

In the Lab

Saving the Current U.S. Weather Map *(continued)*

4. Right-click the weather map and then click Save Image As on the shortcut menu to display the Save Image dialog box. Click the Save in box arrow, click 3½ Floppy (A:), click the File name text box, type U.S. Weather map, and then click the Save button to save the picture on a floppy disk.

5. Click the Close button to close the Mozilla Firefox window.

6. Hand in the disk to your instructor.

6 Copying and Pasting a Picture and Text

Problem: To complete an assignment in history class, you must locate The Internet Movie Database (IMDB) Web site and select an individual whose biography is on the Web site. When you find the biography of an individual you like, you need to copy his or her picture and the text of the biography into WordPad, and then print the WordPad document.

Instructions: Perform the following tasks.

Part 1: *Retrieving a Web Page*

1. If necessary, connect to the Internet and start Firefox.

2. Type www.imdb.com on the Location bar and then click the Go button to display the home page of The Internet Movie Database (IMDb) Web site (Figure 1-71).

3. Using the links on the Web site, search for the biography of an actor or actress in whom you are interested.

FIGURE 1-71

In the Lab

Part 2: *Copying a Picture and Text to Microsoft WordPad*

1. If a picture of the individual is available, copy the picture to the Clipboard.
2. Start Microsoft WordPad.
3. Paste the picture on the Clipboard into the WordPad document, click anywhere off the picture, and then press the ENTER key.
4. Click the Mozilla Firefox button on the taskbar.
5. Click the link that displays the biography.
6. Copy the biography text to the Clipboard.
7. Click the Document - WordPad button on the taskbar.
8. Paste the text on the Clipboard into the WordPad document.
9. Save the WordPad document on a floppy disk using the file name IMDB Assignment.
10. Print the WordPad document.
11. Click the Close button to close the WordPad and Mozilla Firefox windows.
12. Hand in the WordPad document to your instructor.

7 Copying, Pasting, and Saving a Picture

Problem: You are currently taking a political science class and must find the names and pictures of both senators from your state. You are then to copy the names and pictures into WordPad and print the WordPad document.

Instructions: Perform the following tasks.

1. If necessary, connect to the Internet and start Firefox.
2. Click the Location bar, type www.senate.gov on the Location bar, and then click the Go button to display the U. S. Senate Web page (Figure 1-72 on the next page).
3. Using links on the Web page, find a picture of one of the two senators who represent the state of Florida.
4. Start Microsoft WordPad.
5. Copy and paste the picture from the Web page into a blank WordPad document, click anywhere off the picture, and then press the ENTER key.
6. Find a picture of the other senator who represents the state of Florida.
7. Copy and paste the picture from the Web page into the WordPad document, click anywhere off the picture, and then press the ENTER key.
8. Save the document on a floppy disk using an appropriate file name.
9. Print the document.
10. Click the Close button on the WordPad window.
11. Click the Close button on the Mozilla Firefox window.
12. Hand in the document to your instructor.

(continued)

Mozilla
Firefox

In the Lab

Copying, Pasting, and Saving a Picture *(continued)*

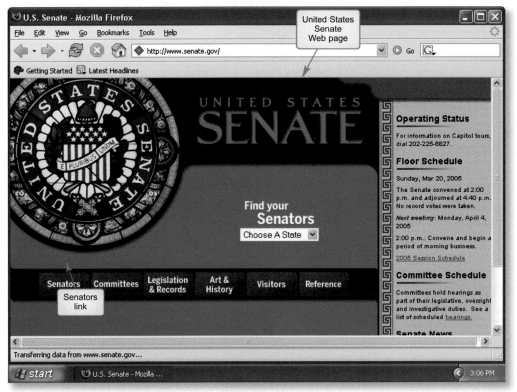

FIGURE 1-72

8 Planning a Trip on the Web

Problem: You are planning a trip from Miami to Las Vegas exactly one month from today. You plan to stay in Las Vegas seven days, including travel days. You want to use Expedia.com to summarize your options for flights, hotels, car rentals, and areas of interest, and you also want directions from your hotel to the Hoover Dam.

Instructions: Perform the following tasks.

Part 1: Summarizing Flight Information

1. If necessary, connect to the Internet and start Firefox.
2. Click the Location bar, type www.expedia.com on the Location bar, and then click the Go button to display the Expedia.com home page (Figure 1-73).

In the Lab

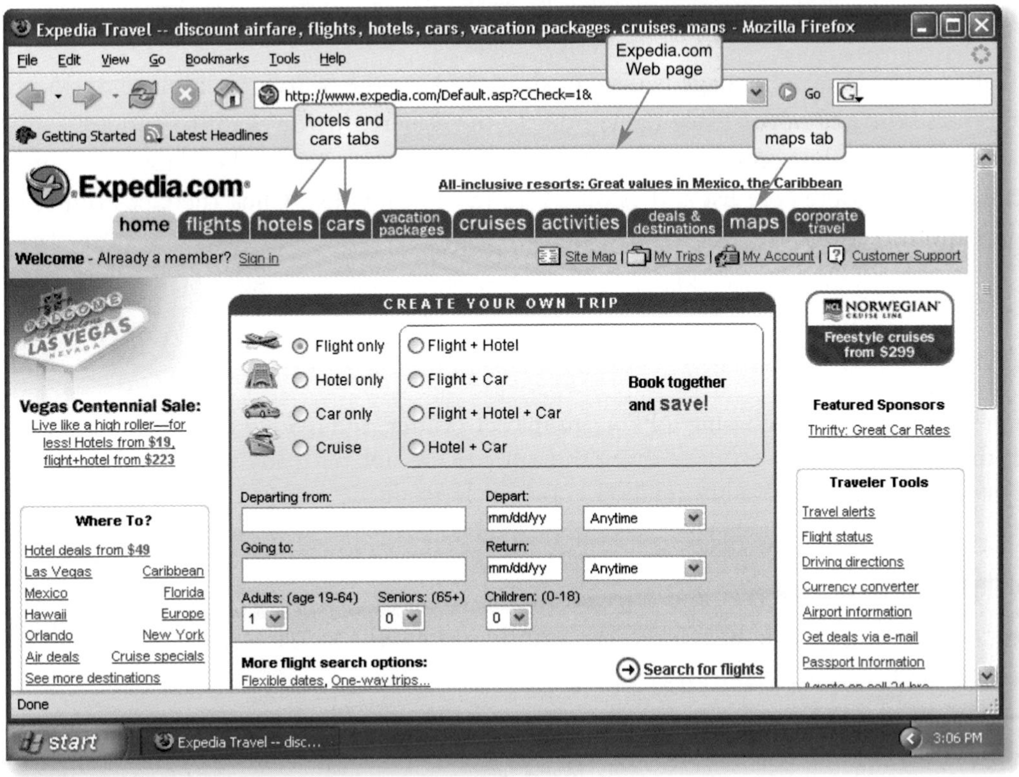

FIGURE 1-73

3. Type Miami in the Departing from box; type Las Vegas in the Going to box; select 2 in the Adults box; enter the date and select the time (i.e., July 7 noon) in the Depart boxes; and seven days from the date of departure, including the date of departure (i.e., July 13 noon) in the Return boxes. Click the Search for flights button.
4. Scroll through the flight information and then print it.

Part 2: *Summarizing Hotel Information*

1. With the Expedia.com page displayed, click the hotels tab at the top of the page.
2. If necessary, click the Las Vegas option button or type Las Vegas in the Other city box. If necessary, enter the same dates and number of adults as described in Step 3 of Part 1. Click the Search button.
3. When the Search results page is displayed, scroll through the page and find the Hard Rock Hotel and Casino. If it is not on the page displayed, then request the next group of hotels by clicking the Next button. Print the page that includes the Hard Rock Hotel and Casino.

Part 3: *Summarizing Car Rental Information*

1. With the Expedia.com page displayed, click the cars tab at the top of the page.
2. If necessary, type Las Vegas, NV in the Pick-up location box and then select Midsize in the Car class list. Click the Search button. Print the page.

Part 4: *Maps and Directions*

1. With the Expedia.com page displayed, click the maps tab. Click the Get Driving Directions link.

(continued)

In the Lab

Planning a Trip on the Web *(continued)*

2. When the Get Driving Directions page is displayed, make sure the Search for a place option button is selected, and then type LAS in the Place name box. In the Where do you want to end area, make sure the Search for a place option button is selected, and then type Hoover Dam in the Place name box. If necessary, select Quickest in the Route type list and select Miles in the Units list. Click the Get driving directions link.

3. Print the map and directions.

Comparing Prices Online

Problem: You are interested in purchasing a PDA, an ink-jet printer, and a Sony digital camera. A friend suggested that you look on the Web for the lowest prices even though you are not yet ready to buy online. You decide to use the Web to find prices and obtain more information about each product.

Instructions: Perform the following tasks.

1. If necessary, connect to the Internet and start Firefox.

2. Click the Location bar, type www.bestbuy.com, and then press the ENTER key to display the Best Buy home page (Figure 1-74).

FIGURE 1-74

3. Point to the Computers tab and click PDAs & Handhelds from the list. When the next page is displayed, click the PDAs link. Print the page.

4. Point to the Cameras & Camcorders tab and click Digital Cameras from the list. When the next page is displayed, click the Sony Digital Cameras link. Print the page. Scroll down and click a digital camera model. Print the page.

5. Point to the Computers tab and click Printers from the list. When the next page is displayed, click the Inkjet Printers link. Print the page. Scroll down and click an inkjet model. Print the page.

In the Lab

10 Job Hunting on the Web

Problem: You are job hunting and your area of expertise is e-commerce. Instead of using the newspaper to find a job, you decide to search for jobs on the Internet. You decide to visit three Web sites in hopes of finding the perfect job.

Instructions: Perform the following tasks.

1. If necessary, connect to the Internet and start Firefox.
2. Click the Location bar, type `www.computerjobs.com`, and then press the ENTER key to display the computerjobs.com home page (Figure 1-75).

FIGURE 1-75

3. When the computerjobs.com home page is displayed, type `e-commerce` in the keyword search text box and then press the ENTER key. When the first page of the e-commerce listings is displayed, print it.
4. Type `www.monster.com` on the Location bar and then press the ENTER key.
5. When the Monster home page is displayed, click the Search Jobs link. If you are asked to sign up for a Monster account, click "Not today, thanks," and then click the Next button. Type `e-commerce` in the Enter Key Words box and then press the ENTER key. When the first page of the e-commerce listings is displayed, print it.
6. Type `www.careerbuilder.com` on the Location bar and then press the ENTER key.
7. When the careerbuilder.com page is displayed, type `e-commerce` in the Enter Keyword(s): box, and then press the ENTER key. When the first page of the e-commerce listings is displayed, print it.

In the Lab

11 Finding a Person and a Business on the Web

Problem: You are concerned about what personal information is available on the Web. You decide to search the Web for any personal information about yourself. In addition, you would like to locate antique dealers near your hometown.

Instructions: Perform the following tasks.

Part 1: *Finding a Person*

1. If necessary, connect to the Internet and start Firefox.
2. Click the Location bar, type www.switchboard.com, and then press the ENTER key.
3. When the Switchboard.com home page is displayed (Figure 1-76), click the Find a Person option button, type your first name in the First Name box, and then type your last name in the Last Name box and your state in the State box. Leave the remaining boxes empty. Click the Search button. If necessary, locate the page with your name on it by using the Next link. Print the page with your name on it. If you cannot find your name, print the page on which your name should have been displayed.

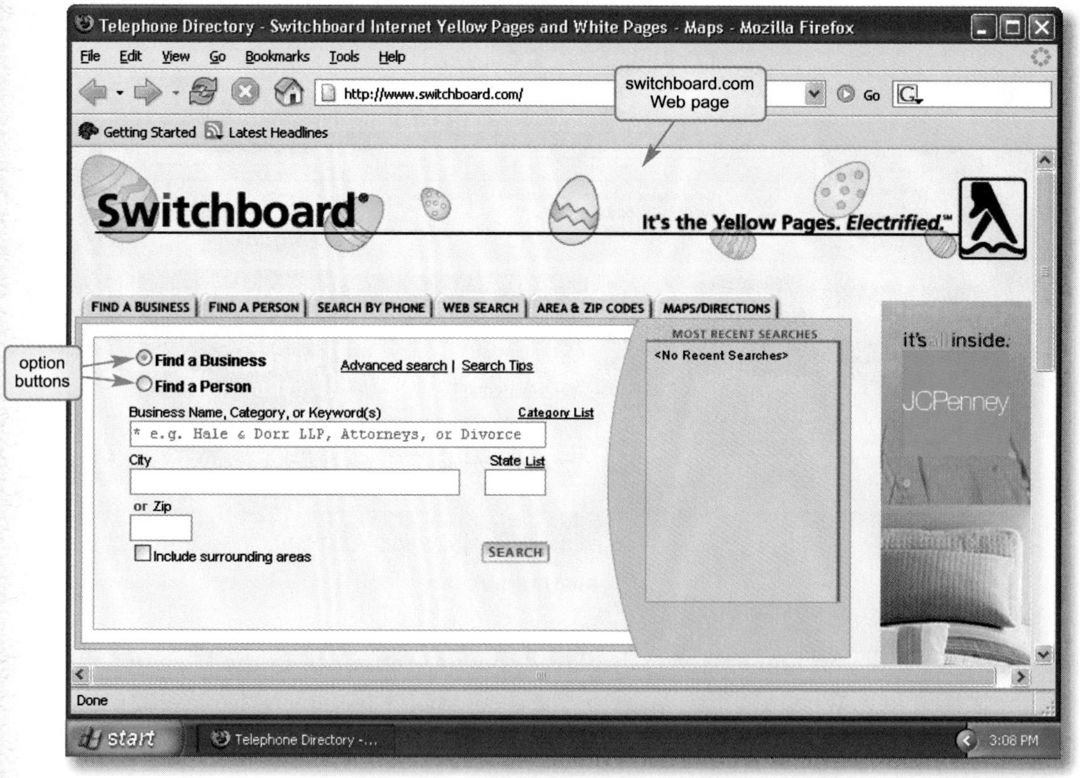

FIGURE 1-76

Part 2: *Finding a Business*

1. With the home page of the Switchboard.com Web site displayed, click the Find a Business option button.
2. Locate antique dealers near your hometown. You must enter a city and state or Zip code. Print the page with the list of antique shops.

In the Lab

12 Working with Toolbars

Problem: Toolbars, toolbars, toolbars. What's the big deal? You don't understand what the big deal is, so you decide to learn more about toolbars. You want to know how to hide a toolbar, how to search for information on the Internet using the Location bar, and how to customize a toolbar.

Instructions: Perform the following tasks.

Part 1: *Hiding a Toolbar*

1. If necessary, connect to the Internet and start Firefox.
2. Right-click an area on the Navigation toolbar to display a shortcut menu.
3. Click Bookmarks Toolbar on the shortcut menu to remove the Bookmarks toolbar from the Mozilla Firefox window.

Part 2: *Search for Information on the Internet Using the Location Bar*

1. Type national weather on the Location bar.
2. Click the Go button to display the National Weather Service Web page in the display area.

Part 3: *Customizing the Navigation Toolbar*

1. Display the Bookmarks toolbar by clicking View on the menu bar, pointing to Toolbars, and selecting Bookmarks Toolbar from the Toolbars submenu.
2. Right-click an area of the Navigation toolbar and then click Customize on the shortcut menu to display the Customize Toolbar dialog box (Figure 1-77).

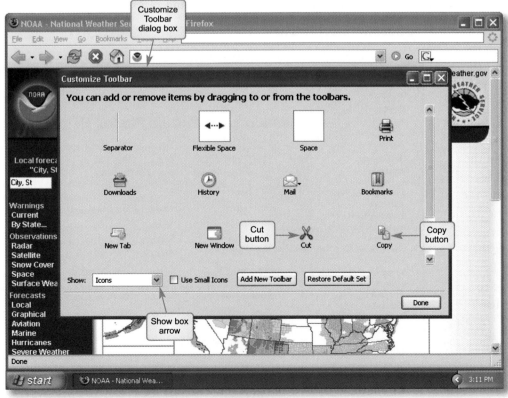

FIGURE 1-77

(continued)

In the Lab

Working with Toolbars *(continued)*

3. Drag the Copy button from the Customize Toolbar dialog box to the Navigation toolbar, between the Stop and Home buttons.
4. Drag the Cut button from the Customize Toolbar dialog box to the Navigation toolbar, between the Stop and Copy buttons.
5. Drag the Paste button from the Customize Toolbar dialog box to the Navigation toolbar, between the Copy and Home buttons.
6. Click the Show box arrow in the Customize Toolbar dialog box and then click Icons and Text in the list.
7. Click the Done button in the Customize Toolbar dialog box. The buttons on the Navigation toolbar are displayed with text labels.

Part 4: *Returning the Toolbar to Its Original Configuration*

1. Right-click a blank area of the Navigation toolbar, click Customize, and then click the Restore Default Set button.
2. Click the Done button in the Customize Toolbar dialog box.
3. Click the Close button in the Mozilla Firefox window.

13 Using the Firefox Help Contents Sheet

Problem: Not knowing much about the Contents sheet in Firefox Help, you decide to learn more about the organization of the Contents sheet, how to use the Contents sheet to search for information on navigating Web pages.

Instructions: Use Firefox Help and Contents to perform the following tasks.

1. If necessary, connect to the Internet and start Firefox.
2. Click Help on the menu bar and then click Help Contents.
3. If the Contents sheet is not displayed, click the Contents tab. Help topics in the Contents sheet are organized into the categories shown in Figure 1-78.
4. Double-click the Using Mozilla Firefox topic to expand the list.
5. Click the Navigating Web Pages topic. List two ways to navigate to Web pages on the Internet.

FIGURE 1-78

14 Using the Firefox Help Index

Problem: Not knowing much about the Index sheet in Firefox Help, you decide to learn more about the Index sheet by using it to search for the following topics: cookies, certificates, privacy, and shortcuts.

Instructions: Use Firefox Help to perform the following tasks.

1. If necessary, connect to the Internet and start Firefox.
2. Click Help on the menu bar and then click Help Contents.
3. If the Index sheet is not displayed, click the Index tab. The Index sheet contains an extensive index of Firefox Help topics (Figure 1-79).

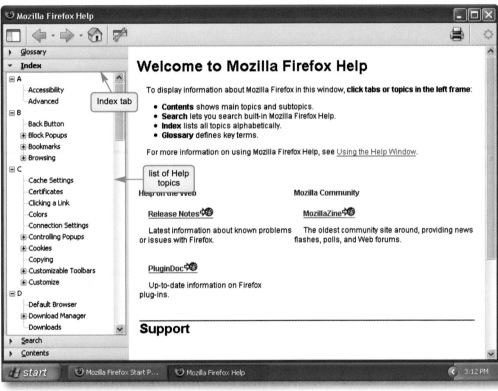

FIGURE 1-79

4. Locate and click Cookies on the Help sidebar, and then answer the following questions.
   a. What is a cookie? _____
   b. What does a cookie store? _____
5. Locate and click Certificates on the Help sidebar, and then answer the following questions.
   a. What is the function of certificates? _____
   b. Explain Client Certificate Selection. _____
6. Locate and click Privacy on the Help sidebar, and then answer the following question.
   a. List five options related to your privacy in Mozilla Firefox. _____
   _____
   _____

(continued)

Using the Firefox Help Index *(continued)*

7. Locate and click Shortcuts, and then answer the following questions.
   a. What is the Firefox shortcut key to go to the Home Page? _____
   b. What is the Firefox shortcut key to reload the current Web page? _____
   c. What is the Firefox shortcut key to stop downloading a Web page? _____

8. Click the Close button in the Mozilla Firefox Help window.

9. Click the Close button in the Mozilla Firefox window.

10. Hand in the answers to the questions to your instructor.

Cases and Places

The difficulty of these case studies varies:
■ are the least difficult and ■■ are more difficult. The last exercise is a group exercise.

1 ■ Your old car broke down and you are in the market for a new one. Type autos.msn.com as the URL to display the MSN Autos home page. Select your favorite make and model from the Find a Car area to search for a new car. Check the availability and prices for two additional models of the same make. Print a page for each car showing your search results.

2 ■ Your uncle would like to invest in the stock market. He has asked you to find fundamental stock information about Microsoft Corporation (msft), NetFlix (nflx), XM Satellite Radio (xmsr), Fuelcell Energy Inc. (fcel), and TiVo Inc. (tivo). Use the Yahoo! Web site (finance.yahoo.com) to obtain today's stock price, today's range, volume, 52-week range, and the P/E (price/earnings ratio). To display this information, enter the stock symbol and click the Go button. Print the detailed results for each stock. In addition, when the information is displayed for TiVo Inc., scroll down and click the first topic under Headlines. Print the page.

3 ■ You are planning a vacation to Orlando, Florida. You want to leave exactly one month from today and plan to stay seven days, including the travel days. Check with Northwest Airlines (nwa.com), Continental Airlines (continental.com), Delta Airlines (delta.com), and Southwest airlines (southwest.com) for travel specials to Orlando. Print any Web pages containing travel specials and then summarize the information you find in a brief report.

4 ■■ You have decided to purchase a computer online. You plan to spend between $800 and $1,200 for a computer with a monitor and a printer. Visit three online computer stores, such as HP (hp.com), Dell (dell.com), and Gateway (gateway.com). On each site, find a computer that sells for the amount you plan to spend. For each site, print the page that indicates the computer and price. Compare the three computers. Which one is the best buy? Why?

5 ■■ Firefox is not the only browser program in use today. Using the Internet, computer magazines and newspapers, or other resources, prepare a brief report about three other Web browsers in use today. Describe their features, differences, and similarities.

6 ■■ **Working Together** Have each member of your group visit a daily newspaper Web site, such as the *New York Times* (nytimes.com), *Chicago Tribune* (chicagotribune.com), *Los Angeles Times* (latimes.com), *Miami Herald* (miamiherald.com), and a local newspaper's Web site. Print at least one page from each newspaper site. Compare the latest headline news. Navigate through each site. How are the newspaper sites similar and dissimilar? Which newspaper has the best Web site? Why? Present your findings to the class.

MOZILLA
Firefox

Web Research Techniques and Search Engines

CASE PERSPECTIVE

After taking a short college course to better understand how to search for information on the Internet, you feel confident you can find the appropriate resources on the World Wide Web to use for an upcoming English class research paper. The topic you chose for the paper is the discovery of the Perseid meteor shower.

You decide the first step in researching the meteor shower should be to search the Web for authoritative Web sites. You recall from taking an Internet class that Web sites are classified into nine different categories and that there are three basic types of search tools.

While talking to your English instructor, he emphasizes that it is very important to evaluate each Web site for its reliability, significance, and content. From the bottom drawer of his file cabinet, he retrieves a document titled "Web Resource Evaluation Worksheet," which he suggests you use to simplify the process of evaluating Web sites.

Next, you talk to the instructor of the Internet course you just completed. She had several good ideas about searching the Web for specific topics and reminds you that you should be as specific as possible while performing a search. From a bookshelf in the back of the room, she retrieves a book titled *The Value of Boolean Expressions and Internet Searching* for you to read. As you were leaving, she reminds you that using WordPad is an easy way to create a working bibliography.

With the information gathered from your instructors and the knowledge from your Internet class, you are confident you can find valid Web sites and perform the research necessary to write the research paper on the discovery of the Perseid meteor shower.

As you read through this project, you will learn how to locate information on the World Wide Web and evaluate the information for its usefulness as a Web resource.

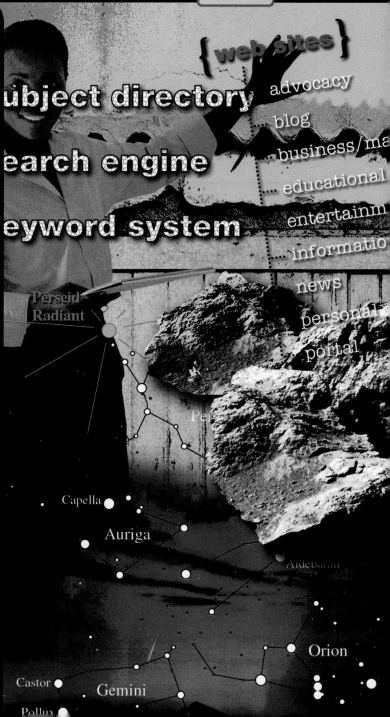

Web Research Techniques and Search Engines

Objectives

You will have mastered the material in this project when you can:

- Describe the nine general categories of Web sites
- List the criteria for evaluating a Web resource
- Describe the three basic types of search tools
- Search the Web using either a directory or keywords
- Use tabbed browsing to view multiple Web pages in one window
- Customize and refine a search

- Describe the techniques used for successful keyword searches
- Describe how to create a working bibliography
- Compile a list of works cited for Web resources
- Search the Web for addresses, maps, definitions, and pictures
- Use the Location bar to search for a Web page or view folders on the computer

Introduction

Research is an important tool for success in an academic career. Writing papers, preparing speeches, and doing homework assignments all rely heavily on research. When researching, you are trying to find information to support an idea or position, to prove a point, or to learn about a topic or concept. Traditionally, research was accomplished using books, papers, periodicals, and other materials found in libraries. The World Wide Web provides a new and useful resource for supplementing the traditional print materials found in the library. There are currently trillions of Web pages, up from just a few million pages in 1994.

While the Web is a valuable resource, you should not rely solely on the Web for research information. Web sites change quite frequently, which means Web pages may become unavailable. In addition, the information found on Web pages is not always up-to-date, accurate, or verifiable.

This project demonstrates successful techniques for locating information on the Web and then evaluating the information for its usefulness as a source.

Types of Web Resources

Web sites are organized by content into nine categories: advocacy, blog, business/marketing, educational, entertainment, informational, news, personal, and portal. In addition, the Web provides other resources whereby you can access useful information when doing research. The next several sections describe the types of Web sites and other resources.

Advocacy Web Sites

An **advocacy Web site** contains content that describes a cause, opinion, or idea (Figure 2-1a on the next page). The purpose of the advocacy Web page is to convince the reader of the validity of a cause, opinion, or idea. These Web sites usually present views on a particular group or association. Sponsors of advocacy Web sites include the American Association of Retired Persons (AARP), the Democratic National Committee, the Republican National Committee, the Society for the Prevention of Cruelty to Animals, and the American Civil Liberties Union.

Blog Web Sites

A **blog Web site**, short for Web log, uses a regularly updated journal format to reflect the interests, opinions, and personalities of the author and sometimes Web site visitors (Figure 2-1b on the next page). A blog has an informal style (similar to a diary) that consists of a single individual's ideas or a collection of ideas and thoughts among visitors.

Business/Marketing Web Sites

A **business/marketing Web site** contains content that tries to promote or sell products or services (Figure 2-1c on the next page). Nearly every business maintains a business/marketing Web site. Dell Inc., 21st Century Insurance Company, General Motors Corporation, Kraft Foods Inc., and Walt Disney Company all have business/marketing Web sites. Many of these companies also allow you to purchase their products or services online.

Educational Web Sites

An **educational Web site** offers exciting, challenging avenues for formal and informal teaching and learning (Figure 2-1d on the next page). On the Web, you can learn how to sail a boat or how to cook a meal. For a more structured learning experience, companies provide online training to employees, and colleges offer online classes and degrees. Instructors often enhance classroom teaching by publishing course materials, grades, and other pertinent class information on the Web.

Entertainment Web Sites

An **entertainment Web site** offers an interactive and engaging environment (Figure 2-1e on the next page). Popular entertainment Web sites offer music, videos, sports, games, ongoing Web episodes, sweepstakes, chats, and more. Sophisticated entertainment Web sites often partner with other technologies. For example, you can cast your vote about a topic on a television show.

More About

Advocacy Web Pages

Other advocacy Web pages include the Maine Democratic Party and National Rifle Association. For more information about advocacy Web pages, visit the Firefox More About Web page (scsite.com/firefox/more) and click Advocacy Web Pages.

More About

Business/Marketing Web Pages

Other business/marketing Web pages include Chevron and DuPont. For more information about business/marketing Web pages, visit the Firefox More About Web page (scsite.com/firefox/more) and click Business/Marketing Web Pages.

More About

Educational Web Pages

Other educational Web pages include Scuba.com and WebCT.com. For more information about educational Web pages, visit the Firefox More About Web page (scsite.com/firefox/more) and click Educational Web Pages.

More About

Entertainment Web Pages

Other entertainment Web pages include MLB.com and Fox. For more information about entertainment Web pages, visit the Firefox More About Web page (scsite.com/firefox/more) and click Entertainment Web Pages.

Figure 2-1 (a) Advocacy

(b) Blog

(c) Business/Marketing

(d) Educational

(e) Entertainment

(f) Informational

(g) News

(h) Personal

(i) Portal

FIGURE 2-1

Informational Web Sites

An **informational Web site** contains factual information (Figure 2-1f). Many United States government agencies have informational Web sites providing information such as census data, tax codes, and the congressional budget. Other organizations provide information such as public transportation schedules and published research findings.

News Web Sites

A **news Web site** contains newsworthy material including stories and articles relating to current events, life, money, sports, and the weather (Figure 2-1g). Many magazines and newspapers sponsor Web sites that provide summaries of printed articles, as well as articles not included in the printed versions. Newspapers and television and radio stations are some of the media that maintain news Web sites.

Personal Web Sites

A private individual or family not usually associated with any organization may maintain a **personal Web site** or just a single Web page (Figure 2-1h). People publish personal Web pages for a variety of reasons. Some are job hunting. Others simply want to share life experiences with their family, friends, and others around the world.

Portal Web Sites

A **portal Web site** offers a variety of Internet services from a single, convenient location (Figure 2-1i). Most portals offer the following free services: search engine and/or subject directory; news; sports and weather; Web publishing services; reference tools such as yellow pages, stock quotes, and maps; shopping malls and auctions; and e-mail and other forms of online communication. See Table 2-1 for a list of popular portals.

Many portals have Web communities. A **Web community** is a Web site that joins a specific group of people with similar interests or relationships. These communities may offer online photo albums, chat rooms, and other services to facilitate communications among members.

More About

Informational Web Pages

Other informational Web pages include the Internal Revenue Service, American Airlines, and Amtrak Railroads (though the last two are obviously also business/marketing Web pages). For more information about informational Web pages, visit the Firefox More About Web page (scsite.com/firefox/more) and click Informational Web Pages.

More About

News Web Pages

Other news Web pages include CNN, Fox News, and Orlando Sentinel. For more information about news Web pages, visit the Firefox More About Web page (scsite.com/firefox/more) and click News Web Pages.

Table 2-1 Popular Portals and Their URLs

PORTAL	URL	PORTAL	URL
AltaVista	altavista.com	HotBot	hotbot.com
America Online	aol.com	LookSmart	looksmart.com
Euroseek.com	euroseek.com	Lycos	lycos.com
Excite	excite.com	Microsoft Network	msn.com
Go.com	go.com	Netscape	netscape.com
Google	google.com	Yahoo!	yahoo.com

Other Web Resources

The Web provides a number of other resources where you will find useful tools and information. File transfer protocol (FTP) sites, newsgroups, and for-profit database services all contain information and files that you can use for research purposes.

Papers, documents, manuals, and complete ready-to-execute programs are available using FTP. **File transfer protocol (FTP)** is an Internet standard that permits file uploading and downloading (transferring) with other computers on the Internet. Uploading is the opposite of downloading; that is, **uploading** is the process of transferring documents, graphics, and other objects from your computer to another computer on the Internet.

Gopher started out as a document retrieval system to assist people in getting help for computing problems. Today, it has become a directory-based method of retrieving files. Many government agencies have organized gopher sites to provide information and distribute documents and forms.

A **newsgroup** is an online area in which users have written discussions about a particular subject. To participate in a discussion, or **thread**, a user sends a message to the newsgroup, and other users in the newsgroup read and reply to the message. Some major topic areas include news, recreation, society, business, science, and computers.

A number of **database services**, such as Dow Jones and LexisNexis (Figure 2-2), have been developed. These services, for a small fee, allow you to perform searches for information. Some schools subscribe to these database services and make the searching services available to the faculty, staff, and students. Ask a librarian how to access these database services.

More About

Newsgroups

Newsgroups provide a forum for finding current information on a topic. Many experts and professionals read the threads in newsgroups pertaining to their areas of expertise and are willing to answer questions and supply information. For more information about newsgroups, see Project 3 of this book.

LexisNexis
database services
Web page

FIGURE 2-2

Summary of Types of Web Resources

Determining the exact category into which a Web resource falls is sometimes difficult because of the overlap of information on the page. You will find advertising on news Web pages. Personal Web pages may advocate some cause or opinion. A business/marketing Web page may contain factual information that is verifiable from other sources. In spite of this overlapping, identifying the general category in which the Web page falls can help you evaluate the usefulness of the Web page as a source of information for a research paper.

Evaluating a Web Resource

Once a promising Web page is found, you should evaluate it for its reliability, significance, and content. Remember, anyone can put a page on the Web, and Web pages do not have to be reviewed for accuracy or verified by editors. It is up to you to ensure the information and other materials you use from the Web are accurate, attributable, and verifiable.

Just as criteria exist for evaluating printed materials, criteria also exist for evaluating Web pages. These criteria include authorship, accuracy of information, currency of information, and topic and scope of coverage. Table 2-2 shows the information you should look for within each criterion when evaluating Web resources.

More About

Evaluating Resources

Although a single evaluating tool does not exist, several colleges and universities have Web sites that contain information about evaluating Web sites. Three such sites are maintained by Cornell University, Western Illinois University, and Michigan State University. For more information about evaluating Web resources, visit the Firefox More About Web page (scsite.com/firefox/more) and click Evaluating Resources.

Table 2-2 Criteria for Evaluating Web Pages

CRITERION	INFORMATION TO EVALUATE
Authorship	• Is the name of the person or organization publishing the page legitimate? • Does a link exist to a page that describes the goals of the organization? • Does the page include a statement of official approval from the parent organization? • Is there a copyright notice? • What are the author's qualifications? • Are any opinions and biases clearly stated? • Does the page contain advertising? If so, is it differentiated from content? • Is the information provided as a public service?
Accuracy of Information	• Are any sources used and are they listed on the page? • Does the page contain links to other Web sites that verify the information on the page? • Are data and statistics clearly displayed and easy to read? • Is the page grammatically correct?
Currency of Information	• When was the page written? • When was the page placed on the Web? • When was the page last updated? • Does the page include dates associated with the information on the Web page?
Topic and Scope of Coverage	• What is the purpose of the Web page? • Does the page declare a topic? • Does the page succeed in describing or discussing the declared topic? • Are points clear, well-stated, and supported? • Does the page contain links to related resources? • Is the page under construction?

You may want to create an evaluation worksheet to use as an aid in consistently evaluating the Web pages you find as potential resources. Figure 2-3 shows a sample evaluation worksheet created from the criteria listed in Table 2-2 on the previous page. You can copy this worksheet or create your own to use each time you find a possible research source.

Web Resource Evaluation Worksheet

Web Page Title:

Web Page URL:

Type of Web Resource

Advocacy Business/Marketing Educational Entertainment Informational News Personal Portal

Reasons?

Authorship

What are the author's qualifications?

Is there a sponsoring organization? Does the page link to the organization?

Are any opinions and biases clearly stated?

Does the page contain a copyright notice?

Accuracy of Information

What sources verify the information on the Web page? Does the page link to those sources?

Is the page grammatically correct?

Currency of Information

What date was the page placed on the Web?

What date was the page last updated?

What date did you visit the page?

Topic and Scope

What is the purpose of the page?

Does the page succeed in describing and discussing the topic?

Are points clear, well-stated, and supported?

Does the page include links to other related pages?

FIGURE 2-3

Finding a valuable resource among the trillions of Web pages available on the World Wide Web, however, can be quite a challenge. The most efficient way to find a probable resource from among all those pages is to use the special search tools created specifically for use on the Web. They will guide you to the information you are seeking.

Web Search Resources

The World Wide Web has trillions of Web pages, and bibliographic control does not exist. To find information for a term paper, learn more about a topic of interest, or display the home page of a governmental agency, you must either know the URL of the specific Web page or you must use a search tool. A **search tool** is a software program that helps you find Web pages containing certain information. Search tools fall into three general categories.

- Subject directory
- Search engine
- Keyword system

The first type of search tool, called a **subject directory**, uses a directory to organize related Web resources. Figure 2-4 shows a directory (Yahoo! directory) that is organized into broad categories. You must decide into which category the search topic falls and then click the corresponding link. When you click the link, another page of links is displayed that contains more specific categories from which to choose. You continue following the links until you find the information you want.

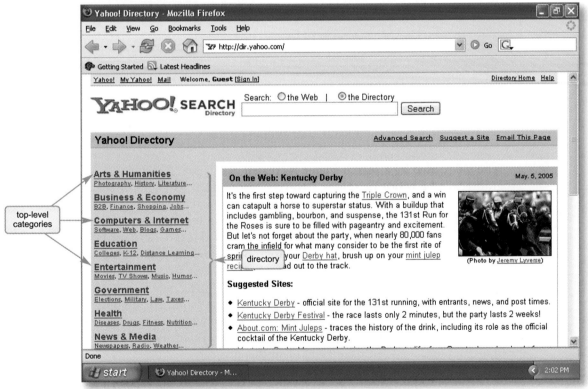

FIGURE 2-4

Because directories allow you to choose from a list of categories, you do not have to provide keywords to find information. You may have to spend considerable time traveling through several levels of categories, however, only to discover that no pages on the topic are available.

A second type of search tool, called a **search engine**, retrieves and displays a list of links to Web pages based on a query. A **query** is a **keyword** or **search term** (a word, set of words, or phrase) you enter to tell the search engine the topic about which you want information. The search engine uses the keyword to search an index of Web resources in its database. Some of the more popular search engines are Google, Yahoo!, MSN Search, Ask Jeeves, AltaVista, and Excite.

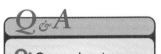

Q: Can search engines provide access to more than just Web pages?

A: Yes. Some search engines allow you to search a newsgroup, periodical or newspaper, business directory, or personal directory.

Figure 2-5 shows a typical **keyword search form** (Google Advanced Search) used to enter keywords to search the Web. You provide one or more relevant keywords about the topic, and the search engine will return links that point directly to Web pages that contain those keywords.

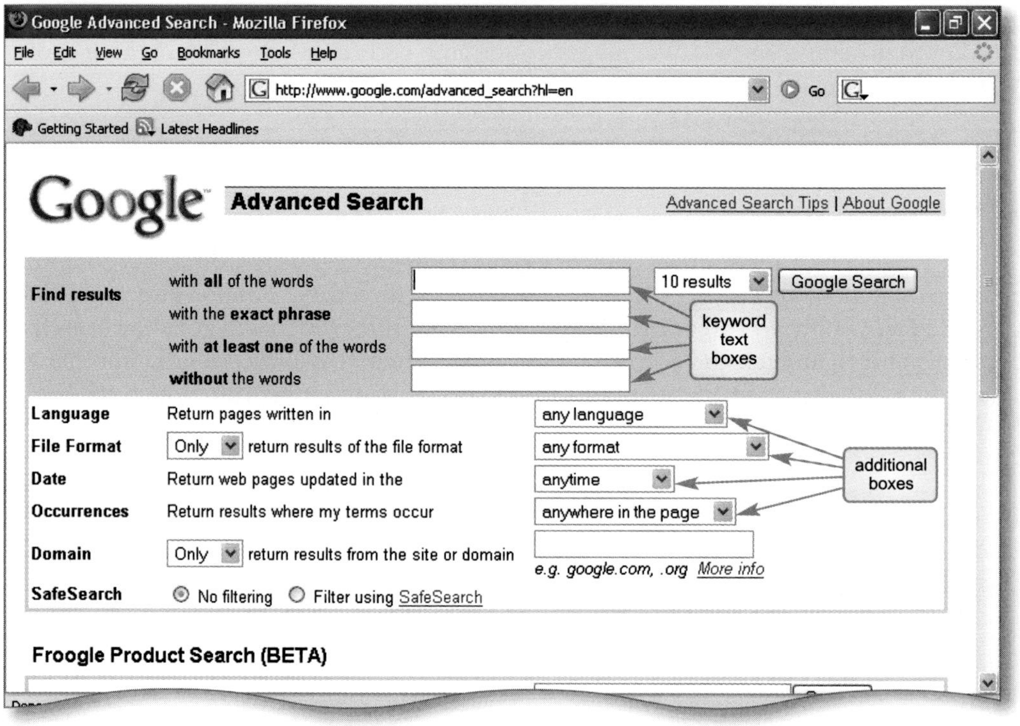

FIGURE 2-5

The index used by a search engine is created using several techniques. An automated program, called a **robot** or **spider**, "travels" around the Web, automatically following links and adding entries to the index. Individuals also can request that their Web pages be added to a directory or index, usually for a fee.

Most of the popular portal Web sites listed in Table 2-1 on page FX 71 have both a search engine and a subject directory. Most portals also include specialized search tools that display maps and directions (Expedia), provide information about businesses (Yellow Pages), and help find people (People Finder).

The third type of search tool, a Keyword system, is part of the Firefox browser. A **Keyword system** allows you to enter a name or word on the Location bar to display a corresponding Web page. The Keyword system is shown in detail in Figures 2-63 and 2-64 on page FX 111 in this project.

Why study different search tools? Just as it is impossible for a card catalog to contain an entry for every book in the world, it is impossible for each search tool to catalog every Web page on the World Wide Web. In addition, different search tools on the Web perform different types of searches. Some search for keywords in the title of a Web page, while others scan links for the keywords. Still others search the entire text of Web pages. Because of the different searching techniques, the results of a search vary surprisingly.

When developing Firefox, Mozilla realized the importance of using search tools and made several accessible via the Search bar. To practice doing research on the Web, assume you want to find information on the discovery of the Perseid meteor shower. The following sections show how to start Firefox and use the Yahoo! directory to search for information on the discovery of the Perseid meteor shower.

Starting Firefox

The following steps illustrate how to start Firefox using the procedure you used at the beginning of Project 1 on pages FX 8 and FX 9.

To Start Firefox

1

• **Click the Start button on the Windows taskbar, point to All Programs on the Start menu, point to Mozilla Firefox on the All Programs submenu, and then click Mozilla Firefox on the Mozilla Firefox submenu.**

• **If the Default Browser dialog box is displayed, click the No button to not make Firefox the default browser.**

• **If the Mozilla Firefox window is not maximized, double-click its title bar to maximize it.**

Firefox starts. After several seconds, Firefox displays the Mozilla Firefox Start Page - Mozilla Firefox window and displays the Firefox Start page in the display area (Figure 2-6). The home page may look different on your computer.

FIGURE 2-6

Searching the Web Using a Directory

Yahoo! is famous for its directory. Starting with general categories and becoming increasingly more specific as links are selected, the Yahoo! directory provides a menu-like interface for searching the Web. Because the Yahoo! directory uses a series of menus to organize links to Web pages, you can perform searches without entering keywords. The following step illustrates how to display the Yahoo! home page.

More About

Directory and Keyword Search Engines

Today, most search engines provide both a directory and a keyword search tool.

To Display the Yahoo! Home Page

1

• **Click the Location bar, type** www.yahoo.com **as the URL, and then click the Go button.**

Firefox displays the URL for the Yahoo! home page (http://www.yahoo.com/) on the Location bar and displays the Yahoo! home page (Figure 2-7).

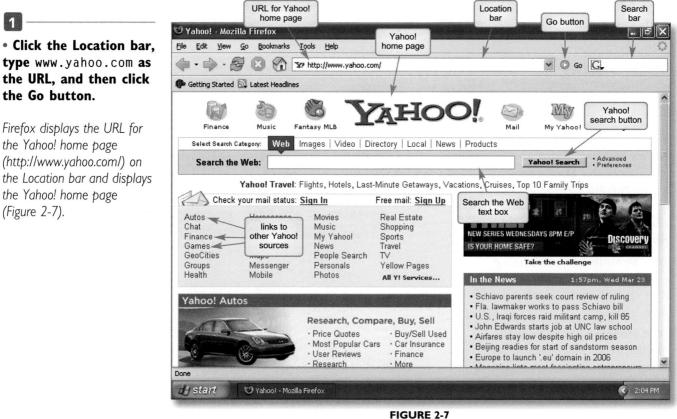

FIGURE 2-7

When you type a URL on the Location bar and then click the Go button, Firefox remembers the URL you typed. As a result, when you type the URL for the Yahoo! home page on the Location bar in Figure 2-7, a box may display below the Location bar displaying a list of previously entered items. If this happens, you can select a URL from the box beneath the Location bar by clicking the URL, or you can continue to type the URL from the keyboard.

You use the Search the Web text box and Yahoo! Search button below the Yahoo! title to perform a keyword search. Several links display below the text box. Scroll the Web page to see the Yahoo! directory (Figure 2-8). Web pages in the Yahoo! directory are organized into the broad categories.

Because astronomy is part of the major category, Science, this category is appropriate to start the search. The steps in Figures 2-8 through 2-14 on pages FX 79–82 illustrate how to navigate through the Yahoo! directory to retrieve information about the discovery of the Perseid meteor shower.

More About

Yahoo!

Two graduate students at Stanford University accumulated lists of their favorite Web sites and started Yahoo!. Yahoo!, which became a corporation in 1996, is now a household name among Web users.

To Search Using the Yahoo! Web Directory

1

• **Scroll the display area to display the Science link in the Yahoo! Web Directory area.**

The Science link is displayed in the Yahoo! Web Directory area (Figure 2-8).

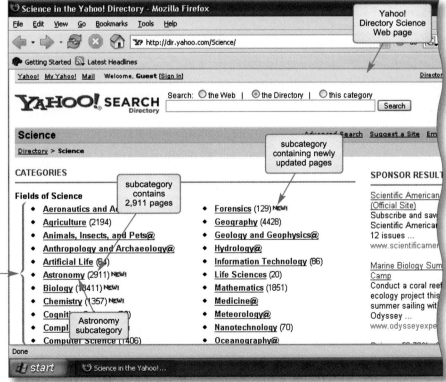

FIGURE 2-8

2

• **Click Science to view the links in the Science category.**

The Science in the Yahoo! Directory Web page is displayed (Figure 2-9). The number in parentheses next to a subcategory indicates how many Web page listings you will find if you click the subcategory. For example, the Astronomy subcategory contains 2,911 listings. The word NEW! to the right of a link indicates the link recently has been updated with new Web pages. The number of Web page listings and/or search results may be different on your computer.

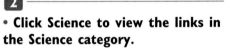

FIGURE 2-9

3

• **Click Astronomy to view the links in the Astronomy subcategory.**

• **Scroll the display area to view the Solar System subcategory.**

The Astronomy in the Yahoo! Directory Web page is displayed (Figure 2-10). The Solar System subcategory contains 934 listings. An @ symbol next to a link indicates a link to another Yahoo! subcategory.

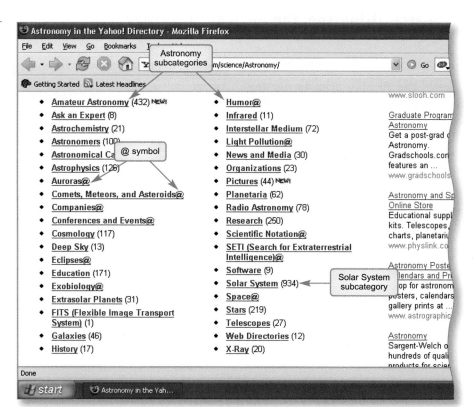

FIGURE 2-10

4

• **Click Solar System to view the links in the Solar System subcategory.**

The Solar System in the Yahoo! Directory Web page is displayed (Figure 2-11). The Comets, Meteors, and Asteroids subcategory contains 191 listings.

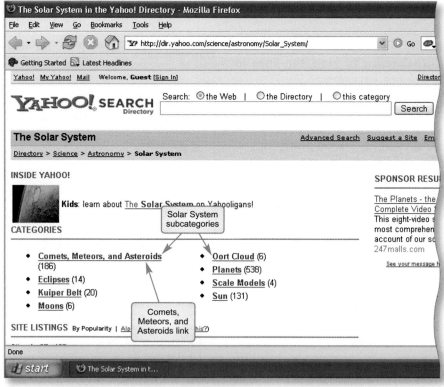

FIGURE 2-11

5

• **Click Comets, Meteors, and Asteroids to view the links in the Comets, Meteors, and Asteroids subcategory.**

The Comets, Meteors, and Asteroids in the Yahoo! Directory Web page is displayed (Figure 2-12). The Perseid Meteor Shower subcategory contains 13 listings.

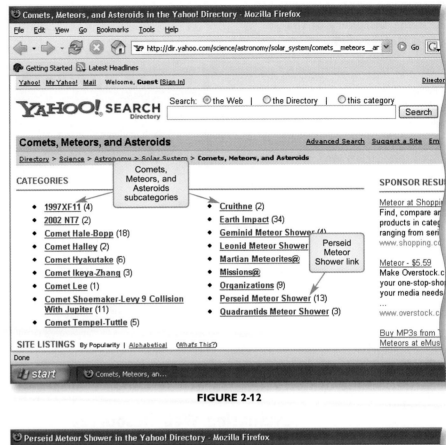

FIGURE 2-12

6

• **Click Perseid Meteor Shower to view the listings in the Perseid Meteor Shower subcategory.**

• **Scroll the display area to display the Discovery of the Perseid Meteors link.**

The Perseid Meteor Shower in the Yahoo! Directory Web page is displayed (Figure 2-13). The Discovery of the Perseid Meteors link is displayed in the list.

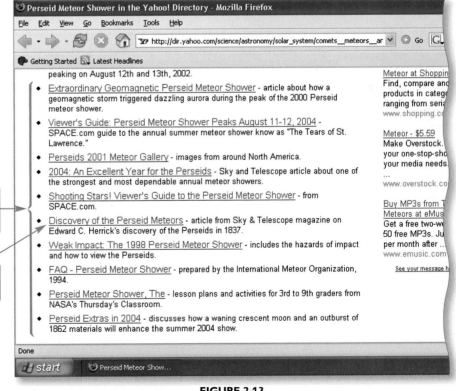

FIGURE 2-13

7

• **Click the Discovery of the Perseid Meteors link.**

The Sky and Telescope - The Discovery of the Perseid Meteors Web page containing The Discovery of the Perseid Meteors article is displayed (Figure 2-14). The Web page contains the Web page URL, link to the sponsoring organization, Web page title, and author name.

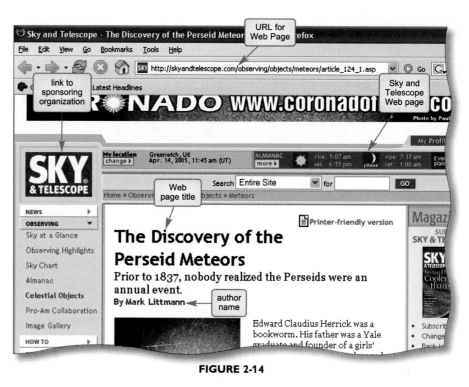

FIGURE 2-14

Evaluating Web Resources

Now that you have a potentially useful Web page, you should apply the criteria discussed earlier on page FX 73 to evaluate the Web page to see if it can be used as a source for research. The following steps show how to use the sample worksheet template as shown in Figure 2-3 on page FX 74 to evaluate the Sky and Telescope page.

To Evaluate a Web Resource

1

• **Scroll the display area to display the bottom of the Web page.**

The bottom of the Web page, containing the 1, 2, 3, and 4 page numbers, is displayed (Figure 2-15).

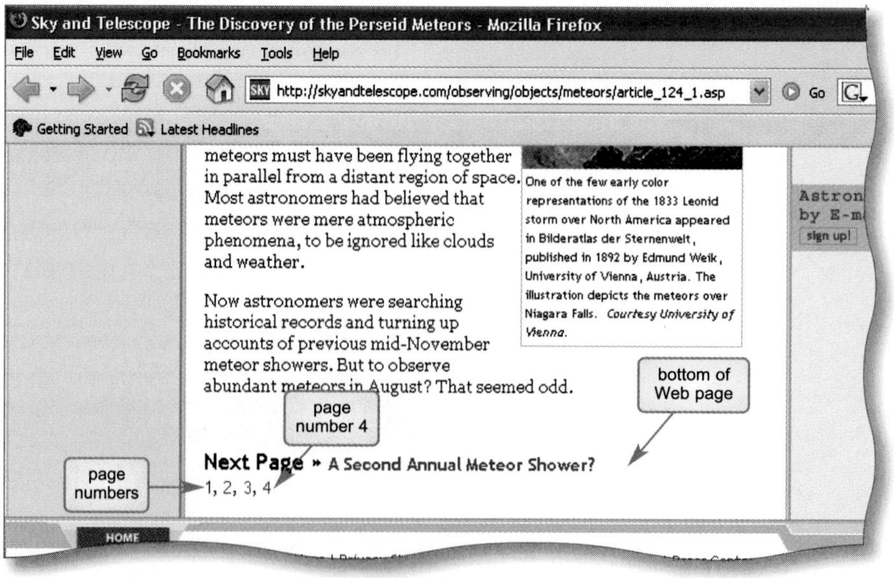

meteors must have been flying together in parallel from a distant region of space. Most astronomers had believed that meteors were mere atmospheric phenomena, to be ignored like clouds and weather.

Now astronomers were searching historical records and turning up accounts of previous mid-November meteor showers. But to observe abundant meteors in August? That seemed odd.

One of the few early color representations of the 1833 Leonid storm over North America appeared in Bilderatlas der Sternenwelt, published in 1892 by Edmund Weik, University of Vienna, Austria. The illustration depicts the meteors over Niagara Falls. *Courtesy University of Vienna.*

Next Page » A Second Annual Meteor Shower?
1, 2, 3, 4

page numbers

page number 4

bottom of Web page

FIGURE 2-15

2

• **Click 4 at the bottom of the Web page to display page 4 in the article.**

• **Scroll the display area to display the bottom of the Web page.**

The bottom of page 4 contains the author qualifications, author acknowledgements, and copyright notice (Figure 2-16).

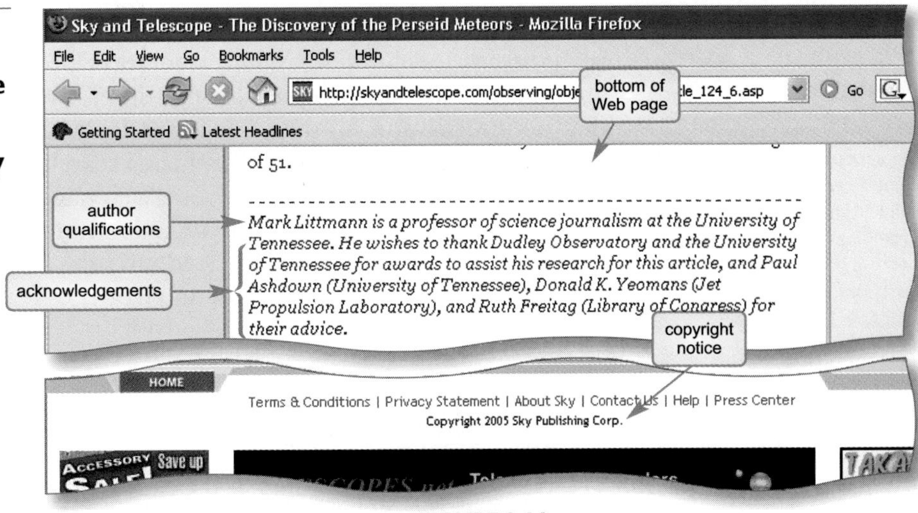

Sky and Telescope - The Discovery of the Perseid Meteors - Mozilla Firefox

File   Edit   View   Go   Bookmarks   Tools   Help

http://skyandtelescope.com/observing/obje... bottom of Web page ...le_124_6.asp   Go

Getting Started   Latest Headlines

of 51.

author qualifications → *Mark Littmann is a professor of science journalism at the University of Tennessee. He wishes to thank Dudley Observatory and the University of Tennessee for awards to assist his research for this article, and Paul Ashdown (University of Tennessee), Donald K. Yeomans (Jet Propulsion Laboratory), and Ruth Freitag (Library of Congress) for their advice.*

acknowledgements →

copyright notice →

HOME

Terms & Conditions | Privacy Statement | About Sky | Contact Us | Help | Press Center
Copyright 2005 Sky Publishing Corp.

FIGURE 2-16

The information gathered so far is summarized on the worksheet illustrated in Figure 2-17. Based on the current worksheet criteria, The Discovery of the Perseid Meteors page is an exceptionally strong resource.

Instead of manually recording evaluation information on a printed copy of the worksheet, you can create an electronic version of the worksheet using a word processor. Then, for each Web resource you select, you can open a new copy of the worksheet document, record the entries, and save the document using a document name that reflects the Web resource being evaluated. Use one worksheet document per Web resource.

Web Resource Evaluation Worksheet

Web page title: **The Discovery of the Perseid Meteors**

Web page URL: **http://skyandtelescope.com/observing/objects/meteors/article_124_1.asp**

Type of Web Resource

Advocacy Business/Marketing Educational Entertainment (Informational) News Personal Portal

Reasons? **Resource on origins of Perseid meteors**

Authorship

What are the author's qualifications? **Mark Littmann - Prof. of Science Journalism**

Is there a sponsoring organization? Does the page link to the organization?
Yes - Sky and Telescope magazine; Yes
Are any opinions and biases clearly stated?

Does the page contain a copyright notice? **Yes - Copyright 2005 Sky Publishing Corp.**

Accuracy of Information

What sources verify the information on the Web page? Does the page link to those sources?

Is the page grammatically correct? **Yes**

Currency of Information

What date was the page placed on Web?

What date was the page last updated?

What date did you visit the page? **May 4, 2007**

Topic and Shape

What is the purpose of the page? **Discovery of Perseid meteors**

Does the page succeed in describing and discussing the topic? **Yes**

Are points clear, well-stated, and supported? **Yes**

Does the page include links to other related pages? **Yes**

FIGURE 2-17

More About

Evaluating a Web Resource

Many Web pages do not have the necessary criteria for being a research source. You will find that you discard many promising Web pages simply because you cannot find the necessary evaluation criteria.

The steps on pages FX 79 through FX 82 showed how to search the World Wide Web using a directory (in this case, Yahoo!). By selecting from a list of categories, such directories eliminate the need for keywords. You may have to spend considerable time, however, traveling through several levels of categories, only to discover that no information on the topic is available.

Using a search engine that performs searches based on keywords, you can explore the Web and display links to Web pages without having to maneuver through any intermediate pages. You provide one or more relevant words, or **keywords**, about the topic in which you are interested, and the search engine returns links that point directly to pages containing those keywords.

Searching the Web

Firefox allows you to search the Web using either the Location bar or Search bar. The Location bar allows you to search for Web pages and search for files and folders on the computer. The Search bar allows you to search for Web pages using search engines such as Yahoo!, Google, and Creative Commons. In addition, you can search for items on sites such as Amazon.com and eBay, or look up the definition of a word on Dictionary.com. Table 2-3 illustrates the default search engines available on the Search bar.

Table 2-3 Default Search Engines Available on the Search Bar	
Google	Search for Web pages, groups, images, news, and more using the Google search engine.
Yahoo!	Search for Web pages, groups, images, news, and more using the Yahoo! search engine.
Amazon.com	Search for products for sale on the Amazon.com Web site.
Creative Commons	Search for publicly licensed works on the Web.
Dictionary.com	Search for definitions, synonyms, and antonyms.
eBay	Search for auctions on the eBay Web site.

Adding a Search Engine to the Search Bar

In the next section, you will use the Search bar to search the Web. In some cases, the six default search engines on the Search bar may not be sufficient to find what you are looking for. Firefox allows you to add hundreds of additional search engines to the Search bar such as A9 Search, AltaVista, Ask Jeeves, CDDB, LEO, IMDB, Merriam-Webster, and Wikipedia. The Ask Jeeves search engine finds answers to questions entered by users. The following steps illustrate how to add the Ask Jeeves search engine to the Search bar.

To Add a Search Engine to the Search Bar

1

• **Click the Google logo on the Search bar and then point to Add Engines.**

Six search engine names and the Add Engines link are displayed on the Search bar menu (Figure 2-18).

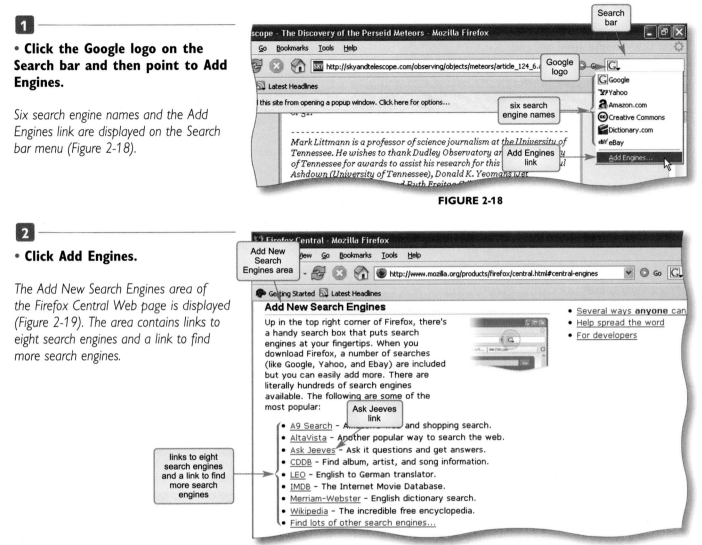

FIGURE 2-18

2

• **Click Add Engines.**

The Add New Search Engines area of the Firefox Central Web page is displayed (Figure 2-19). The area contains links to eight search engines and a link to find more search engines.

Add New Search Engines

Up in the top right corner of Firefox, there's a handy search box that puts search engines at your fingertips. When you download Firefox, a number of searches (like Google, Yahoo, and Ebay) are included but you can easily add more. There are literally hundreds of search engines available. The following are some of the most popular:

• A9 Search – A_____ _____ and shopping search.
• AltaVista – Another popular way to search the web.
• Ask Jeeves – Ask it questions and get answers.
• CDDB – Find album, artist, and song information.
• LEO – English to German translator.
• IMDB – The Internet Movie Database.
• Merriam-Webster – English dictionary search.
• Wikipedia – The incredible free encyclopedia.
• Find lots of other search engines...

• Several ways **anyone** can
• Help spread the word
• For developers

FIGURE 2-19

3

• **Click the Ask Jeeves link.**

Firefox displays the Add Search Engine dialog box containing the name (jeeves), search category (General), and source (http://mycroft.mozdev.org/plugins/jeeves.src) of the Ask Jeeves search engine (Figure 2-20).

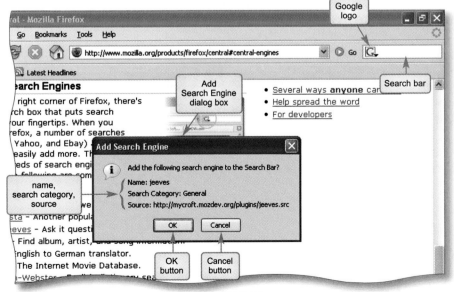

Add Search Engine

Add the following search engine to the Search Bar?

Name: jeeves
Search Category: General
Source: http://mycroft.mozdev.org/plugins/jeeves.src

OK   Cancel

FIGURE 2-20

4

• **Click the OK button in the Add Search Engine dialog box.**

• **Click the Google logo on the Search bar.**

The Search bar menu is displayed and the Ask Jeeves search engine name is added to the menu (Figure 2-21).

5

• **Click the Google logo on the Search bar to close the Search bar.**

The Search bar menu closes.

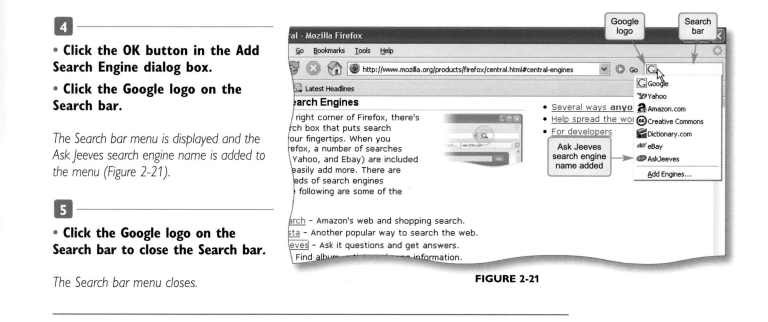

FIGURE 2-21

The following section illustrates how to search the Web using the Ask Jeeves search engine.

Searching the Web Using the Ask Jeeves Search Engine

As previously mentioned, one method to search the Web is to use the Search bar. The Search bar allows you to search for Web pages using a variety of search engines by typing a word, phrase, statement, or question on the Search bar and then pressing the ENTER key.

For instance, you can enter a statement (Give me a list of the planets in the solar system.) or a question (How many planets are in the solar system?). The search engine searches for and displays a list of links to Web pages that pertain to the words, phrase, statement, or question. The following steps illustrate how to use the Ask Jeeves search engine to search for Web pages containing information about the dates of the 2003 Perseid meteor shower.

To Search for Web Pages Using the Ask Jeeves Search Engine

1

• **Click the Google logo on the Search bar and then point to Ask Jeeves.**

A menu containing seven search engines and the Add Engines option is displayed (Figure 2-22).

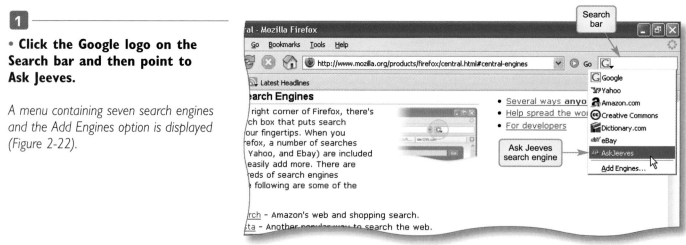

FIGURE 2-22

• **Click Ask Jeeves.**

The Search bar menu closes and the Ask Jeeves logo is displayed on the Search bar (Figure 2-23).

FIGURE 2-23

3

• **Type** In 2003, what were the dates of the perseid meteor shower? **on the Search bar.**

Firefox displays the last part of the question on the Search bar (Figure 2-24).

FIGURE 2-24

4

• **Press the ENTER key.**

Ask Jeeves searches for and finds hundreds of Web pages (Figure 2-25). The Ask Jeeves Results -in 2003, what were the dates of the perseid meteor shower? Web page displays the two links. The number of Web pages found may be different on your computer.

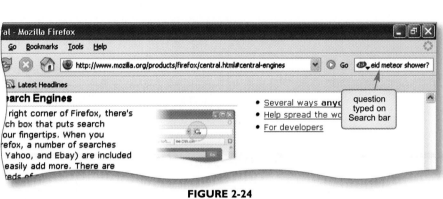

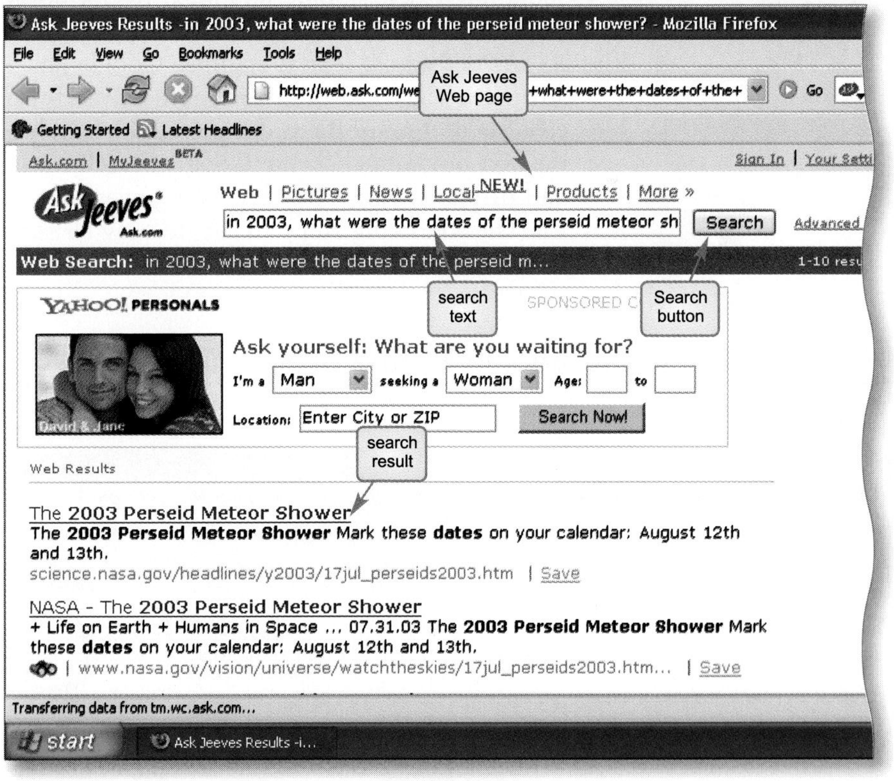

FIGURE 2-25

Other Ways

1. Press CTRL+K, type question, press ENTER

More About

Web Search Engines

Fierce competition exists among search engines. Each search engine claims to have the largest index of Web resources. This competition is healthy and ensures that there are large, up-to-date indexes of Web resources.

The Ask Jeeves search engine displays the question (in 2003, what were the dates of the perseid meteor shower?) in the text box at the top of the Web page. The Ask Jeeves search engine uses keywords from the question to search for Web pages and display the corresponding links in the display area.

The first link (The 2003 Perseid Meteor Shower) contains the dates (August 12th and August 13th) of the 2003 Perseid meteor shower. Clicking this link displays a Web page with more information about The 2003 Perseid Meteor Shower.

In addition to performing an Internet search using a question, you also can search the Internet using one or more keywords. A search engine uses a keyword to find relevant Web pages. The following section discusses how to search the Web using keywords and how to use tabs in Firefox while doing so.

Using Tabbed Browsing to Help Search the Web

Searching the Web for an exact topic is not always easy when search engines return numerous hits. A **hit** results when a search engine returns a Web page that matches the search criteria. The **tabbed browsing** feature provides a way to navigate between the search results and associated Web page(s) in a single browser window.

Simple Search Forms

Google is one of the more widely used search engines. It has an index of billions of Web pages. Each day, its robots visit millions of sites, capturing URLs and corresponding text to update its index. Robot programs also check for **dead links**, which are URLs that no longer work.

As with most search engines, Google has both a simple search form and an advanced search form. The simple search form is displayed on its home page and consists of a text box and the Google Search button. When you type a keyword in the text box and click the Google Search button, Google will search for the keyword and display a list of links to Web pages that contain the keyword.

The following steps illustrate how to search for Web pages that contain the keywords "meteor shower."

To Search Using the Google Simple Search Form

1

• **Click the Location bar, type** www.google.com, **and then click the Go button.**

The URL for the Google home page (http://www.google.com/) is displayed on the Location bar (Figure 2-26).

FIGURE 2-26

2

• **Type** meteor shower **in the search text box.**

Firefox displays the words, meteor shower, in the text box (Figure 2-27).

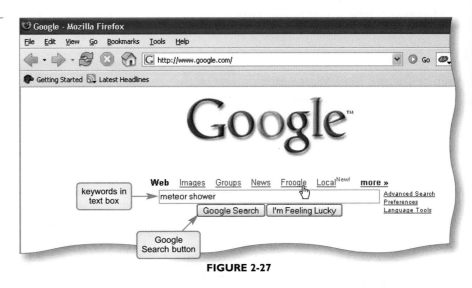

FIGURE 2-27

3

• **Click the Google Search button.**

Google performs the search for "meteor shower" (Figure 2-28). The search results in 369,000 links and several links are displayed in the display area. The number of links and the links in the display area may be different on your computer.

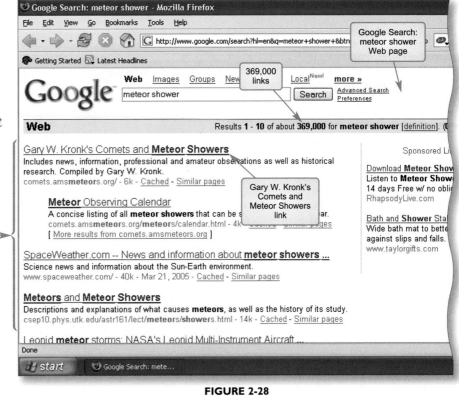

FIGURE 2-28

Opening a Link in a New Tab

Since you may not find the exact topic you are looking for the first time you try, it may be necessary to return to the Google Search page to continue evaluating additional Web pages. Firefox's tabbed browsing feature allows you to open multiple Web pages without requiring a separate browser window for each page. The following steps illustrate how to open a link in a new tab.

To Open a Link in a New Tab

1

• **Right-click the Gary W. Kronk's Comets and Meteor Showers link in the display area and then point to the Open Link in New Tab command.**

A shortcut menu containing the highlighted Open Link in New Tab command is displayed (Figure 2-29).

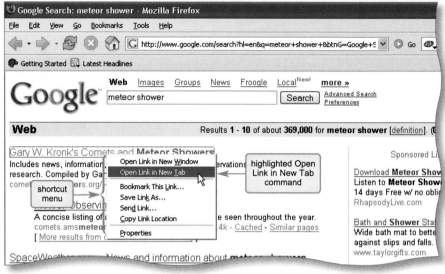

FIGURE 2-29

2

• **Click Open Link in New Tab.**

Firefox creates two tabs on the tab bar below the Bookmarks toolbar (Figure 2-30). The tab bar contains the Google Search: meteor shower tab and the Gary W. Kronk's Comets and Meteor Showers tab. The Google Search: meteor shower tab page is displayed in the display area.

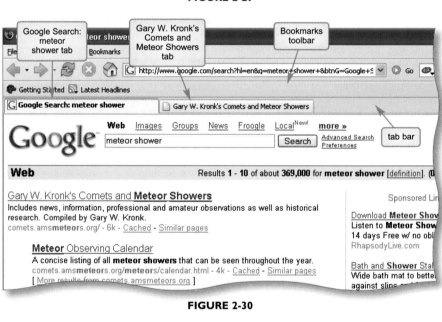

FIGURE 2-30

Other Ways

1. Middle-click Gary W. Kronk's Comets and Meteor Showers link
2. While holding down CTRL, click Gary W. Kronk's Comets and Meteor Showers link

Switching Between Tabs

Currently, the Gary W. Kronk's Comets and Meteor Showers tab is inactive and the Google Search: meteor shower tab is active. When you want to switch to another tab, click the tab. The clicked tab becomes the active tab and the contents of the tab is displayed in the display area. The following steps illustrate how to switch to the Gary W. Kronk's Comets and Meteor Showers tab.

To Switch Between Tabs

1

• **Click the Gary W. Kronk's Comets and Meteor Showers tab.**

The Gary W. Kronk's Comets and Meteor Showers tab is the active tab and the Gary W. Kronk's Comets and Meteor Showers Web page is displayed in the display area (Figure 2-31).

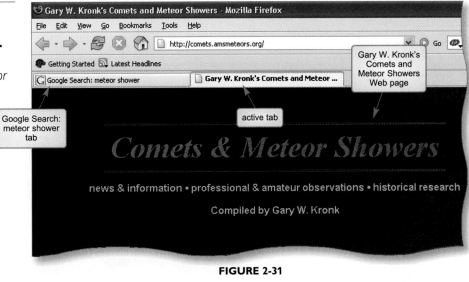

FIGURE 2-31

2

• **When you are finished viewing the Gary W. Kronk's Comets and Meteor Showers Web page, click the Google Search: meteor shower tab.**

The Google Search: meteor shower tab becomes the active tab and the Google Search: meteor shower Web page is displayed in the display area (Figure 2-32).

FIGURE 2-32

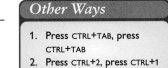

Other Ways

1. Press CTRL+TAB, press CTRL+TAB
2. Press CTRL+2, press CTRL+1

Closing a Tab

When you are finished viewing the contents of a Web page in a tab, you should close the tab to keep the tab bar free from clutter. Having too many tabs open simultaneously makes it difficult to locate a particular tab. The following steps illustrate how to close a tab.

To Close a Tab

1

• **Click the Gary W. Kronk's Comets and Meteor Showers tab on the tab bar.**

Firefox displays the Gary W. Kronk's Comets and Meteor Showers Web page in the display area (Figure 2-33).

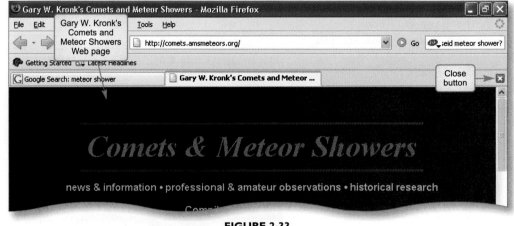

FIGURE 2-33

2

• **Click the Close button on the right side of the tab bar.**

The Gary W. Kronk's Comets and Meteor Showers Web page closes, the tab bar closes, and the Google Search: meteor shower Web page is displayed in the display area (Figure 2-34).

FIGURE 2-34

Other Ways

1. Middle-click Gary W. Kronk's Comets and Meteor Showers tab
2. Right-click the Gary W. Kronk's Comets and Meteor Showers tab, click Close Tab
3. Right-click the Google Search: meteor shower tab, click Close Other Tabs

The Google search results in approximately 369,000 links (Figure 2-28 on page FX 89). In comparison, a search using another search engine, MSN Search, returned approximately 250,000 links. As you can see, different search engines return different numbers of links.

If you spent just one minute looking at each Web page the Google search returned, it would take over a year to view all of them. You can obtain more reasonable results by refining the search. The next section illustrates how to refine a search.

Refining a Web Search

You **refine** a search by providing more information the search engine can use to select a smaller, more useful list of links. Most search engines will search for multiple keywords as if each word carries the same weight. This means Web pages containing any one of a set of multiple keywords or any combination of a set of multiple keywords will satisfy the search engine and be returned as a successful match. Web pages that contain the word "meteor," for example, are included in the 369,000 links returned by the search, even though some of those pages have nothing to do with a meteor shower. To eliminate these Web pages, the keywords need to be more selective and better organized.

In addition to entering keywords, in Google you also can use operators, advanced operators, and some compound search criteria to refine a search. The following paragraphs describe the operators, advanced operators, and compound search criteria.

Operators are symbols that increase the accuracy of a search by fine-tuning the keywords in the search. Operators include the +, -, and ~ symbols and the OR logical operator. Placing the **+ symbol** before a keyword guarantees the keyword will be included in the search. In place of using the + symbol, placing quotation marks around two or more keywords also includes the keywords in the search. Placing the **– symbol** to the left of a keyword guarantees that the keyword is excluded from the search. Placing the **~ symbol** immediately preceding a keyword causes a search for the keyword and its synonym.

The **OR logical operator**, also referred to as a **Boolean operator**, is a compound search criterion that allows you to control how individual words in a keyword phrase are used. For example, the phrase "peanut OR butter" finds Web pages containing either "peanut" or "butter." The Web pages found also can contain both words, but do not have to.

Although the Google search engine allows only the OR logical operator, other search engines allow the use of OR and other Boolean operators. The logical operators include AND, OR, NOT, and NEAR. The **AND operator** and the **OR operator** allow you to create keyword searches containing compound conditions. The **NOT operator** is used to find pages that do not contain certain keywords. The **NEAR operator** is used to find pages in which two keywords are within 10 words of each other.

Table 2-4 describes the Boolean operators and gives an example of each one.

More About

Refining the Search

You can instruct some search engines to search for two or more words that are physically close to each other by using the NEAR operator. If the keywords are within 10 words of each other, the search engine adds the Web page to the list of Web pages found during the search.

Q: How can I get help while using Google?

A: The Google Help Central Web page contains many helpful topics. To view the topics, type `www.google.com/help/index.html` on the Location bar and then click the Go button.

Table 2-4 Boolean Operators and Examples

BOOLEAN OPERATOR	EXAMPLE
AND	Finds only Web pages containing all of the specified words or phrases. "Peanut AND butter" finds Web pages with both the word "peanut" and the word "butter."
OR	Finds Web pages containing at least one of the specified words or phrases. "Peanut OR butter" finds Web pages containing either "peanut" or "butter." The Web pages found can contain both words, but do not have to.
NOT	Excludes Web pages containing the specified word or phrase. "Peanut AND NOT butter" finds Web pages with "peanut" but not containing "butter." With some search engines, NOT cannot stand alone. You must use it with another operator, such as AND. For example, the AltaVista search engine does not accept "peanut NOT butter," but does accept "peanut AND NOT butter."
NEAR	Finds Web pages containing both specified words or phrases within 10 words of each other. "Peanut NEAR butter" finds documents with "peanut butter," but probably not any other kind of butter.
( )	Use parentheses to group complex Boolean phrases. For example, "(peanut AND butter) AND (jelly OR jam)" finds Web pages with the words "peanut butter and jelly" or "peanut butter and jam" or both.

More About

**Advanced
Searches**

If you use Boolean operators
in a search query, you can
substitute symbols for the
operators. The symbol equiv-
alents for the Boolean
operators are AND (&), OR
(|), AND NOT (!), and
NEAR (~).

Advanced operators are query words that have special meaning in Google. The advanced operators modify a search or perform a different type of search. The advanced operators include: cache, link, related, info, define, stocks, site, allintitle, intitle, allinurl, and inurl. For example, typing link:www.google.com finds all Web pages that have links to the www.google.com Web site.

Most search engines have a link on their search pages to access advanced search options. The Google Advanced search link is displayed to the right of the Google Search text box on the Google home page (Figure 2-26 on page FX 88) and to the right of the Search button on other pages. In addition, clicking the Advanced Search Tips link on the Google Advanced Search page displays information about advanced searching.

The following step shows how to refine a search using the Google advanced search capability.

To Display the Google Advanced Search Form

1

• **Click the Advanced Search link to the right of the Search button.**

Google displays the Advanced Search form containing the highlighted Find results area and Language, File Format, Date, Occurrences, Domain, and SafeSearch entries (Figure 2-35).

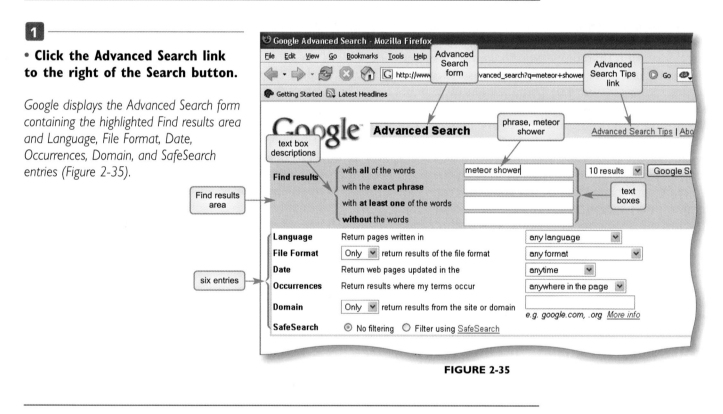

FIGURE 2-35

The Find results area contains four descriptions and four text boxes. Table 2-5 describes the text box descriptions and gives an example of each Web page rule.

Table 2-5 Find Results Area	
TEXT BOX DESCRIPTIONS	**WEB PAGE RULES**
with all of the words	Web pages must contain all the words you typed in the text box.
with the exact phrase	Web pages must contain the exact words in the order you typed them in the text box.
with at least one of the words	Web pages must contain at least one of the words in the text box.
without the words	Web pages must not contain the word or words in the text box.

The following steps show how to use the Google Advanced Search form to refine the search.

To Search Using Google Advanced Search

1

- **Delete the phrase, meteor shower, in the with all of the words text box.**
- **Type** Edward Herrick **in the with all of the words text box.**
- **Click the with the exact phrase text box.**
- **Type** perseid meteor shower **in the text box.**

The Google Advanced Search form contains the words, Edward Herrick, in the with all of the words text box and the phrase, perseid meteor shower, in the with the exact phrase text box (Figure 2-36).

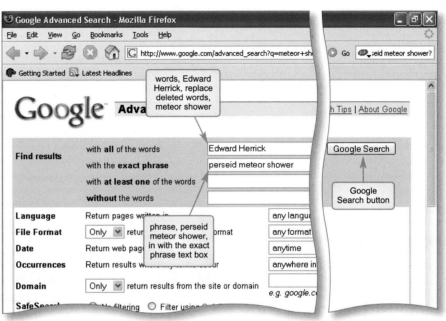

FIGURE 2-36

2

- **Click the Google Search button.**
- **If necessary, scroll down to display the Perseid Meteor Shower in the Yahoo! Directory link.**

Google performs the search and finds 46 links (Figure 2-37). The Perseid Meteor Shower in the Yahoo! Directory link is displayed in the display area. The number of search results that display on your computer may be different.

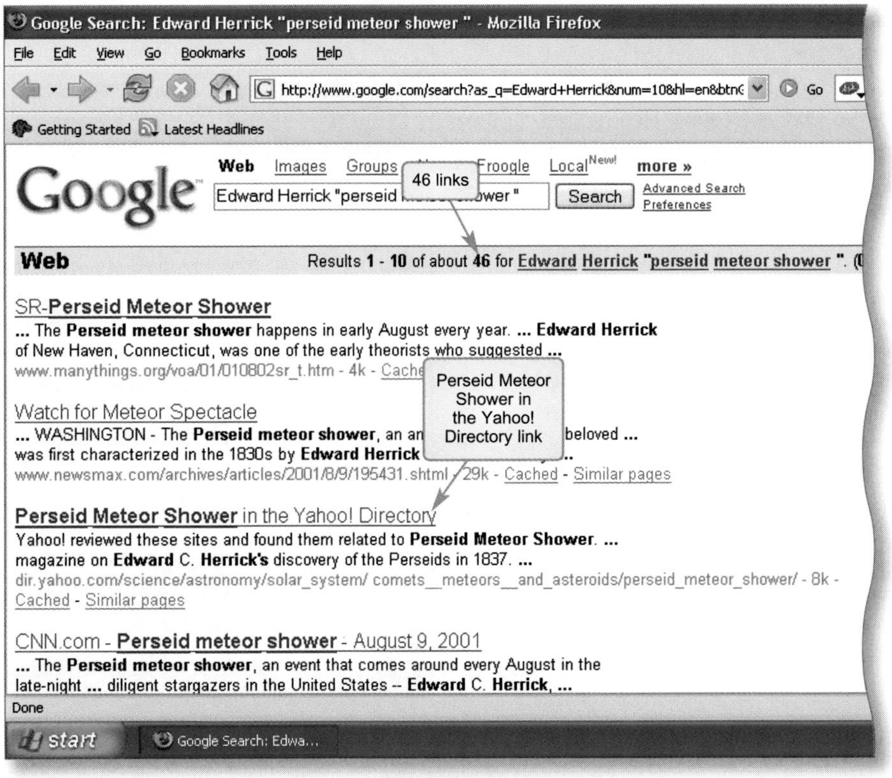

FIGURE 2-37

3

• **Click the Perseid Meteor Shower in the Yahoo! Directory link in the display area.**

• **If necessary, scroll down to display the Discovery of the Perseid Meteors link.**

Related links, including the Discovery of the Perseid Meteors link, are displayed (Figure 2-38).

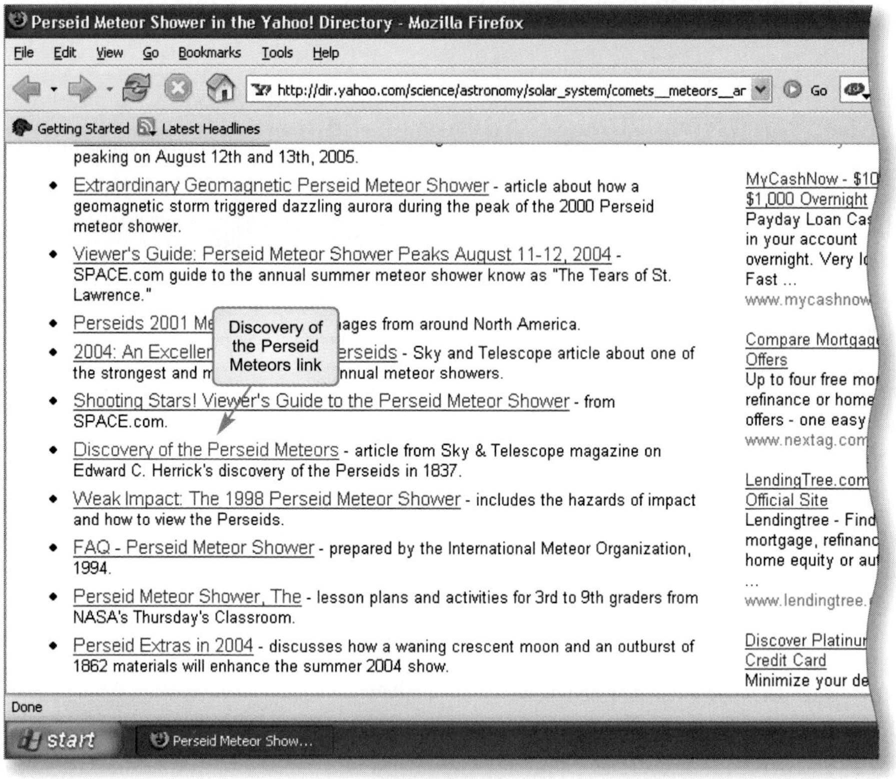

FIGURE 2-38

4

• **Click the Discovery of the Perseid Meteors link in the Yahoo! Search directory.**

The Sky and Telescope - The Discovery of the Perseid Meteors Web page containing The Discovery of the Perseid Meteors article is displayed (Figure 2-39). This is the same Web page found by searching the Yahoo! directory (Figure 2-14 on page FX 82).

FIGURE 2-39

In Figure 2-36 on page FX 95, the first name, Edward, and last name, Herrick, are displayed in the with all of the words text box. Searching using the names in the text box causes a search for both names (first name and last name) and displays Web pages that contain both names. The phrase "perseid meteor shower" in the with the exact phrase text box causes a search for the exact phrase "perseid meteor shower," and displays Web pages that contain the exact phrase.

Using keywords and advanced searching techniques, you have refined a search to locate many useful Web resources successfully.

Successful Searching Techniques

Recall that the initial search for meteor showers using the Google simple search form returned 369,000 links (Figure 2-28 on page FX 89). The second attempt using the Google Advanced Search form returned 46 links (Figure 2-37 on page FX 95) and the pages were more useful. This illustrates the first successful searching technique: be as specific as possible with keywords. Put some thought into what small group of words most represents the topic or is used frequently with it. Choose the best from this group of words to use with the search engine.

If you receive only a few or no useful links, make the keywords slightly more general and try again. For example, assume you want to find information about tax-exempt municipal bonds. A specific-to-very-general list of keywords might be: tax-exempt bonds, municipal bonds, tax-free bonds, tax-free investments, bonds, or investments.

Try to match as many relevant words as possible. This returns more links with better odds that something useful will be among them, although you may have to spend some time looking through all of them. Most search engines support the use of Boolean operators, such as AND, OR, NOT, and NEAR, and parenthesis for grouping. Use the operators to specify complex phrases and conditions. For example, you might use the keywords "(rocket OR shuttle) AND experiment" to search for experiments that were performed in outer space. Use the search engine's Help feature to learn which Boolean operators are available and how to use them.

Another useful technique offered by most search engines is to indicate that certain keywords must display on the Web page, or that certain keywords cannot appear on the Web page. A plus sign (+) indicates inclusion and a minus sign (–) indicates exclusion. You place the + or – sign immediately before a particular keyword. You can use the **inclusion or exclusion capability** to help narrow the search. For example, searching for the keywords "gold –motorcycle" will return links containing the keyword "gold," but not those containing the keyword "motorcycle," thus eliminating any Goldwing motorcycle links.

Another useful feature is the wildcard character. Several search engines allow you to use the **wildcard character** (*) to indicate zero, one, or more characters in a word. For example, searching for immun* will return hits for immune, immunology, immunologist, and any other word beginning with the letters, i-m-m-u-n. Use wildcards if the spelling of a keyword is unknown or may be incorrectly specified on the Web page. Table 2-6 on the next page provides a guide for useful search tips, including the use of wildcard characters.

Table 2-6 Successful Search Techniques	
TIP	**EXAMPLE**
Use parentheses to group items	Use parentheses ( ) to specify precedence in a search. For example, to search for Web pages that contain information about both President Clinton and President Bush, try this advanced query: president AND ((George NEAR Bush) AND ((Bill OR William) NEAR Clinton)).
Use wildcard character	Use an asterisk (*) to broaden a search. To find any words that start with gold, use gold* to find matches for gold, goldfinch, goldfinger, golden, and so on. Use this character if the word you are searching for could have different endings (for example, do not search for dog, search for dog* if it may be plural).
Use quotes to surround a phrase	If you know a certain phrase will display on the page you are looking for, put the phrase in quotes (for example, try entering song lyrics such as "you ain't nothin' but a hounddog").
Use either specific or general keywords	Carry out searches using specific keywords to obtain fewer, more precise links, or general keywords to obtain numerous, less precise links.

Creating a Working Bibliography

Once you find a good Web source, how do you record it? A **working bibliography** will help you organize and compile the resources you find, so that you can cite them as sources in the list of works cited. For Web resources, you should note the author or authors, title of the page, URL, date of publication, date of the last revision, date you accessed the resource, heading of any part or section where the relevant information is located, navigation instructions necessary to find the resource, and other pertinent information.

When you are compiling the information, you often will need to look for an e-mail address on the Web page to find the author. You may have to write to the person responsible for the Web site, or **Webmaster**, and ask for the author's name. First, display the home page of the Web site to see if a directory or contact section is listed. If you do not find a directory or contact section, display the bottom of the Web page or other pages in the Web page. Many Web pages include the e-mail address of the Webmaster at the bottom of the page.

Traditionally, index cards have been used to record relevant information about a work, and you still can use index cards to record Web research. Several electronic means, however, are now available for keeping track of the Web sites you visit and the information you find.

- You can e-mail pertinent information to yourself and store the messages in separate folders. Use one folder for each point or category you are researching.
- You can store the pertinent information in separate document files using copy and paste techniques. Use a separate file for each point or category you research.
- You can create a folder in the Favorites list and then place related favorites you find on the Web in that folder.
- You can print the promising Web page.

To demonstrate how to record relevant information about a Web resource, the following steps illustrate how to copy information from the Sky and Telescope - The Discovery of the Perseid Meteors Web page and paste it into a WordPad document. The copy and paste technique you will use was illustrated in Project 1 on pages FX 35–36.

To Record Relevant Information About a Web Research Source

1

• **Click the Start button on the Windows taskbar, point to All Programs on the Start menu, point to Accessories on the All Programs submenu, and then click WordPad on the Accessories submenu.**

Windows starts the WordPad application and the Document - WordPad window is displayed (Figure 2-40). The Document - WordPad button is displayed on the taskbar.

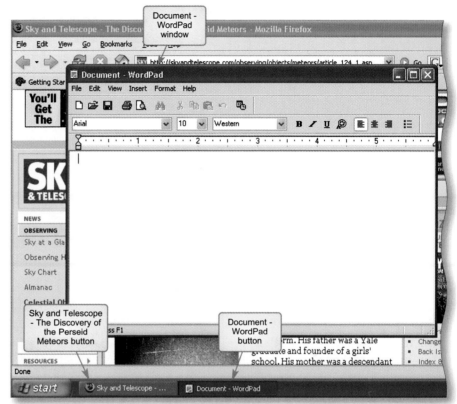

FIGURE 2-40

2

• **Click the Sky and Telescope button on the taskbar to display the Sky and Telescope - The Discovery of the Perseid Meteors window.**

• **Scroll to display the beginning of the article.**

The Sky and Telescope - The Discovery of the Perseid Meteors window, containing the Sky and Telescope Web page, is displayed (Figure 2-41).

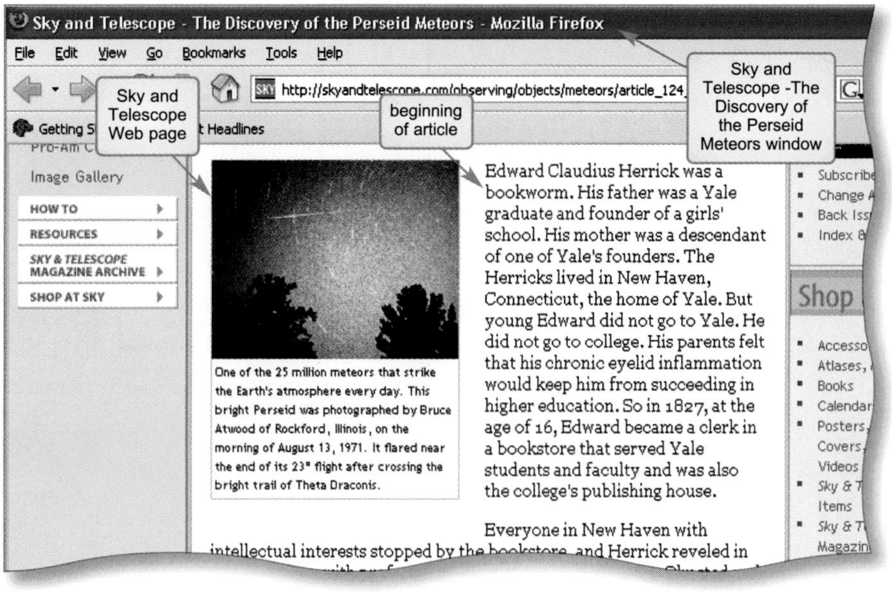

FIGURE 2-41

3

• **Point to the left of the first line of the article.**

• **Drag to select the first paragraph in the article.**

• **Right-click the selected text.**

The text is selected and a shortcut menu is displayed (Figure 2-42).

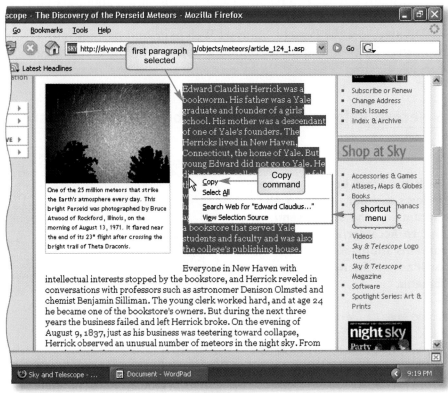

FIGURE 2-42

4

• **Click Copy on the shortcut menu.**

• **Click the Document - WordPad button on the taskbar.**

Windows copies the highlighted text to the Clipboard and the Document - WordPad window is displayed (Figure 2-43).

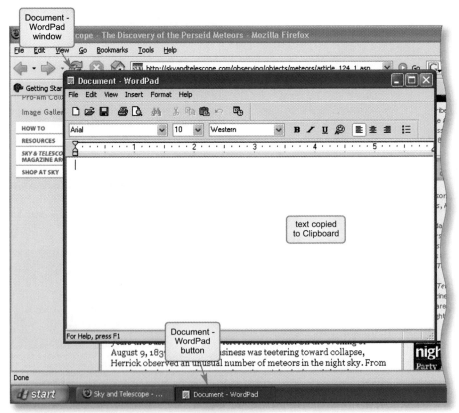

FIGURE 2-43

5

- **Type** http://skyandtelescope.com/observing/objects/meteors/article_124_1.asp **in the WordPad document.**

- **Press the ENTER key and then type** Sky & Telescope Magazine **in the WordPad document.**

- **Press the ENTER key and then type today's date in the WordPad document.**

- **Press the ENTER key twice.**

The URL, organization name, and today's date appear in the WordPad window (Figure 2-44). These are some of the pieces of information needed when citing the work in a research paper.

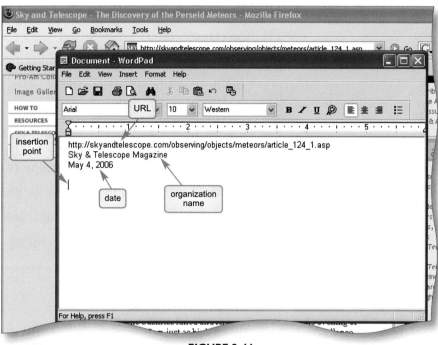

FIGURE 2-44

6

- **Right-click a blank area of the document and then click Paste on the shortcut menu.**

Windows pastes the contents of the Clipboard in the WordPad window at the location of the insertion point (Figure 2-45).

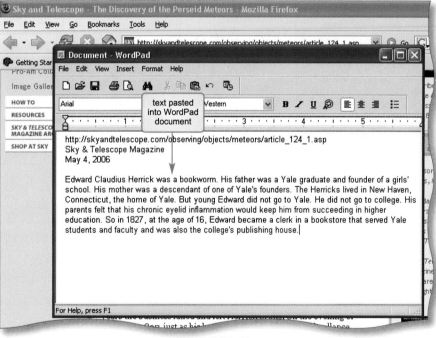

FIGURE 2-45

Saving a WordPad Document

To prevent the accidental loss of the WordPad document, you should formulate an appropriate file name, such as "Discovery of Perseid Meteors," for the document and save it on a 3½-inch floppy disk in drive A, or to an alternate location. After saving the file, quit WordPad.

The next steps show how to save the WordPad document using the file name "Discovery of Perseid Meteors" and quit WordPad.

Mozilla
Firefox

To Save a WordPad Document

1 **If necessary, insert a formatted floppy disk in drive A.**

2 **Click the Save button on the toolbar.**

3 **Type** Discovery of Perseid Meteors **in the File name box.**

4 **Click the Save in box arrow.**

5 **Click 3½ Floppy (A:) in the Save in list. If you are saving the Web page to another location or onto another media, navigate to that location and substitute the location for 3½ Floppy (A:).**

6 **Click the Save button in the Save As dialog box.**

7 **If necessary, remove the floppy disk from drive A.**

8 **Click the Close button on the WordPad title bar to quit WordPad.**

WordPad saves the WordPad document using the Discovery of Perseid Meteors file name, closes the WordPad window, and quits WordPad.

If you are using the electronic technique for evaluating a Web source, you can save the research information at the bottom of the worksheet document. Then, both the evaluation criteria and the research information for a particular Web page are stored in the same document.

Citing Web Sources

Most of the preferred style authorities, such as Modern Language Association (MLA) and American Psychological Association (APA), publish standards for citing Web resources. You can find these guides at a library or on the Web. Online information about these style guides can be found at www.mla.org and www.apa.org.

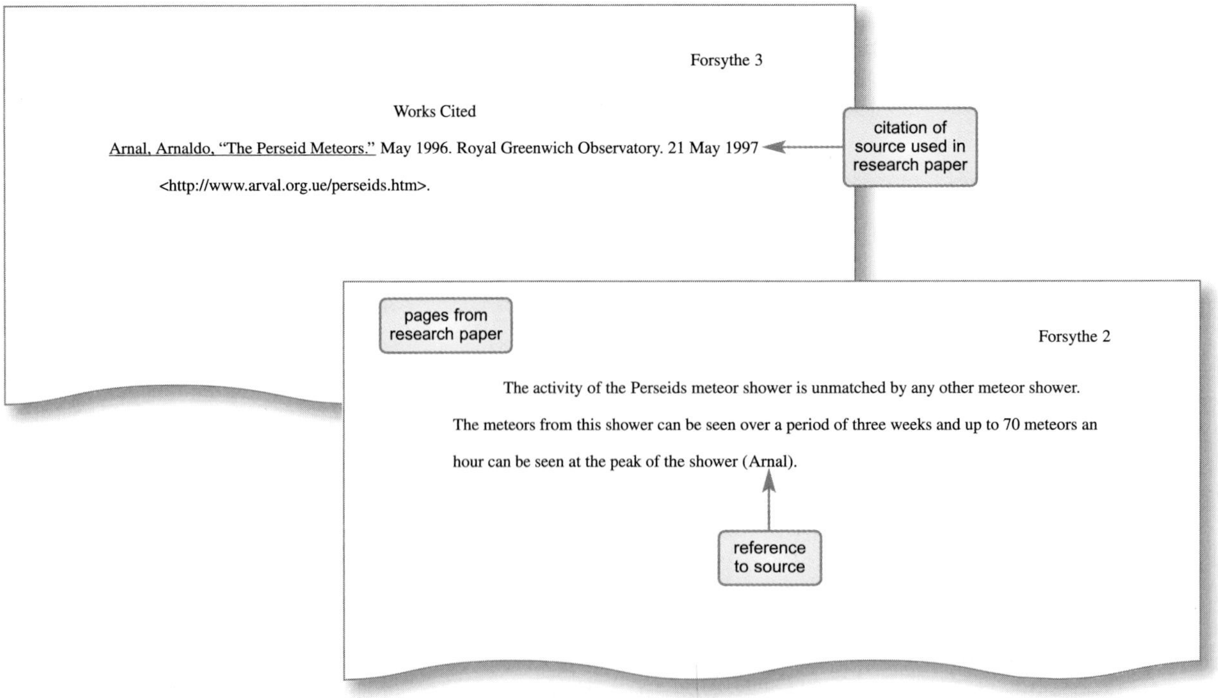

More About

Citing Web Sources

All of the style guides mentioned in the text differ slightly from one another on the format of the citation used to cite a Web source. Check with your instructor for the accepted format your school uses. Check out on the Web the two most widely used style guides: the Modern Language Association and the American Psychological Association.

Forsythe 3

Works Cited

Arnal, Arnaldo, "The Perseid Meteors." May 1996. Royal Greenwich Observatory. 21 May 1997 ◄——— citation of source used in research paper

<http://www.arval.org.ue/perseids.htm>.

pages from research paper

Forsythe 2

The activity of the Perseids meteor shower is unmatched by any other meteor shower. The meteors from this shower can be seen over a period of three weeks and up to 70 meteors an hour can be seen at the peak of the shower (Arnal).

reference to source

FIGURE 2-46

Figure 2-46 contains an example of using and citing a Web resource using the MLA style. The example documents the source of the criteria for the activity of the Perseid meteor shower.

As you have learned in this project, the World Wide Web can be an informative and valuable source of information. By using proper searching and note-taking techniques, and asking the right questions about the usefulness of a Web resource, you can add to the information base you use to write a paper or speech. Always remember, however, that Web sources should complement, not replace, printed sources for locating information.

Searching the Web for Other Information

In this project, you first searched for Web pages using the Yahoo! directory and then searched for Web pages using the Google search engine. You also can use Google and other search engines on the Web to search for mailing addresses and e-mail addresses, business names and business categories, maps, words, encyclopedia articles, and pictures. The following sections illustrate how to search for a mailing address, a landmark, a word in a dictionary, and a picture.

Searching the Web for an Address

You can use the InfoSpace or BigFoot Web sites to find the address of an individual. The following steps illustrate how to search for the address of one of the authors of this book when you know only the author's first and last name and the state in which he lives. Sometimes you will find that you need to specify a city as well.

To Search the Web for an Address

• **If necessary, maximize the Sky and Telescope - The Discovery of the Perseid Meteors - Mozilla Firefox window.**

• **Type** www.infospace.com **on the Location bar and then click the Go button.**

The URL for the Yellow Pages and White Pages - Infospace home page is displayed on the Location bar and the Yellow Pages and White Pages - Infospace home page is displayed in the display area (Figure 2-47). The display area contains the selected Find a Business by Type option button, a text box containing the words, Type of Business, a text box containing the word, City, and a box containing the State* entry.

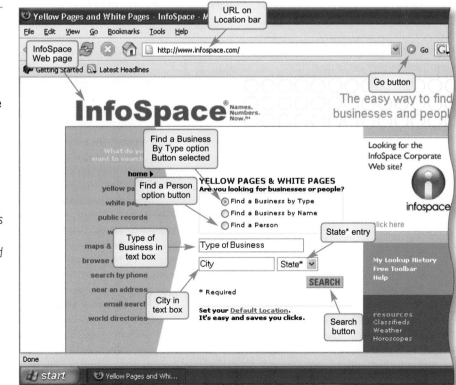

FIGURE 2-47

2

• **Click the Find a Person option button. Click the LastName*,FirstName text box to remove the text and then type** Forsythe, Steven **in the text box.**

• **Click the arrow in State* box to display a list of state names and then click CA in the list.**

The Find a Person option button is selected, the LastName, FirstName text box contains the author's name (Forsythe, Steven), and the California state abbreviation (CA) is displayed in the State menu (Figure 2-48).*

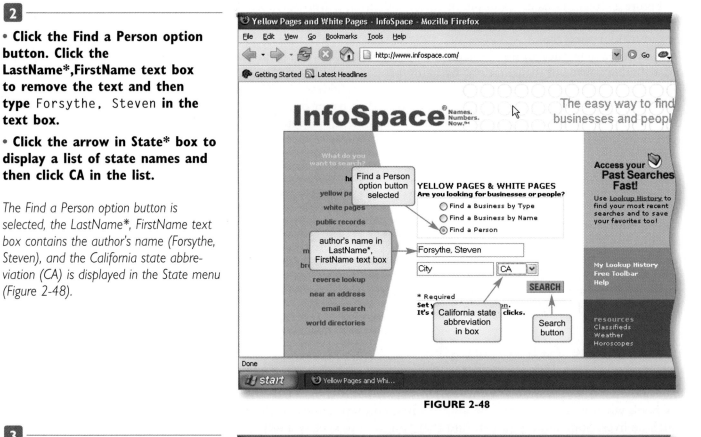

FIGURE 2-48

3

• **Click the Search button.**

• **Scroll the display area to display the search results.**

InfoSpace searches for the address of the author and the display area displays the search results (Figure 2-49). The links may be different on your computer.

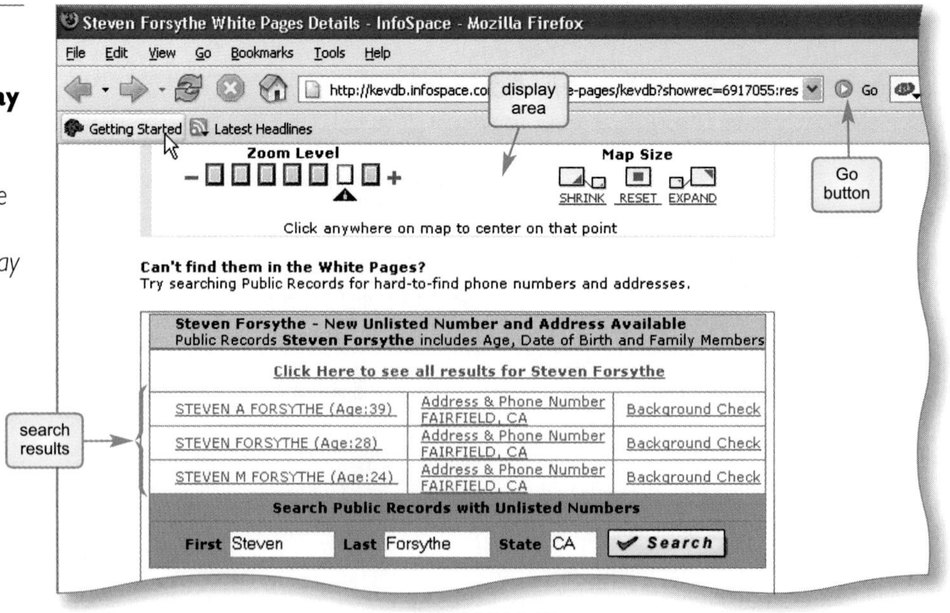

FIGURE 2-49

Searching the Web for a Map

When you plan to visit a new landmark, city, or state, you can use the Internet to provide a map of the area you plan to visit. Many people like the Expedia.com Web site for finding maps. The next steps show how to search for a map of the University of Central Florida Arena in Orlando, Florida.

To Search the Web for a Place or Landmark

1

• **Type** www.expedia.com **in the Location bar and then click the Go button.**

The URL for the Expedia Travel home page (http://www.expedia.com) is displayed on the Location bar, and the Expedia Travel home page is displayed in the display area (Figure 2-50).

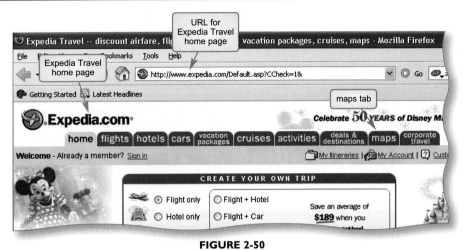

FIGURE 2-50

2

• **Click the maps tab near the top of the display area.**

The Maps page on the Expedia.com Web site is displayed (Figure 2-51).

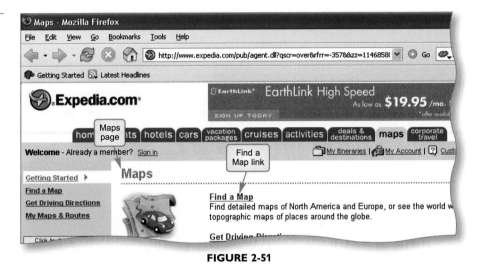

FIGURE 2-51

3

• **Click the Find a Map link.**

• **If necessary, scroll the Find a map page to display the Search for a place option button and the Find a map link.**

Firefox displays the Find a map page, containing the Search for an address or intersection option button and the Search for a place option button (Figure 2-52).

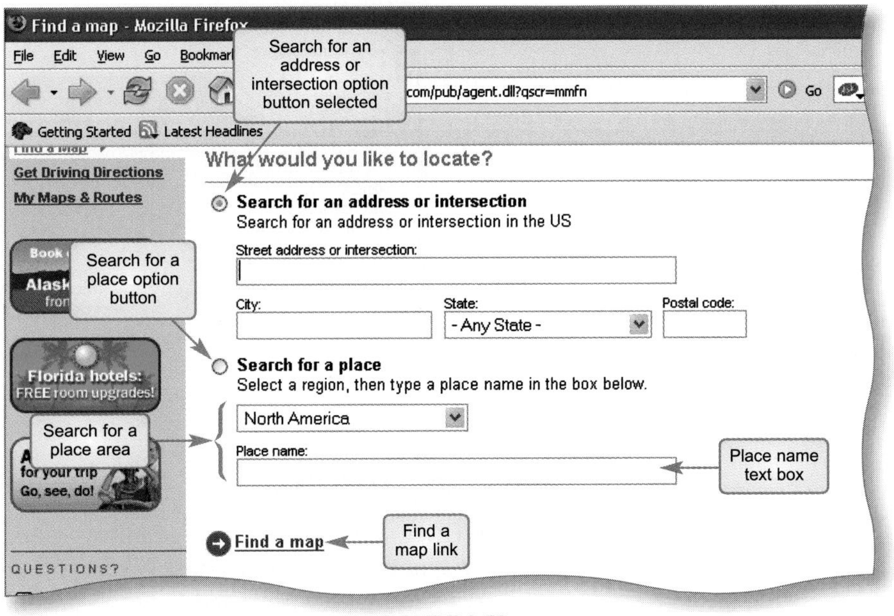

FIGURE 2-52

4

• **Click the Search for a place option button.**

• **Type** University of Central Florida Arena **in the Place name text box.**

The Search for a place option button is selected and University of Central Florida Arena is displayed in the Place name text box (Figure 2-53).

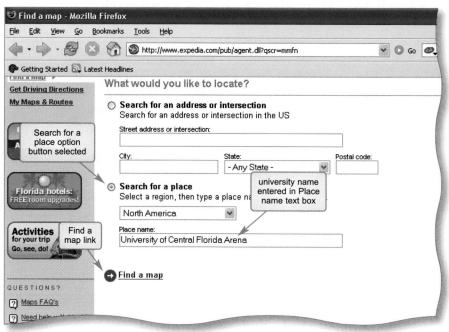

FIGURE 2-53

5

• **Click the Find a map link.**

Expedia.com searches for and displays a map of the University of Central Florida Arena in the Search Results page (Figure 2-54).

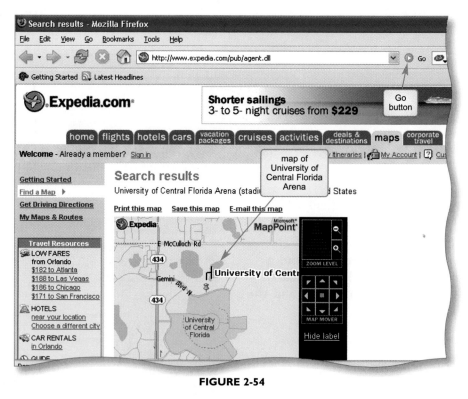

FIGURE 2-54

Other Ways

1. On Location bar type www.mapquest.com, click Go button, type address or intersection, city, state, and zip code, click Get Map button

Searching the Web for the Definition of a Word

The Dictionary.com Web page allows you to search for an encyclopedia article, word, or synonym and antonym. When you enter a word and then click the Search button, the Web site is searched for the appropriate word and a definition is displayed. The next steps show how to find the definition of the abbreviation "DVD."

To Search the Web for the Definition of a Word

1

• **Type** www.dictionary.com **on the Location bar and then click the Go button.**

The URL for the Dictionary.com home page (http://dictionary.reference.com) is displayed on the Location bar and the Dictionary.com Web page is displayed in the display area (Figure 2-55).

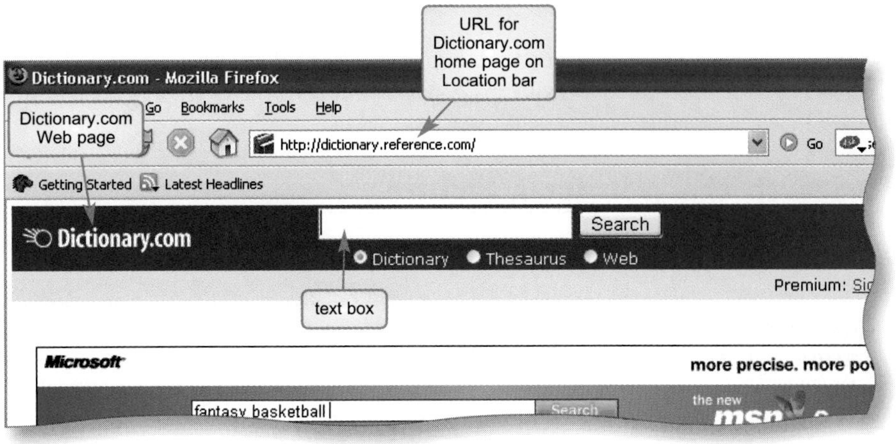

FIGURE 2-55

2

• **Type** DVD **in the text box at the top of the Dictionary.com home page and then point to the Search button.**

The abbreviation, DVD, is displayed in the text box at the top of the page (Figure 2-56).

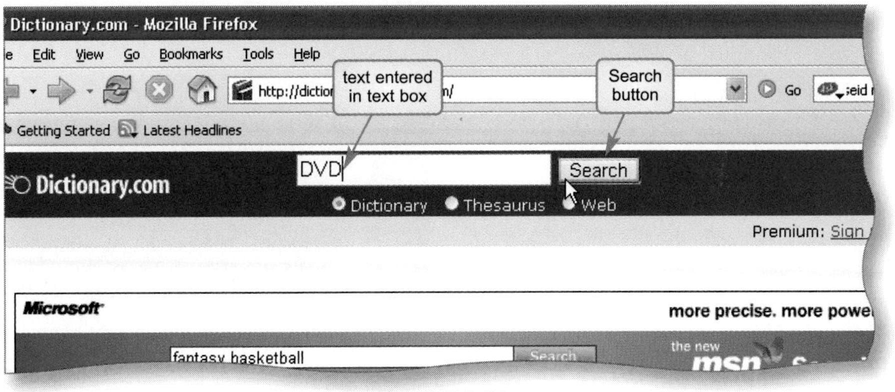

FIGURE 2-56

3

• **Click the Search button.**

• **If necessary, scroll down to display the first entry.**

Dictionary.com searches for and displays four entries in the display area (Figure 2-57). The first entry in the list comes from The American Heritage® Dictionary of the English Language, Fourth Edition. The search results may be different on your computer.

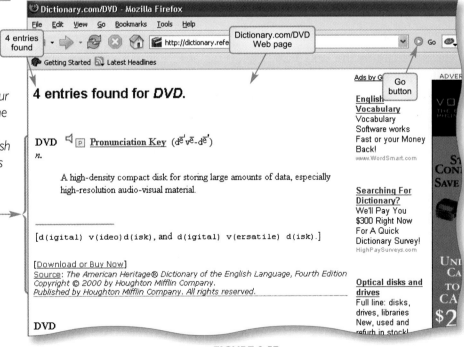

FIGURE 2-57

Searching the Web for a Picture

When you want to search for a picture, the Corbis Web site is a good choice because it provides convenient access to digital pictures and stock photography. The following steps illustrate how to search for surfing pictures.

To Search the Web for a Picture

 1

• **Type** www.corbis.com **on the Location bar and then click the Go button.**

The URL for the Corbis home page (http://www.pro.corbis.com) is displayed on the Location bar and the Corbis home page is displayed (Figure 2-58).

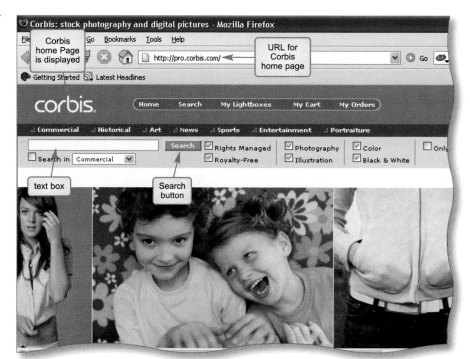

FIGURE 2-58

2

• **Type** surfing **in the text box and then point to the Search button.**

The word "surfing" is displayed in the text box near the top of the Corbis home page (Figure 2-59).

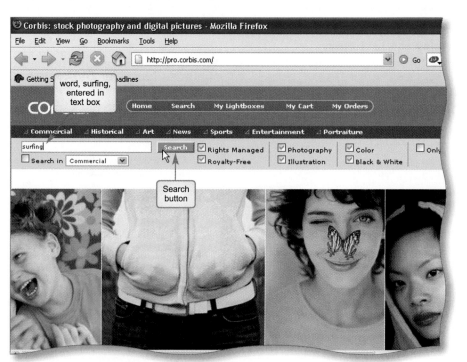

FIGURE 2-59

3

• **Click the Search button.**

Searching the Corbis Web site results in finding 1,000 pictures (Figure 2-60). Twenty-five pictures and their titles is displayed per page. Clicking the right arrow displays the next set of twenty-five pictures. The list of pictures may be different on your computer.

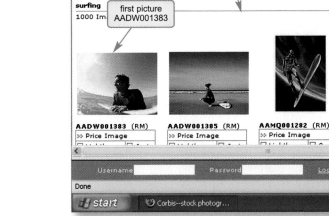

FIGURE 2-60

4

• **Click the first picture (AADW001383) in the first row.**

Firefox displays a new window containing the enlarged picture (Figure 2-61).

5

• **When you are done viewing the picture, click the Close button.**

FIGURE 2-61

Other Ways to Search the Web

Previously, this project used the Search bar and various search engines to search for information (Web page, address, place or landmark, definitions, pictures, and so on). You also can use the Location bar to search for information on the Web. As mentioned previously, this type of search tool is called a Keyword system. A **Keyword system** allows you to enter a name or word on the Location bar to display a list of corresponding Web pages.

You can use the Location bar to type an address (URL) and display the associated Web page. In addition, you can type a folder location (path) to display the contents of the folder, and type a document name to start an application and display the document in the application window. These operations are illustrated in the following sections.

Using the Location Bar and a URL to Display a Web Page

One method to search for and display a Web page using the Location bar is to type an address (URL) and then click the Go button. For example, the URL for the Kelley Blue Book Web page is www.kelleybluebook.com. The next step illustrates how to type the URL for the Kelley Blue Book Web page on the Location bar and display the Kelley Blue Book Web page.

To Search for a Web Page Using the Location Bar

1

• **Click the Location bar, type** www.kelleybluebook.com **on the Location bar, and then click the Go button.**

The URL for the Kelley Blue Book Web page is displayed on the Location bar, and the Kelley Blue Book Web page is displayed in the display area (Figure 2-62).

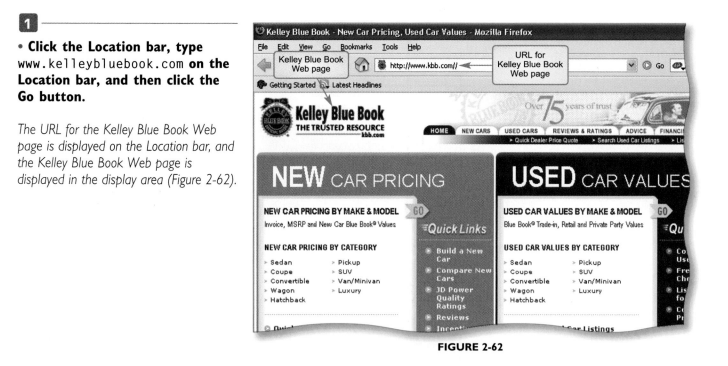

FIGURE 2-62

Using the Location Bar and a Keyword to Display a Home Page

If you type a specific product, trademark, company name, or institution name on the Location bar and then click the Go button, Firefox will use Google's search technology to find the most popular home page that relates to the text on the Location bar.

Assume you want information on the University of Central Florida, but do not know the university's URL. After entering the phrase "university of central florida," Google searches for and displays the University of Central Florida home page.

The following steps show how to display the home page of the University of Central Florida using the Location bar.

To Search for a Home Page Using the Location Bar

1

- **Click the Location bar and then type** university of central florida **on the Location bar.**

The Location bar contains the entry "university of central florida" (Figure 2-63).

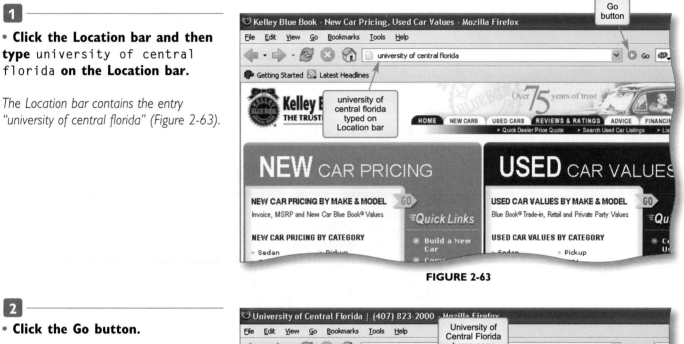

FIGURE 2-63

2

- **Click the Go button.**

Because the university of central florida entry does not contain a www. or .com or .org, Firefox sends the keywords (university of central florida) to the Keyword system. The Keyword system finds the University of Central Florida home page using Google's search technology and Firefox displays the University of Central Florida home page (Figure 2-64).

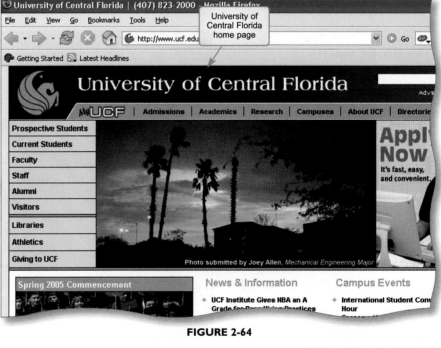

FIGURE 2-64

Other Ways
1. Press CTRL+L, type keyword, press ENTER

This method works well with company names, organization names, association names, and specific products and services.

Using the Location Bar to Search for a Folder on the Computer

To display the contents of a folder using the Location bar, you must type the path of the folder and then click the Go button. A **path** is the means of navigating to a specific location on a computer or network. To specify a path, you must type the drive letter, followed by a colon (:), a backslash (\), and the folder name. For example, the path for the WINDOWS folder on drive C is C:\WINDOWS. The following steps show how to type the path of the WINDOWS folder and display the contents of the WINDOWS folder.

To Search for a Folder and Its Contents Using the Location Bar

1

• **Click the Location bar and then type** c:\windows **on the Location bar.**

The path of the WINDOWS folder is displayed on the Location bar (Figure 2-65).

2

• **Click the Go button.**

A file icon and the path of the WINDOWS folder appear in the Location bar and the Index of file:///c:/windows/ - Mozilla Firefox window containing the files and folders in the WINDOWS folder is displayed (Figure 2-66).

3

• **Click the Close button to close the Index of file:///c:/windows/ - Mozilla Firefox window.**

The Index of file:///c:/windows/ - Mozilla Firefox window closes.

FIGURE 2-65

FIGURE 2-66

In addition to using the Location bar to display a Web page, search for a page on the Web, and display the contents of a folder, you also can use the Location bar to open a document. To display a document, you must know the path (location) of the document as well as the document name. When you type the path of the document on the Location bar and then click the Go button, Firefox will open the document in either the display area, or it will start another application on the computer designed to read and display the document.

Project Summary

In this project, the nine general types of Web pages and the three general types of search tools were described. You learned how to evaluate a Web page as a potential source for research. You learned how to search the Internet using the Yahoo! directory. You learned the techniques for using the Google search engine to enter keywords and for using advanced search techniques. You learned how to record relevant information about a potential source for future reference and how to write a citation for a Web resource. You saw how to use various search engines to search the Internet for an address, a map, a definition, and a picture. In addition, you learned how to search the Web using the Location bar and the Keyword system.

What You Should Know

Having completed the project, you now should be able to perform the tasks below. The tasks are listed in the same order they were presented in this project.

1. Start Firefox (FX 77)
2. Display the Yahoo! Home Page (FX 78)
3. Search Using the Yahoo! Web Directory (FX 79)
4. Evaluate a Web Resource (FX 82)
5. Add a Search Engine to the Search Bar (FX 85)
6. Search for Web Pages Using the Ask Jeeves Search Engine (FX 86)
7. Search Using the Google Simple Search Form (FX 88)
8. Open a Link in a New Tab (FX 90)
9. Switch Between Tabs (FX 91)
10. Close a Tab (FX 92)
11. Display the Google Advanced Search Form (FX 94)
12. Search Using the Google Advanced Search (FX 95)
13. Record Relevant Information About a Web Research Source (FX 99)
14. Save a WordPad Document (FX 102)
15. Search the Web for an Address (FX 103)
16. Search the Web for a Place or Landmark (FX 105)
17. Search the Web for the Definition of a Word (FX 107)
18. Search the Web for a Picture (FX 108)
19. Search for a Web Page Using the Location Bar (FX 110)
20. Search for a Home Page Using the Location Bar (FX 111)
21. Search for a Folder and Its Contents Using the Location Bar (FX 112)

Learn It Online

Instructions: To complete the Learn It Online exercises, start your browser, click the Location bar, enter scsite.com/firefox/learn, and then click the Go button. When the Firefox Learn It Online page is displayed, follow the instructions in the exercises below. Each exercise has instructions for printing your results, either for your own records or for submission to your instructor.

1 Project Reinforcement TF, MC, and SA

Below Firefox Project 2, click the Project Reinforcement link. Print the quiz by clicking Print on the File menu for each page. Answer each question.

Flash Cards

Below Firefox Project 2, click the Flash Cards link and read the instructions. Type 20 (or a number specified by your instructor) in the Number of Playing Cards text box, type your name in the Enter your name text box, and then click the Flip Card button. When the flash card is displayed, read the question and then click the ANSWER box arrow to select an answer. Flip through Flash Cards. If your score is 15 (75%) correct or greater, click Print on the File menu to print your results. If your score is less than 15 (75%) correct, then redo this exercise by clicking the Replay button.

3 Practice Test

Below Firefox Project 2, click the Practice Test link. Answer each question, enter your first and last name at the bottom of the page, and then click the Grade Test button. When the graded practice test is displayed on your screen, click Print on the File menu to print a hard copy. Continue to take practice tests until you score 80% or better.

4 Who Wants To Be a Computer Genius?

Below Firefox Project 2, click the Computer Genius link. Read the instructions, enter your first and last name at the bottom of the page, and then click the PLAY button. When your score is displayed, click the PRINT RESULTS link to print a hardcopy.

5 Wheel of Terms

Below Firefox Project 2, click the Wheel of Terms link. Read the instructions and then enter your first and last name and your school name. Click the PLAY button. When your score is displayed, right-click the scores and then click Print on the shortcut menu to print a hard copy.

6 Crossword Puzzle Challenge

Below Firefox Project 2, click the Crossword Puzzle Challenge link. Read the instructions and then enter your first and last name. Click the SUBMIT button. Work the crossword puzzle. When you are finished, click the Submit button. When the crossword puzzle is displayed, click the Print Puzzle button to print a hard copy.

7 Tips and Tricks

Below Firefox Project 2, click the Tips and Tricks link. Click a topic that pertains to Project 2. Right-click the information and then click Print on the shortcut menu. Construct a brief example of what the information relates to in Firefox to confirm you understand how to use the tip or trick.

8 Newsgroups

Below Firefox Project 2, click the Newsgroups link. Click a topic that pertains to Project 2. Print three comments.

9 Expanding Your Horizons

Below Firefox Project 2, click the Articles for Microsoft Windows XP link. Click a topic that pertains to Project 2. Print the information. Construct a brief example of what the information relates to in Firefox to confirm you understand the contents of the article.

10 Search Sleuth

Below Firefox Project 2, click the Search Sleuth link. To search for a term that pertains to this project, select a term below the Project 2 title and then use the Google search engine at google.com (or any major search engine) to display and print two Web pages that present information on the term.

11 Firefox How-To Article

Below Firefox Project 2, click the Firefox How-To Articles link. When your browser displays the Firefox How-To Articles Web page, scroll down and click one of the links that covers one or more of the objectives listed at the beginning of the project on page FX 68. Print the first page of the How-To article before stepping through it.

12 Getting More from the Web

Below Firefox Project 2, click the Getting More From the Web link. When your browser displays the Getting More from the Web with Firefox Web page, click one of the Top Stories or Featured Contents links. Print the first page.

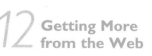

In the Lab

1 Searching the Web Using the Yahoo! Web Directory

Problem: You work full-time for the San Antonio Community Center. Your boss has asked you to search for information on several unrelated topics and print the first page of each Web site.

Instructions: Use Firefox and a computer to perform the following tasks.

Part 1: *Displaying the Yahoo! Directory*

1. If necessary, connect to the Internet and start Firefox.
2. Click the Location bar, type www.yahoo.com and then click the Go button to display the Yahoo! Home page. The Yahoo! Web directory can be found on this page.

Part 2: *Finding Information about Alternative Medicine Using the Yahoo! Directory*

1. Using the Yahoo! Web directory and the Health category, locate information on an alternative form of medicine called rolfing. **Rolfing** involves working the body to improve structural integrity and also is referred to as Body Working. Answer the following questions.
   a. What is rolfing? _____
   b. Who founded and taught rolfing? _____
   c. What is the benefit of rolfing? _____
2. Print the home page for the Guild for Structural Integration and write your name on the printout (Figure 2-67).

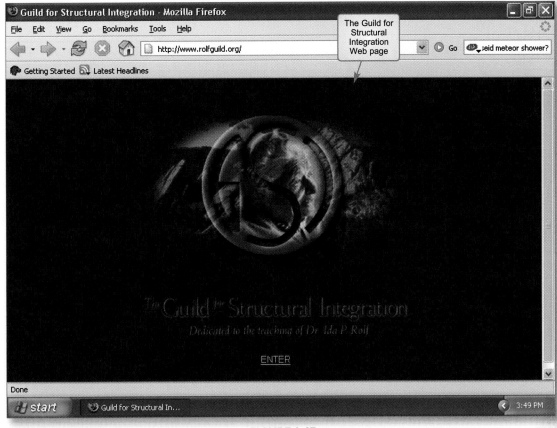

FIGURE 2-67

(continued)

In the Lab

Searching the Web Using the Yahoo! Web Directory *(continued)*

Part 3: *Finding a College Using the Yahoo! Web Directory*

1. Using the Yahoo! Web directory and the Education category, locate the home page of the only private college in Cherokee County, South Carolina. Answer the following questions.
   a. What is the college name? _____
   b. In what city is the college located? _____
   c. What team name does the Athletic Department use? _____
2. Print the home page of the college and write your name on the printout.

Part 4: *Finding Information about Roller Coasters Using the Yahoo! Directory*

1. Using the Yahoo! Web directory and the Recreation category, locate information about amusement parks that have roller coasters and then use the roller coaster database to answer the following questions.
   a. In which city is the Michigan's Adventure Amusement Park located? _____
   b. How many steel roller coasters does the park have? _____
   c. In what amusement park is the oldest indoor roller coaster located? _____
2. Print the roller coaster database Web page and write your name on the printout.

Part 5: *Finding Information about Chemistry Using the Yahoo! Directory*

1. Using the Yahoo! Web directory and the Science category, locate information about the periodic table of elements. Answer the following questions.
   a. What is the symbol for gold? _____
   b. Which element is associated with the symbol Ca? _____
   c. What is the atomic weight of Californium? _____
2. Print the Web page containing the periodic table and write your name on the printout.
3. Hand in all printouts to your instructor.
4. Quit Firefox.

2 Searching the Web Using the Yahoo! Directory

Problem: Your instructor would like you to practice using the Yahoo! directory. She recommends searching for graphic images of different types of artwork. As proof of completing this assignment, you should print the Web page containing the graphic image.

Instructions: Use Firefox and a computer to perform the following tasks.

Part 1: *Displaying the Yahoo! Directory*

1. If necessary, connect to the Internet and start Firefox.
2. Click the Location bar, type www.yahoo.com as the entry, and then click the Go button to display the Yahoo! directory.

Part 2: *Finding Art Work Using the Yahoo! Web Directory*

1. Using the Yahoo! directory and the Arts category, search for and print the Web page containing a graphic image that is representative of each of the following types of artwork: animation, body art, computer-generated, public art, graffiti, and stone sculpture. Figure 2-68 shows a collection of Alabaster bowls created by Ron Christie.

In the Lab

2. On each printout, write your name and the type of artwork the Web page represents. Hand in the pages to your instructor.

3. Quit Firefox.

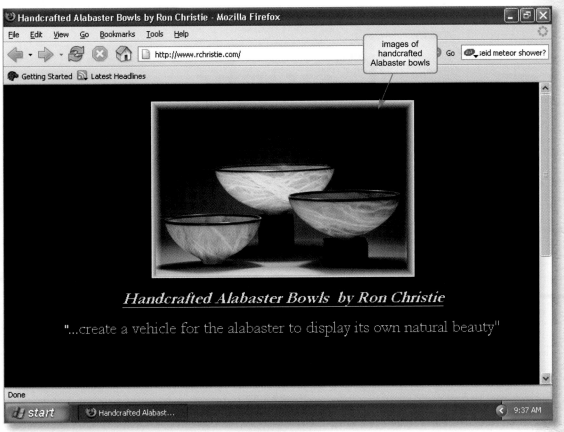

FIGURE 2-68

3 Searching the Web Using the Google Directory

Problem: Your instructor would like you to practice searching Web sites using the Google directory. He would like you to focus on finding Web pages that contain antiques, rules of card games, and images of birds. As proof of completing this assignment, print out the first page of each Web site you visit.

Instructions: Use Firefox and a computer to perform the following tasks.

Part 1: *Displaying the Google Directory*

1. If necessary, connect to the Internet and start Firefox.
2. Click the Location bar, type `www.google.com` as the entry, and then click the Go button to display the Google home page.
3. Click the more link and then click Directory on the resulting page (Figure 2-69 on the next page).

(continued)

In the Lab

Searching the Web Using the Google Directory *(continued)*

FIGURE 2-69

Part 2: *Finding Antiques Using the Google Directory*

1. Using the Google directory and the Arts category, locate a Web page that contains information on antique Nikon cameras. Print the Web page and write your name on the printout.
2. Locate a Web page that contains information about antique salt and pepper shakers. Print the Web page and write your name on the printout.
3. Locate a Web page that contains information about antique stamps. Print the Web page and write your name on the printout.

Part 3: *Finding Games Using the Google Directory*

1. Using the Google directory and the Games category, locate a Web page that contains the rules for the Hearts card game. Print the Web page and write your name on the printout.
2. Locate a Web page that contains the rules for the Canasta card game. Print the Web page and write your name on the printout.
3. Locate a Web page that contains rules for the Euchre card game. Print the Web page and write your name on the printout.

Part 4: *Finding Recreational Activities Using the Google Directory*

1. Using the Google directory and the Recreation category, locate a Web page that contains images of Hot Air Ballooning. Print the Web page and write your name on the printout.

In the Lab

2. Locate a Web page that contains images of birds. Print the Web page and write your name on the printout.
3. Locate a Web page that contains images of miniature trains. Print the Web page and write your name on the printout.
4. Hand in all printouts to your instructor. Quit Firefox.

4 Searching the Web Using AltaVista and Keywords

Problem: Your instructor would like you to practice using the AltaVista search engine. He wants you to search for two interesting articles and then record the URL for each article and develop a short report on each article using WordPad.

Instructions: Use Firefox and a computer to perform the following tasks.

Part 1: *Displaying the AltaVista Home Page*

1. If necessary, connect to the Internet and start Firefox.
2. Click the Location bar, type www.altavista.com as the entry, and then click the Go button to display the AltaVista home page. The home page contains the AltaVista simple search form.

Part 2: *Performing an AltaVista Simple Search*

1. Use the text box and the Find button in the AltaVista simple search form to search for two of the following topics: virtual reality, computer generated graphics, Java applets, MLA style, APA style, or any extreme sport. Figure 2-70 on the next page shows a Web page about bungee jumping from the Bridge To Nowhere in Southern California.
2. Find one or more informative Web pages about each topic you select.
3. Using WordPad, copy information about each topic from the Web pages into a WordPad document and develop a short report about each topic. Add the URLs of the Web sites you used and your name to the end of the report.
4. Print the WordPad document.

Part 3: *Performing an AltaVista Advanced Search*

1. Click the Advanced Search link in the AltaVista simple search form.
2. Use the Advanced Search form to find three Web pages that contain information about three different universities that are not public universities. Sort the resulting Web pages using the word "university."
3. Print the three Web pages and write your name on each printout.
4. Hand in all printouts to your instructor. Quit Firefox.

(continued)

In the Lab

Searching the Web Using AltaVista and Keywords *(continued)*

FIGURE 2-70

5 Searching the Web Using Google and Keywords

Problem: You want to use both the Google simple search and advanced search to find Web pages relating to several of your hobbies. You decide to print out the first page of each Web page you visit.

Instructions: Use Firefox and a computer to perform the following tasks.

Part 1: *Starting the Google Search Engine*

1. If necessary, connect to the Internet and start Firefox.
2. Click the Location bar, type www.google.com as the entry, and then click the Go button to display the Google home page.

Part 2: *Searching for a Web Page*

1. Find a Web page containing inspirational quotations about children. Print the Web page and write your name on the printout.

2. Find the Web page containing the address, phone number, and e-mail address of your representative in the U.S. House of Representatives. Print the Web page and write your name on the printout.

3. Find the Official Web site of Tiger Woods. Print the Web page and write your name on the printout.

Part 3: *Searching for Information*

1. Find the current temperature in Moscow, Russia. Print the Web page, circle the temperature, and write your name on the printout.
2. Use the keywords "movie database" to find who played Harvey Pell in the classic movie *High Noon*. Print the Web page and write the actor name and your name on the printout.
3. What is the URL and physical address of the University of Chicago? Print the Web page and write your name on the printout.

Part 4: *Using the Google Advanced Search*

1. Click Advanced Search on the Google home page to display the Google Advanced Search form (Figure 2-71).
2. Find the number of Web pages that contain the keyword "motorcycle." Print the Web page and write the number of Web pages found and your name on the printout.
3. Find the number of Web pages that contain the keywords "motorcycle" and "Harley-Davidson." Print the Web page and write the number of Web pages found and your name on the printout.
4. Find the number of Web pages that contain the keywords "motorcycle," "Harley-Davidson," and "parts." Print the Web page and write the number of Web pages found and your name on the printout.
5. Find the number of Web pages that contains the exact phrase "geographic map." Print the Web page and write the number of Web pages found and your name on the printout.

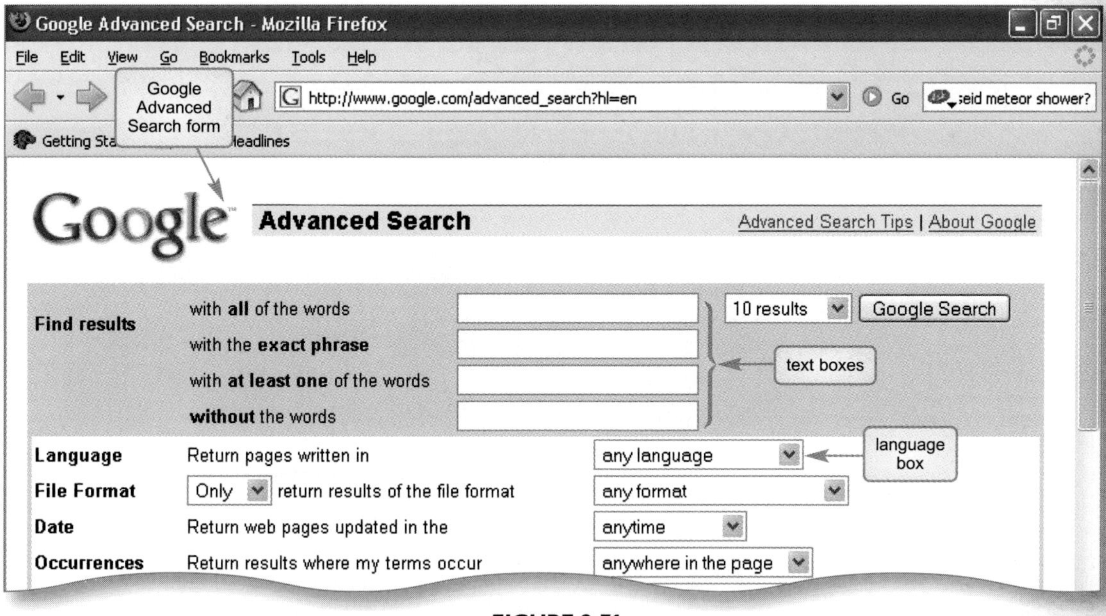

FIGURE 2-71

6. Find the number of Web pages that contain the exact phrase "geographic map" and the keyword "France." Print the Web page and write the number of Web pages found and your name on the printout.
7. Find the number of Web pages that contain an exact phrase "geographic map", the keyword "France," and are written in the French language. Print the Web page and write the number of Web pages found and your name on the printout.
8. Hand in all printouts to your instructor. Quit Firefox.

Mozilla
Firefox

In the Lab

6 Searching the Web Using Excite and Keywords

Problem: Your instructor would like you to practice using the Excite search engine and keywords. He wants you to find one or more interesting topics, copy information about the topic(s) into a WordPad document, and develop a short report. Add the URLs of each Web site you used and your name to the end of the report.

Instructions: Use Firefox and a computer to perform the following tasks.

Part 1: *Displaying the Excite Home Page*

1. If necessary, connect to the Internet and start Firefox.
2. Click the Location bar, type www.excite.com as the entry, and then click the Go button to display the Excite home page. The home page contains the Excite simple search form.
3. Perform a search using Excite and any one of the following topics: government spending, a historical event, the life of a current political figure, an extreme weather event, asteroid collisions with the earth, an extraterrestrial sighting, or genetic engineering. Figure 2-72 shows the Web page of an organization that explores, understands, and explains the origin, nature, and prevalence of life in the universe.
4. Find one or more informative Web pages about the topic you select. Using WordPad, copy information about the topic from the Web pages into a WordPad document and develop a short report about the topic.
5. Add the URLs of the Web sites you used and your name to the end of the report.
6. Print out the WordPad document and hand in the report to your instructor. Quit Firefox.

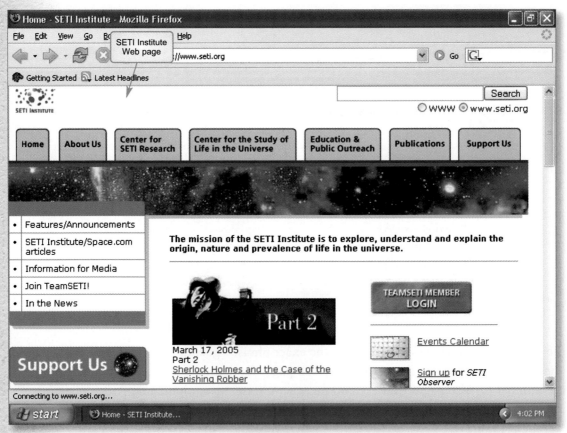

FIGURE 2-72

In the Lab

7 Searching the Web Using Multiple Search Engines

Problem: You would like to become more familiar with search engines and be able to search for pictures, business addresses, and maps. You decide to print out the first page of each Web page you visit.

Instructions: Use Firefox and a computer to perform the following tasks.

Part 1: Starting Firefox

1. If necessary, connect to the Internet and start Firefox.

Part 2: Searching for Web Pages Using Google

1. Locate a Web page for each of the topics listed in Steps 3, 4, and 5 below.
2. Click the Location bar, type www.google.com as the entry, and then click the Go button to display the Google home page.
3. Search for a Web page containing a picture of the northern lights (aurora borealis). Print the Web page and write your name on the printout.
4. Search for a Web page containing a picture of a porcupine puffer fish (diodon nicthemerus). Print the Web page and write your name on the printout.
5. Search for a Web page containing a picture of Brad Pitt or Elle MacPherson. Print the Web page and write your name on the printout.

Part 3: Searching for a Business Address

1. Click the Location bar, type www.infospace.com as the entry, and then click the Go button to display the Infospace home page.
2. Use WordPad to create a list of business names, addresses, and telephone numbers for each of the following businesses: Course Technology (Massachusetts), Microsoft Corporation (Washington), Flagler Museum (Florida), and Recreational Equipment, Inc. (Seattle, Washington). Click the New button after completing each search.
3. Print out the WordPad document and write your name on the printout.

Part 4: Searching for a Map

1. Click the Location bar, type www.expedia.com as the entry, and then click the Go button to display the Expedia home page.
2. Find and print a map for each of the following places or landmarks: Eiffel Tower (France), Key West (Florida), and White House (District of Columbia). Click the Back button after completing each search.
3. Circle the place or landmark on the map and write your name on each map.

Part 5: Searching for a Picture

1. Click the Location bar, type www.corbis.com as the entry, and then click the Go button to display the Corbis home page.
2. Find and print a picture of the Golden Gate Bridge. Write your name on the printout.
3. Find and print a picture of the Seattle Space Needle. Write your name on the printout.
4. Find and print a picture of the Statue of Liberty. Write your name on the printout.
5. Hand in all printouts to your instructor. Quit Firefox.

In the Lab

8 Searching for Home Pages Using the Location Bar

Problem: You are currently performing a search for an educational institution to complete your master's degree. While you know the names of the institutions you wish to research, you also would like to visit their home pages to assist with your research.

Instructions: Use the Location bar in Firefox to find the URL for each of the educational institutions listed below and use the search tools within each institutions Web site to answer the following questions.

Part 1: *Starting Firefox*

1. If necessary, connect to the Internet and start Firefox.

Part 2: *Finding the URL and information about the University of New Hampshire*

1. What is the URL for the University of New Hampshire? _____
2. What are the names of the three colleges in the University of New Hampshire? _____
3. What can a student expect to find in the Memorial Union building? _____

Part 3: *Finding the URL and information about the University of Michigan*

1. What is the URL for the University of Michigan? _____
2. What is the URL for the Ross School of Business? _____
3. In which city is the University of Michigan's central campus located? _____

Part 4: *Finding the URL and information about the University of Miami*

1. What is the URL for the University of Miami? _____
2. What are the names of at least four schools in the University of Miami? _____
3. What is the current student-faculty ratio? _____
4. Quit Firefox.

Cases and Places

The difficulty of these case studies varies:
■ are the least difficult and ■■ are more difficult. The last exercise is a group exercise.

1 ■ Many new bands have their own home pages on the Web. Using the search engine of your choice, find out when and where the Red Elvises will be playing next. Find and print their home page. Next, find out when and where your favorite performer, band, or musical group will be playing next. Find and print their home page. Do these pages qualify as informational Web pages? Write your answer and the reasons supporting your position on one of the printouts and hand it in to your instructor.

2 ■ You have been hired by a local bicycle shop to compare their store prices with the prices available on the Internet. Search the Internet for Web pages that sell bicycles and bicycle parts. Find at least 10 items being sold by 3 different online bicycle stores. Develop a price list to compare the prices of the 10 items and hand in the price list to your instructor.

3 ■ You recently graduated from college and took a job at a small investment firm. Your first job is to search for and compare the services of the major online brokers. Find five online brokers and compare their services, costs to buy and sell stocks, Web sites, and any other pertinent information. Summarize your findings in a report and hand it in to your instructor.

4 ■■ Web search engines use different techniques for searching Web resources. If you were designing a search engine, what would you have the engine look for when determining whether a Web page successfully matches the keywords? Visit the Help page of a few search engines to get an idea of what criteria they use, and then write a list containing the criteria you would have your search engine use to determine whether a Web page is a successful match for keywords. Include an explanation for each item, such as the relative importance assigned, and then hand in the list with the explanations.

Cases and Places

5 ■■ A gopher is a computer system that allows computer users to find files on the Internet. Some federal, state, and local government agencies continue to use a gopher site to provide information and distribute documents and forms. Find one government agency that provides gopher services, learn to use its gopher, and write a brief report about the gopher. Include instructions to use the gopher, documents you found using the gopher, and whether you liked or disliked this method of finding information on the Internet.

6 ■■ **Working Together** Computer security is a major concern for systems administrators. A very important first line of defense is an account name or user name and password. Choosing good passwords is important for security issues. Have each member of your group select a different search engine and then find three different Web sources (Web sites) that describe criteria for creating a good password. Each member should record the relevant information necessary for citing the sources using the MLA or APA style. Print the three Web pages and write the citation on each page using either the MLA or APA style. As a group, each member should present their findings to the class.

Communicating Over the Internet Using Mozilla Thunderbird

CASE PERSPECTIVE

Taking an Internet class at the local community college allowed you to learn more about the Internet. Now you think it would be a good idea to have some real-world experience. A fellow student tells you that you can find information about free seminars on an Internet Web site. You take her recommendation and search the Web for free seminars. You find a seminar entitled "Communicating Over the Internet" and enroll.

Before attending the seminar, you were unsure how to use the Internet to communicate. At the seminar, you watched an impressive presentation that included using Mozilla Thunderbird to send and receive e-mail messages and read and post messages to a newsgroup, and you learned about using Yahoo! Messenger to send instant messages. You also learned proper etiquette for communicating over the Internet, as well as how to define, recognize, and combat spam.

You were careful to make a list of the various ways to communicate over the Internet and the software programs that allow you to communicate. The list also included a reminder to download and install both Mozilla Thunderbird and Yahoo! Messenger.

After downloading and installing your newly acquired software, you are ready to start communicating via the Internet. This presents an alternative to expensive telephone calls to out-of-town friends, family, and business associates. After only one month, you managed to convince the majority of your family and friends to begin communicating over the Internet.

As you read through this project, you will learn how to send and receive e-mail messages and read and post messages to a newsgroup using Mozilla Thunderbird, and how to send instant messages using Yahoo! Messenger.

MOZILLA

Firefox

Communicating Over the Internet Using Mozilla Thunderbird

Objectives

You will have mastered the material in this project when you can:

- Use Mozilla Thunderbird to access your existing electronic mail account
- Open, read, print, reply to, and delete electronic mail messages
- View a file attachment
- Compose, format, and send electronic mail messages
- Add and delete an Address Book card

- Create a connection to a news server
- Search for and display newsgroups
- Read, post, and print newsgroup articles
- Subscribe and unsubscribe to a newsgroup
- Start and sign in to Yahoo! Messenger
- Add and remove a Yahoo! Messenger contact
- Send and receive an instant message

Introduction

In Projects 1 and 2, you used Firefox to search for information on the World Wide Web. In addition to searching for information, you also can use the Internet to communicate with others. Web services designed for communicating over the Internet include two that you'll use in this project: Mozilla Thunderbird, which allows you to send and receive electronic mail and read and post messages to a newsgroup; and Yahoo! Messenger, which allows you to communicate with other Yahoo! Messenger members by sending and receiving instant messages and by engaging in online meetings. Project 3 illustrates the different means of communication available on the Internet.

Electronic (E-Mail) Messages

Electronic mail (e-mail) has become an important means of exchanging messages and files between business associates and friends. Businesses find that using e-mail to send documents electronically saves both time and money. Parents with students away at college or relatives who are scattered across the country find that exchanging e-mail messages is an inexpensive and easy way to stay in touch. In fact, exchanging e-mail messages is one of the more widely used features of the Internet.

One of e-mail's main problem, however, is spam. **Spam** refers to unwanted e-mail that usually solicits a product or service. While it is not possible to completely avoid spam, measures to reduce the amount of spam in your electronic mailbox include never replying to spam, guarding your e-mail address, using spam filters, reporting spam, and changing your e-mail address if the amount of spam in your mailbox gets out of control. Some e-mail providers offer **spam filters**, which are programs that help to separate legitimate e-mail from unwanted junk mail.

Besides exchanging e-mail messages, another popular method of sharing information among individuals is to use Internet newsgroups. An **Internet newsgroup** contains articles and messages about many varied and interesting topics.

Mozilla Thunderbird allows you to receive and store incoming e-mail messages, compose and send e-mail messages, maintain a list of frequently used e-mail addresses, and read and post messages to Internet newsgroups.

Starting Mozilla Thunderbird

Before you send and receive e-mail messages and read and post messages to a newsgroup, you must start Mozilla Thunderbird. For more information about downloading and installing Mozilla Thunderbird, see Appendix B. The following steps show how to start Mozilla Thunderbird.

To Start Mozilla Thunderbird

1

• **Click the Start button on the Windows taskbar, point to All Programs on the Start menu, point to Mozilla Thunderbird on the All Programs submenu, and then point to Mozilla Thunderbird on the Mozilla Thunderbird submenu.**

Windows displays the Start menu, All Programs submenu, Mozilla Thunderbird submenu, and Mozilla Thunderbird command (Figure 3-1).

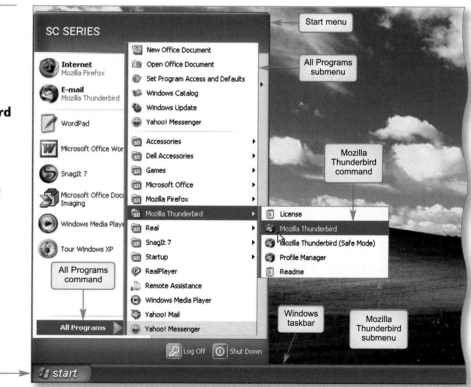

FIGURE 3-1

2

• **Click Mozilla Thunderbird.**

• **If the Mozilla Thunderbird dialog box is displayed, click the No button.**

• **If the Enter your password dialog box is displayed, enter your e-mail account password and then click the OK button. If you do not know your e-mail account password, contact your Internet Service Provider.**

Mozilla Thunderbird starts. After several seconds, Thunderbird displays the Inbox - Mozilla Thunderbird window, containing the Mail toolbar Folders pane, Search bar, status bar, Message list, and Message pane (Figure 3-2). The Welcome to Mozilla Thunderbird! page is displayed in the Message pane.

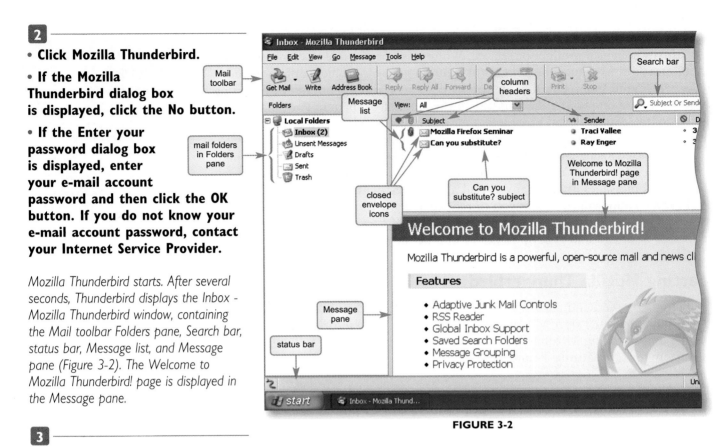

FIGURE 3-2

3

• **If necessary, maximize the Inbox-Mozilla Thunderbird window.**

The Inbox - Mozilla Thunderbird window shown in Figure 3-2 contains a number of elements. The title bar contains the folder name (Inbox) and the program name (Mozilla Thunderbird). Below the title bar and menu bar is a Mail toolbar. Table 3-1 contains the toolbar buttons and a brief explanation of their functions.

The Mail toolbar in Figure 3-2 contains buttons to retrieve new messages (Get Mail), create a new message (Write), display the address book (Address Book), reply to a message (Reply), reply to all messages (Reply All), forward a message (Forward), delete a message (Delete), mark a message as junk mail (Junk), print a message (Print), and stop the transfer of messages (Stop).

Table 3-1   Mail Toolbar Buttons and Functions

BUTTON	FUNCTION
Get Mail	Contacts the mail server, sends the e-mail messages in the Unsent Messages folder, and places new e-mail messages in the Inbox folder.
Write	Composes a new e-mail message.
Address Book	Displays a list of contacts in the Address Book.
Reply	Replies to an e-mail message with a message containing the recipient's name and the subject of the e-mail message preceded by the Re entry.
Reply All	Replies to an e-mail message with a message containing the names of all recipients and the subject of the e-mail message preceded by the Re entry.
Forward	Forwards an e-mail message to another recipient with the subject of the e-mail message enclosed in square brackets and preceded by the Fwd entry.
Delete	Deletes an e-mail message in the Message list by moving the message to the Trash folder.
Junk	Marks an e-mail message as junk and displays the junk icon and message in the Message list.
Print	Prints an e-mail message in the Message list.
Stop	Stops the transfer of e-mail messages.

The Inbox - Mozilla Thunderbird window is divided into three areas. The **Folders pane** contains, in hierarchical structure, the Local Folders folder and five mail folders. Five standard mail folders (Inbox, Unsent Messages, Drafts, Sent, and Trash) are displayed when you start Thunderbird. Although you cannot rename or delete these folders, you can create additional folders.

The highest level in the hierarchy is the Local Folders folder. Five standard mail folder icons are connected by a dotted vertical line below the Local Folders icon.

The **Inbox folder** in Figure 3-2 is the destination for incoming mail. The **Unsent Messages folder** temporarily holds messages until Thunderbird delivers the messages. The **Drafts folder** retains copies of messages not yet ready to send. The **Sent folder** retains copies of messages you have sent. The **Trash folder** contains messages you have deleted. As a safety precaution, you can retrieve deleted messages from the Trash folder if you later decide to keep them. Deleting messages from the Trash folder removes the messages permanently.

Folders can contain e-mail messages and newsgroup articles. Folders in bold type followed by a number in parentheses, **Inbox (2)**, indicate the number of unopened messages in the folder. Additional folders may be displayed on your computer instead of or in addition to the folders shown in Figure 3-2.

The contents of the Inbox folder are displayed in the **Message list** in Figure 3-2 when Thunderbird starts. Seven column headers are displayed above the Message list. A conversation bubble (Message Threads) identifies the first header, a paper clip icon (Attachment) identifies the second header, the word Subject identifies the third header, a glasses icon (Read) identifies the fourth header, the word Sender identifies the fifth header, a No icon (Junk Status) identifies the sixth header. Although not visible in Figure 3-2, the word Date identifies the seventh header. A paper clip icon in the Message list indicates the e-mail message contains an attachment (file or object).

More About

Column Headings

You can change the width of column headers in the Message list by dragging the vertical line between two column headers.

More About

Resizing Areas

You can change the size of the Folders pane, Message list, and Message pane list by dragging the vertical line between the Folders pane and Message list and Message pane, or dragging the horizontal line between the Message list and Message pane.

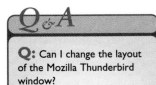

Q: Can I change the layout of the Mozilla Thunderbird window?

A: Yes. To change the layout of the Mozilla Thunderbird window, click the View menu, point to Layout, and select the desired layout (Classic View, Wide View, or Vertical View) from the Layout submenu.

More About

Reading E-Mail Messages

Many people minimize the Inbox - Mozilla Thunderbird window while they work on other tasks. When they receive a new e-mail message, a small window is displayed above the status area on the Windows taskbar and a sound is played.

Entries in the columns below the third header (Subject), fifth header (Sender), and seventh header (Date) indicate the e-mail author's name or e-mail address, subject of the e-mail message, and date and time the message was received. Collectively, these three entries are referred to as the **Message heading**.

A closed envelope icon and a bold message heading in the Subject column identifies an unread e-mail message. In Figure 3-2 on page FX 130, the first e-mail message from Traci Vallee, a business associate, contains a paper clip icon, closed envelope icon, and bold message heading. The closed envelope icon and bold message heading indicate the e-mail message has not been read (opened) and the paper clip indicates the e-mail message has an attachment.

The second e-mail message from Ray Enger, an instructor at a local community college, contains a closed envelope icon and bold message heading. The closed envelope icon and bold message heading indicate the e-mail message has not been read. Other e-mail messages may be displayed on your computer in place of or in addition to these messages.

The closed envelope icon is one of several icons, called **Message list icons**, that are displayed in the Subject column. Different Message list icons may be displayed in the Subject column to indicate the status of the message. The icon may indicate an action that was performed by the sender or one that was performed by the recipient. The actions may include reading, replying to, or forwarding a message. The **Message pane** in Figure 3-2 contains the Welcome to Mozilla Thunderbird! page in the Message pane.

Opening and Reading E-Mail Messages

In Figure 3-2, the message headings for Traci Vallee and Ray Enger are displayed in the Message list. Double-clicking the closed envelope icon in either heading opens the corresponding e-mail message and displays the text of the message in a separate window. The following step illustrates how to open the e-mail message from Ray Enger.

To Open (Read) an E-Mail Message

1

• **Double-click the closed envelope icon to the left of the Can you substitute? subject in the Message list.**

• **Maximize the Can you substitute? - Mozilla Thunderbird window.**

• **If the envelope icon for the Can you substitute? message is not displayed in the Message list, double-click another closed envelope icon.**

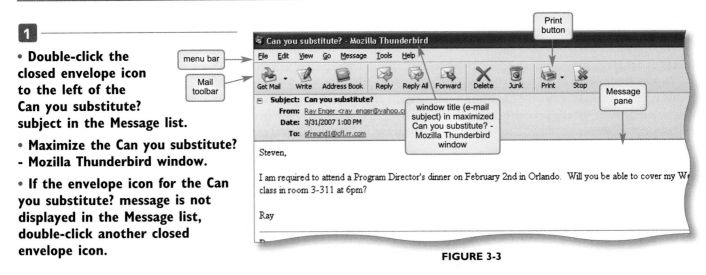

FIGURE 3-3

The maximized Can you substitute? - Mozilla Firefox window is displayed (Figure 3-3). The window contains a menu bar, Mail toolbar, identifying information about the e-mail message (Subject, From, Date, and To), and Message pane. The subject of the e-mail message (Can you substitute?) becomes the window title.

When you double-click a closed envelope icon in the Message list, Thunderbird displays the message in a separate window, changes the closed envelope icon to an opened envelope icon, and no longer displays the message heading in bold type.

Below the title bar and menu bar shown in Figure 3-3 is the Mail toolbar that contains the buttons needed to work with opened e-mail messages (Reply, Reply All, Forward, and so on). Refer to Table 3-1 on page FX 131 for a brief explanation of their functions.

Printing an E-Mail Message

You can print the contents of an e-mail message before or after opening the message. The following steps illustrate how to print an opened e-mail message.

To Print an Opened E-Mail Message

1

• **Click the Print button on the Mail toolbar.**

The Print dialog box is displayed (Figure 3-4).

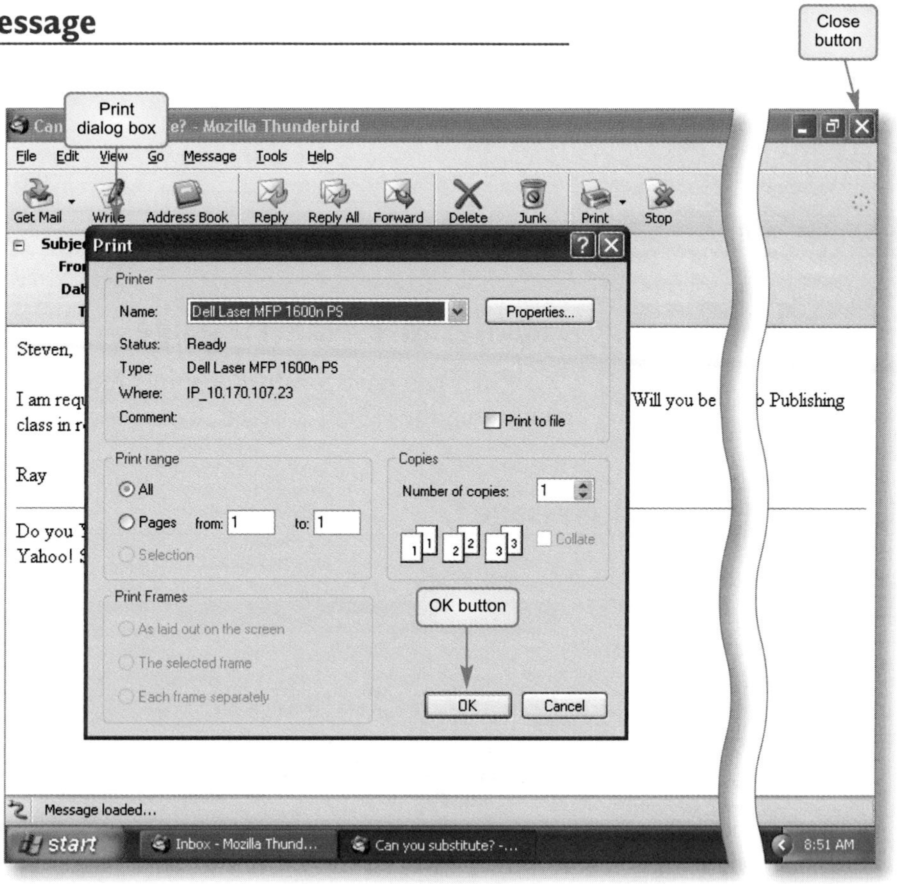

FIGURE 3-4

2

• **Click the OK button in the Print dialog box.**

The printed message consists of a header at the top of the page containing the subject (Can you substitute?). Below the header are the Subject, From, Date, and To entries, and the e-mail message. A footer at the bottom of the page contains the page number, total number of pages, and current date and time (Figure 3-5).

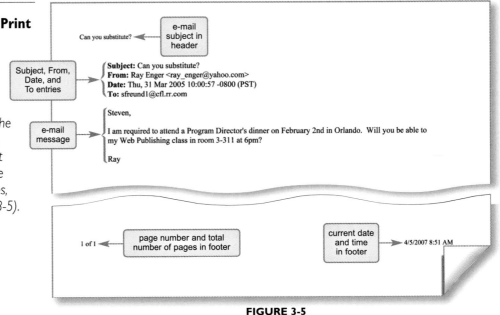

FIGURE 3-5

Closing an E-Mail Message

When you have finished opening and reading an e-mail message, close the window containing the e-mail message by following the step below.

To Close an E-Mail Message

1

• **Click the Close button on the title bar.**

The Can you substitute? - Mozilla Thunderbird window closes and the Inbox - Mozilla Thunderbird window is displayed (Figure 3-6). An open envelope icon replaces the closed envelope icon preceding the Ray Enger message heading and the Inbox entry in the Folders list, Inbox (1), indicates one e-mail message (Traci Vallee) remains unopened.

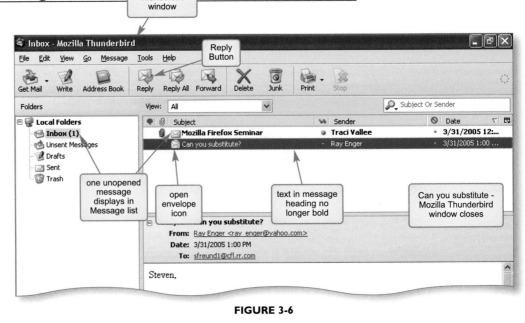

FIGURE 3-6

When you double-click a closed envelope icon in the Message list, Thunderbird opens the message and displays its contents in a separate window. When you close the window, the e-mail message heading in the Message list in the Inbox - Mozilla Thunderbird window no longer is displayed in bold type and the closed envelope icon changes to an open envelope icon to indicate the e-mail message has been opened. In addition, the Inbox entry, Inbox (1), shows only one e-mail message is unopened.

Replying to an E-Mail Message

As mentioned previously, the Address Book is a central location for storing business and personal information about individuals you contact frequently. When you reply to an e-mail message, Thunderbird adds the business and personal information about the original sender to the Address Book. Once a contact is added to the Address Book, Thunderbird can use the Address Book to find the e-mail address needed to reply to the e-mail message or to use when composing a new e-mail message.

The next steps illustrate using the Reply button to compose and send an e-mail reply to a sender—in this case, Ray Enger. The Reply button on the toolbar allows you to reply quickly to an e-mail message without having to find or type the sender's e-mail address. The following steps illustrate how to send an e-mail reply using the Reply button.

More About

Replying to an E-Mail Message

Some people who receive reply e-mail messages find it awkward that the original e-mail message is displayed with the reply message. To remove the original message from all e-mail replies, click Tools on the menu bar, click Account Settings, click the Composition & Addressing option in the left pane, click the Automatically quote the original message when replying check box to deselect it, and then click the OK button.

To Reply to an E-Mail Message

1

• Click the Reply button on the Mail toolbar.

• If necessary, maximize the Compose: Re: Can you substitute? window.

• Type the e-mail reply as shown in Figure 3-7.

The Compose: Re: Can you substitute? window is displayed (Figure 3-7). The Re: entry and subject are displayed in the window title and Subject text box. The e-mail reply and original message are displayed in the Message pane.

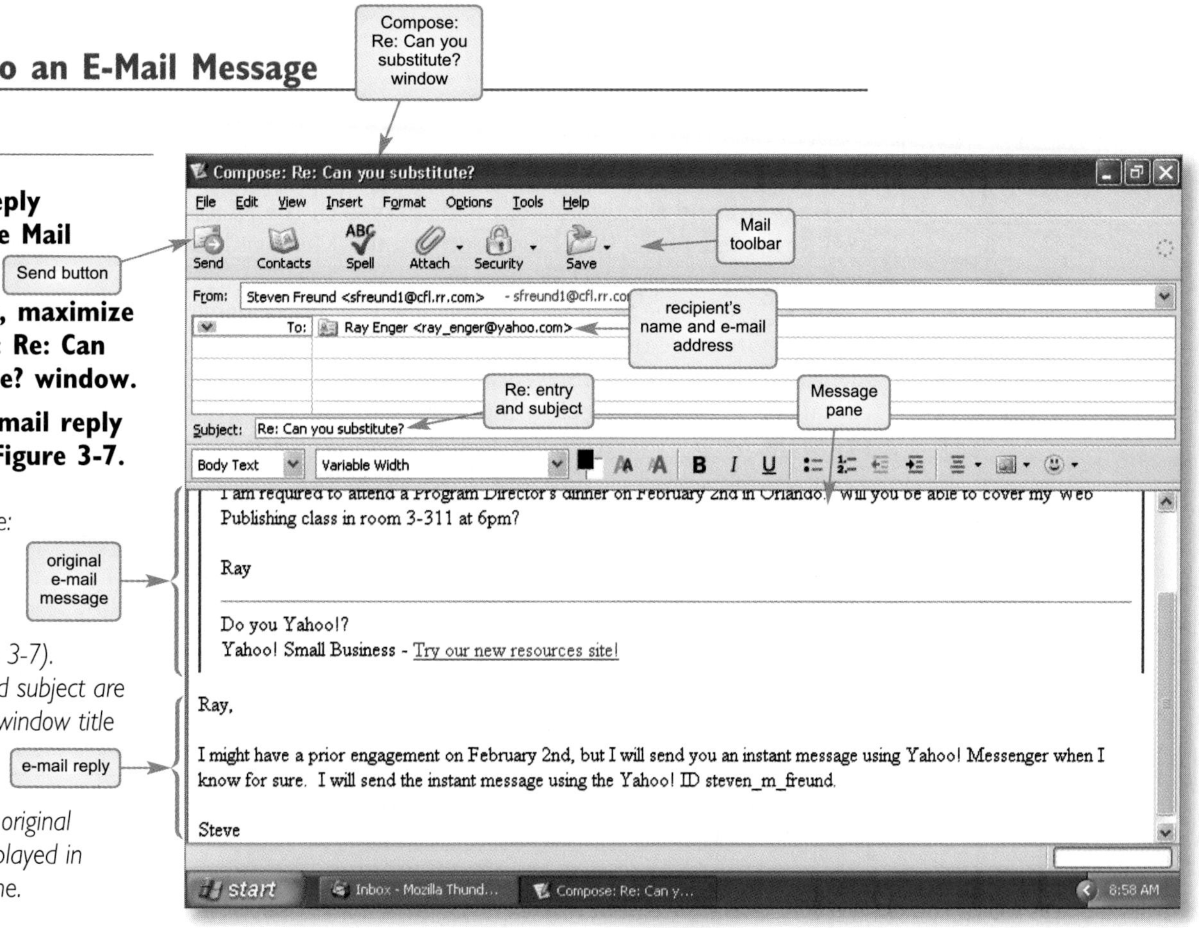

FIGURE 3-7

2

• **Click the Send button on the Mail toolbar.**

• **If the HTML Mail Question dialog box displays, click the Send button in the HTML Mail Question dialog box.**

The Compose: Re: Can you substitute? window closes, Thunderbird stores the reply e-mail message in the Unsent Messages folder while it sends the message, and then moves the message to the Sent folder (Figure 3-8). The Sending Messages - Re: Can you substitute dialog box may be displayed while Mozilla Thunderbird is sending your message.

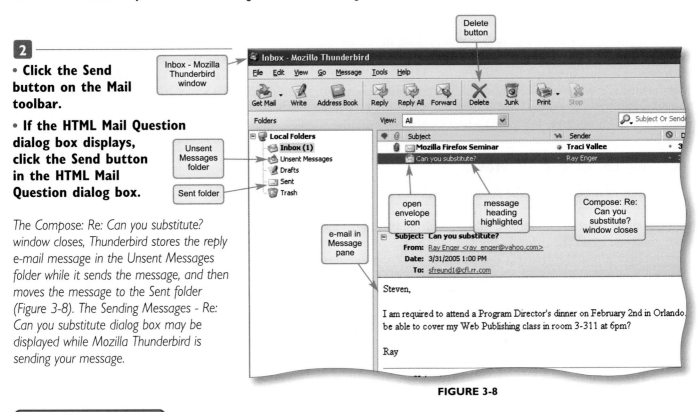

FIGURE 3-8

Other Ways

1. On Message menu click Reply
2. Press CTRL+R

In Figure 3-8, the highlighted Ray Enger message heading is displayed in the Message list and the e-mail text is displayed in the Message pane. The open envelope icon to the left of the Ray Enger entry in the Message list contains an arrow to indicate that you have replied to the message.

In Figure 3-7 on the previous page, the Ray Enger name and <ray_enger@yahoo. com> e-mail address are displayed in the To text box and the original e-mail message is identified by the words "Steven Freund" in the From text box. In addition, the window contains a Mail toolbar below the menu bar. The buttons on this Mail toolbar (Send, Contacts, Spell, Attach, Security, and Save) are useful when replying to a message. Table 3-2 shows the buttons and their functions.

Table 3-2 Compose Mail Toolbar Buttons and Functions	
BUTTON	**FUNCTION**
Send	Stores the e-mail message in the Unsent Mail folder temporarily while the message is sent and then moves the message to the Sent folder.
Contacts	Displays the Contacts sidebar that allows you to select recipients from the Address Book.
ABC Spell	Spell checks the e-mail message.
Attach	Attaches a file to the e-mail message.
Security	Allows you to digitally sign an e-mail message (allowing the recipient to verify the sender's identity), and/or encrypt an e-mail message (preventing someone other than the recipient from reading the message).
Save	Saves the e-mail message as a file, draft, or template.

As you send and reply to messages, the number of messages in the Sent folder increases. To delete an e-mail message from the Sent folder, click the Sent folder icon in the Folders pane, highlight the message in the Message list, and then click the Delete button on the Mail toolbar.

Deleting an E-Mail Message

After reading and replying to an e-mail message, you may want to delete the original e-mail message from the Message list. Deleting a message removes the e-mail message from the Inbox folder. If you do not delete unwanted messages, large numbers of messages will accumulate in the Inbox folder, making it difficult to find and read new messages while wasting disk space. The following step shows how to delete the e-mail message from Ray Enger.

More About

Mail Folders

You can reduce the hard disk space required by a mail folder by clicking File on the menu bar and then clicking the Compact Folders command on the File menu. It may take several minutes to compact all the folders if they contain many messages.

To Delete an E-Mail Message

1

• **Click the Delete button on the toolbar.**

Thunderbird moves the Ray Enger e-mail message from the Inbox folder to the Trash folder and removes the e-mail entry from the Message list. The message header for Traci Vallee is highlighted, and the e-mail message text is displayed in the Message pane (Figure 3-9).

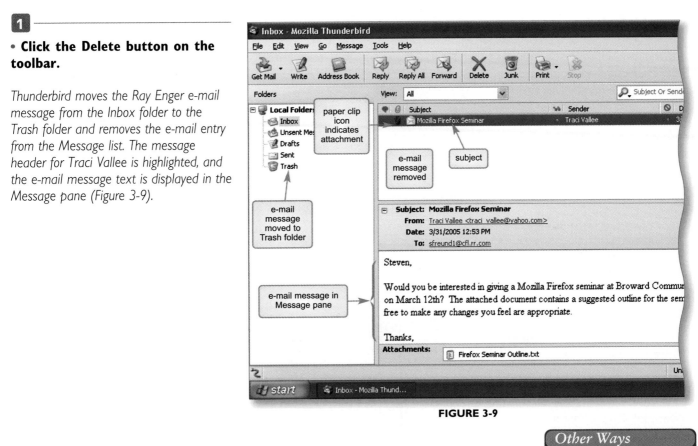

FIGURE 3-9

As you delete messages from the Inbox, the number of messages in the Trash folder increases. To delete an e-mail message from the Trash folder, click the Trash folder icon in the Folders pane, highlight the message in the Message list, and then click the Delete button on the Mail toolbar. This permanently removes the message from your hard drive.

Other Ways

1. Drag e-mail message to Trash folder in Folders pane
2. Highlight message, click Delete Message on Edit menu
3. Right-click e-mail message, click Delete Message on shortcut menu
4. Highlight message, press DELETE

Viewing a File Attachment

The remaining message in the Message list, Traci Vallee, contains a file attachment. An **attachment** is one or more files sent with the e-mail message. A paper clip icon in the column below the second header in Figure 3-9 on the previous page indicates the e-mail message contains a file attachment (file or object). The following steps illustrate how to view the file attachment.

To View a File Attachment

1

• **Double-click the subject to the left of the Traci Vallee name in the Message list.**

• **If necessary, maximize the Mozilla Firefox Seminar - Mozilla Thunderbird window.**

The maximized Mozilla Firefox Seminar - Mozilla Thunderbird window is displayed (Figure 3-10). The Attachments box, containing a text document icon and Firefox Seminar Outline.txt document name, are displayed beneath the Message pane.

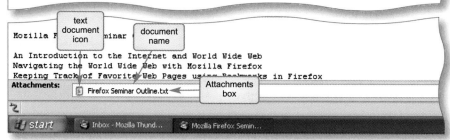

FIGURE 3-10

2

• **Double-click the Firefox Seminar Outline.txt icon in the Attachments box.**

• **If the Opening Firefox Seminar Outline.txt dialog box opens, click the OK button.**

The Firefox Seminar Outline - Notepad window, containing the outline, is displayed (Figure 3-11).

3

• **Click the Close button in the Firefox Seminar Outline - Notepad window.**

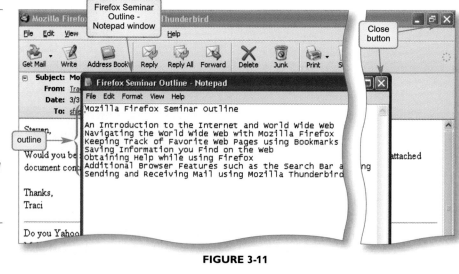

FIGURE 3-11

• **Click the Close button in the Mozilla Firefox Seminar - Mozilla Thunderbird window.**

The Firefox Seminar Outline - Notepad window and Mozilla Firefox Seminar - Mozilla Thunderbird window close.

File attachments can be anything from spreadsheets to pictures. Thunderbird gives you the option of viewing the attachment as you read the e-mail, or you can save it to a location on your computer to view at another time. To prevent possible virus infections on your computer, you only should download and open attachments you expect to receive from people you know.

Composing a New Mail Message

In addition to opening and reading, replying to, and deleting e-mail messages, users want to compose and send new e-mail messages. When composing an e-mail message, you must know the e-mail address of the recipient of the message, enter a brief one-line subject that identifies the purpose or contents of the message, and type the message itself.

You also can format an e-mail message to enhance the appearance of the message. **Formatting** is the process of enhancing the appearance of a document by changing the background of the document, and the style, size, and color of the text in the document.

The next steps show how to compose an e-mail message to one of the authors (Steven Freund) of this book.

To Compose a New E-Mail Message

1

• **Click the Write button on the Mail toolbar.**

• **If necessary, maximize the Compose: (no subject) window.**

The maximized Compose: (no subject) window is displayed (Figure 3-12). The window contains a menu bar, Mail toolbar, text boxes, dimmed Formatting toolbar, and Message area.

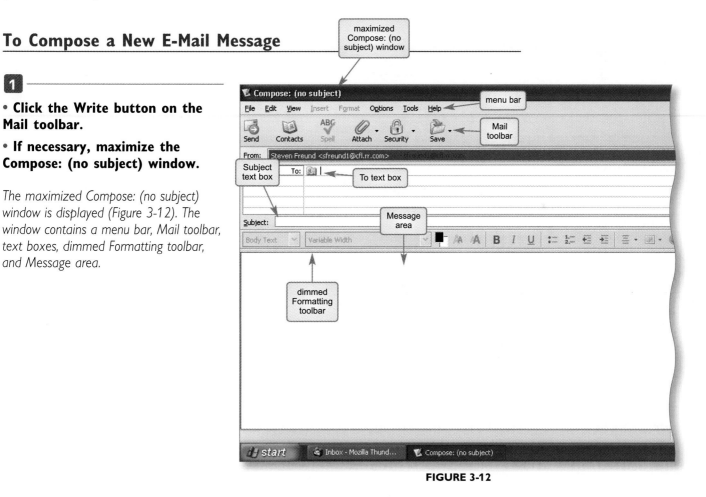

FIGURE 3-12

2

- **Type** sfreund1@cfl.rr.com **in the To text box.**
- **Click the Subject text box.**
- **Type** Internet Bookstore **in the Subject text box.**

The destination e-mail address is displayed in the To text box and the subject of the message is displayed in the Subject text box (Figure 3-13). The window title changes to Compose: Internet Bookstore.

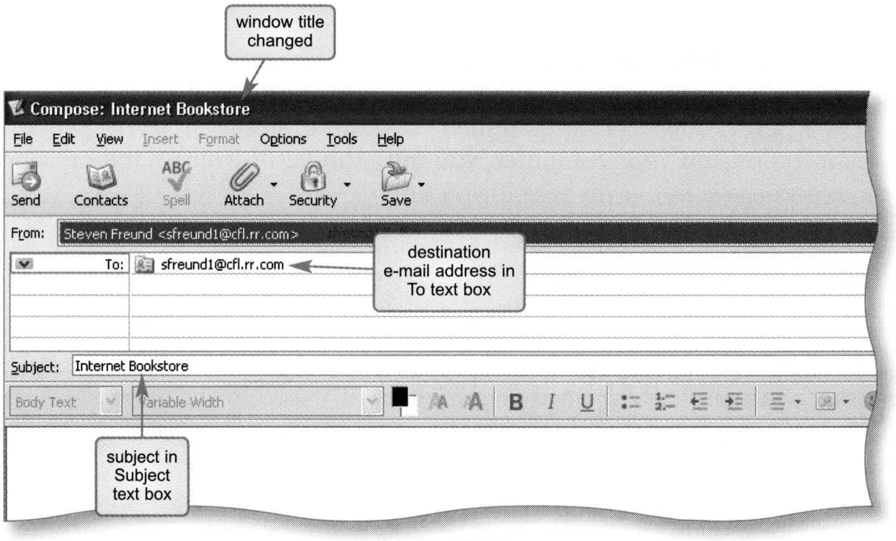

FIGURE 3-13

3

- **Press the TAB key on the keyboard.**
- **Type** Great News! **and then press the ENTER key twice.**
- **Type** Your books are being sold on the Internet. Visit this URL to look for your books: www.amazon.com. **in the Message area and then press the ENTER key twice.**
- **Type your name and then press the ENTER key.**

The Formatting toolbar is no longer dimmed and the e-mail message is displayed in the Message area (Figure 3-14). The text uses a medium-size variable width font. In this case, the sender's name is Steven Freund.

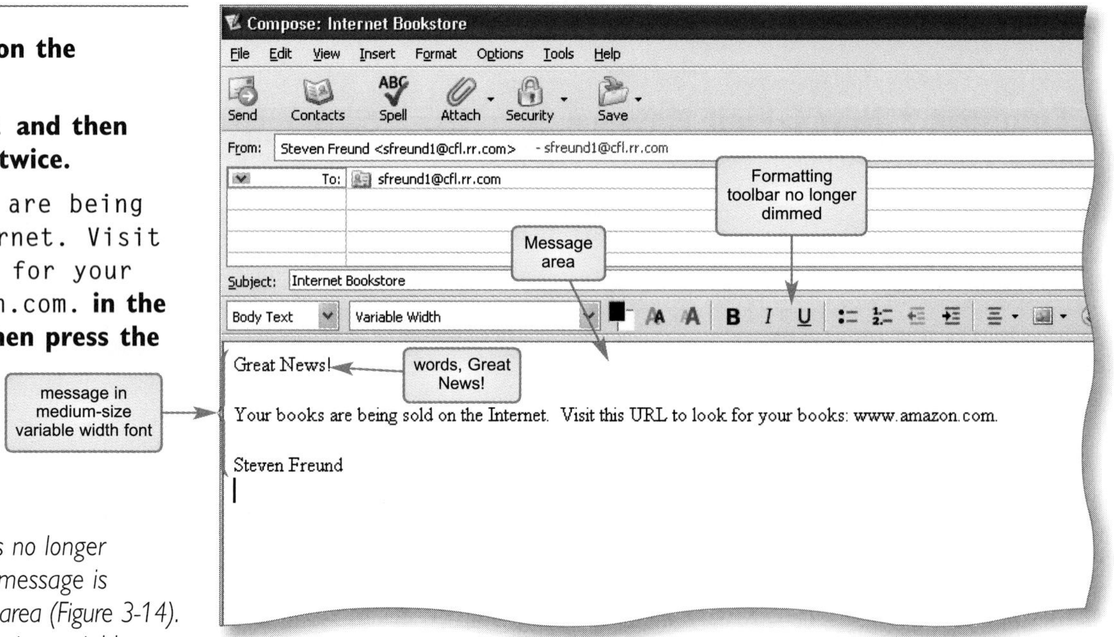

FIGURE 3-14

> *More About*
>
> **Personalizing an E-Mail Message**
>
> You can personalize an e-mail message using smileys (smiley faces) in your message. For example, the :-) smiley means "I am happy" or "I am smiling"; the :-(smiley means "I am sad" or "I am unhappy"; the :-D smiley means "I am laughing"; and the :-O smiley means "I am surprised."

The **Formatting toolbar** shown in Figure 3-14 allows you to change the appearance, size, and color of text; bold, italicize, or underline text; create a numbered or bulleted list; change paragraph indentation or align text; and create a link or insert an image in an e-mail message.

The Compose: Internet Bookstore message window contains two toolbars. The Mail toolbar (containing buttons specific to replying to an e-mail or composing a new e-mail message) is displayed below the menu bar, and the Formatting toolbar is displayed below the Subject text box. The Mail buttons are explained in Table 3-2 on page FX 136. Table 3-3 shows the Formatting toolbar buttons and boxes and their functions.

Table 3-3 Formatting Toolbar Buttons/Boxes and Functions

BUTTON/BOX	FUNCTION	BUTTON/BOX	FUNCTION
Body Text ▼	Changes the style of text in the message.	∷≡	Creates a bulleted list in the message.
Variable Width ▼	Changes the font of text in the message.	1.—2.—	Creates a numbered list in the message.
◼	Changes the foreground and background color of the message.	⇐	Decreases the indentation of a paragraph.
A̲A	Decreases the text size in the message.	⇥	Increases the indentation of a paragraph.
ᴀA	Increases the text size in the message.	≡ ▼	Aligns text in the message.
B	Bolds text in the message.	🖼 ▼	Inserts a link, anchor, image, horizontal line, or table.
I	Italicizes text in the message.	☺ ▼	Inserts a smiley face.
U	Underlines text in the message.		

You change the size of text by selecting a font size. Firefox measures **font size** using the keywords, x-small, small, medium, large, x-large, and xx-large. The following steps show how to center the text "Great News!" and how to increase the font size.

To Format an E-Mail Message

1

• **Select the words, Great News!, in the first line of the e-mail message by pointing to either word (Great or News!) and then triple-click the word.**

The words, Great News!, are highlighted (Figure 3-15).

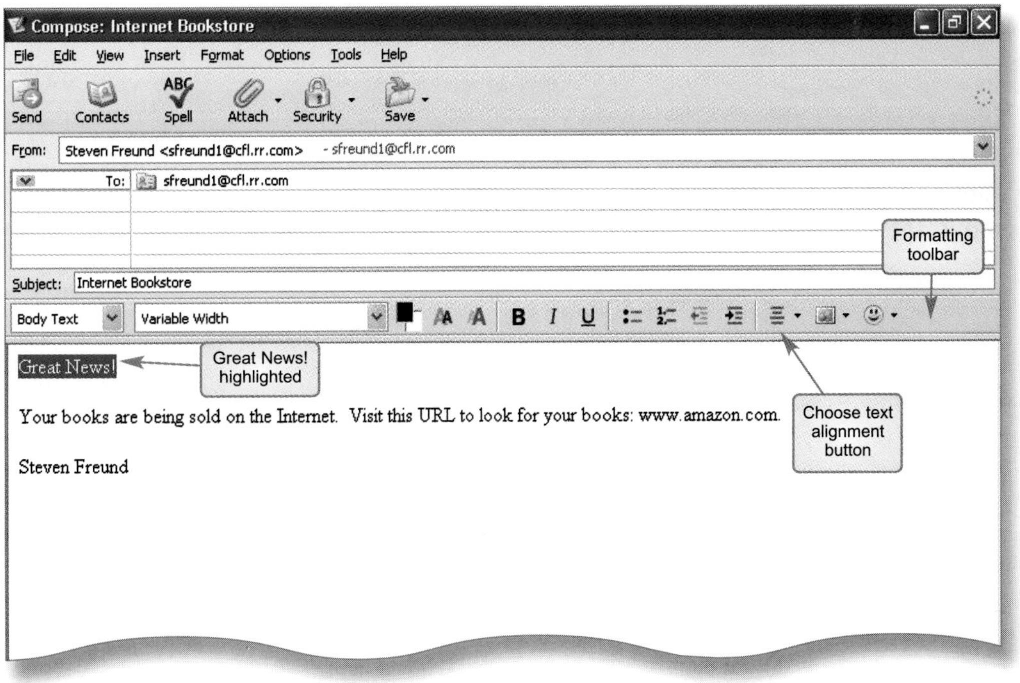

FIGURE 3-15

Mozilla
Firefox

• **Click the Choose text alignment button on the Formatting toolbar.**

• **Click the Center command on the Choose text alignment menu.**

The words, Great News!, are centered in the first line of the e-mail message (Figure 3-16).

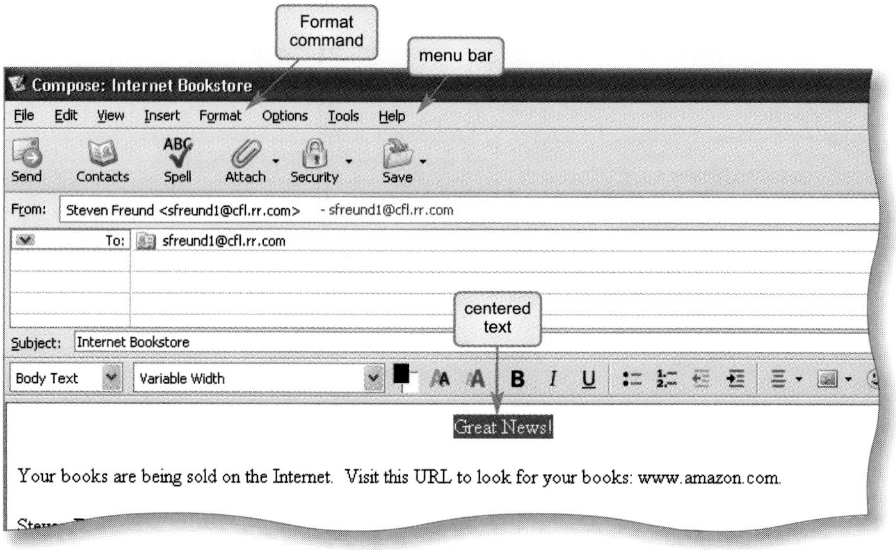

FIGURE 3-16

• **Click Format on the menu bar and then point to Size.**

The Size submenu is displayed, with the medium option selected (Figure 3-17).

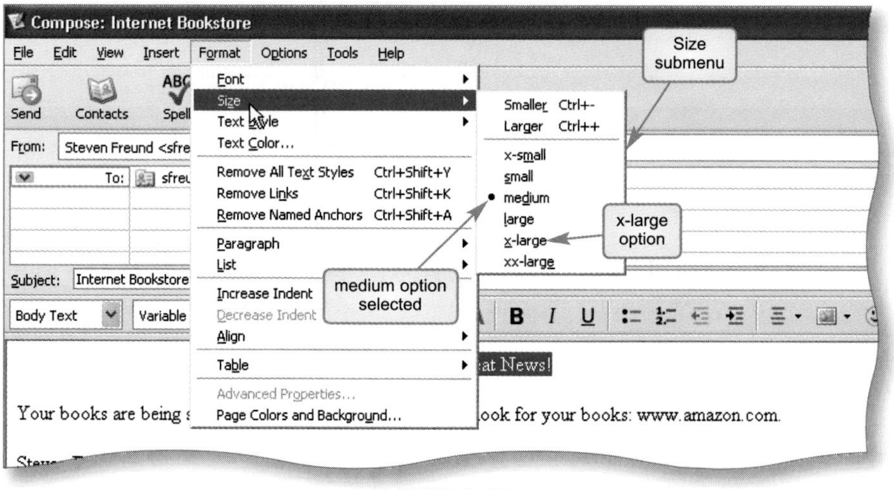

FIGURE 3-17

• **Click x-large on the Size submenu.**

• **Click the highlighted text to remove the highlight.**

The words, Great News!, are displayed in x-large font size (Figure 3-18).

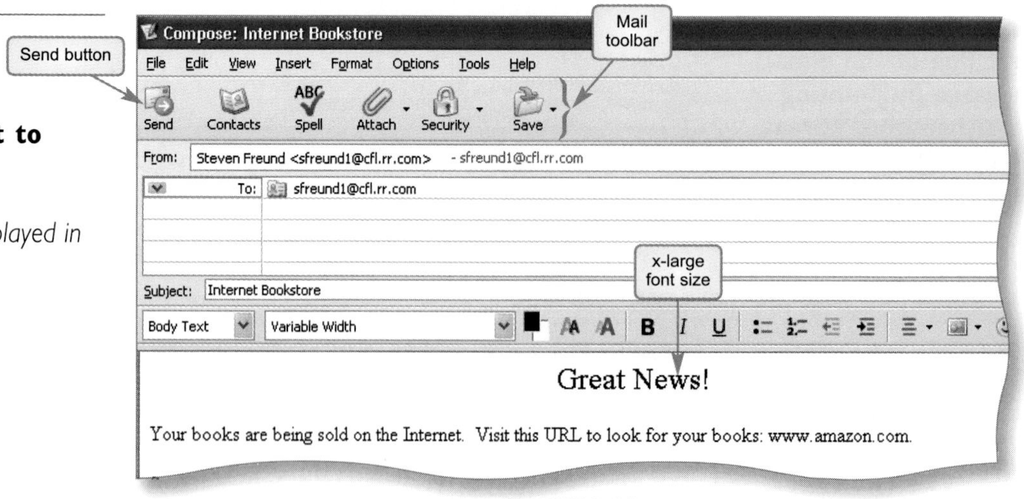

FIGURE 3-18

Other Ways

1. Click the Larger font size button on the Formatting toolbar twice

Sending an E-Mail Message

After composing and formatting an e-mail message, send the message. The following steps illustrate how to send an e-mail message.

To Send an E-Mail Message

1 Click the Send button on the Mail toolbar.

2 If the HTML Mail Question dialog box is displayed, click the Send button.

The Compose: Internet Bookstore window closes, Thunderbird stores the e-mail message in the Unsent Messages folder temporarily while it sends the message, and then it moves the message to the Sent folder (Figure 3-19). The Sending Messages - Internet Bookstore dialog box and/or a window for your anti-virus software may appear while Mozilla Thunderbird is sending your message.

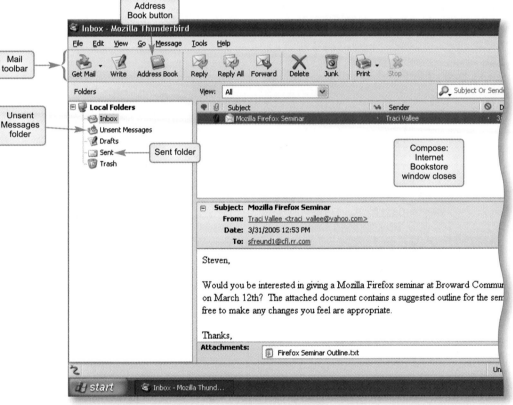

FIGURE 3-19

Address Book

The Address Book program included with Thunderbird allows you to store contact information including e-mail addresses, home and work addresses, telephone and fax numbers, screen names, Web page addresses, and other customized information. The information stored in the Address Book about an individual is referred to as a **card**.

Although most contact information is stored in the **Personal Address Book**, you also are able to create other address books in which to store groups of cards, making it easy to send an e-mail message to a group of people, such as business associates, relatives, or friends.

Earlier, you composed, formatted, and sent an e-mail message to one of the authors of this textbook. You had to type his e-mail address in the To text box (see Figure 3-13 on page FX 140). If you had a card for him in your Address Book, however, you could have selected his name from a list instead of typing the address. The following sections show you how to add a card to the Address Book, edit and print the card information, send an e-mail to the contact, and delete the card.

Adding a Card to the Address Book

Before using the Address Book to send an e-mail to an individual, you should add the contact information to the Address Book. The following steps illustrate how to add the contact information (first name, last name, e-mail address, home telephone, and business telephone) for Annie Meyer.

To Add a Card to the Address Book

1

• **Click the Address Book button on the Mail toolbar in the Inbox - Mozilla Thunderbird window.**

• **If necessary, maximize the Address Book window.**

The maximized Address Book window is displayed (Figure 3-20). The window contains the menu bar, Address Book toolbar, Search bar, status bar, and Card Summary pane. The Address Books pane contains the Personal Address Book and Collected Addresses address books, and the Card list contains five column headers and contact information for five contacts. The card for Ray Enger is displayed in the Card Summary pane.

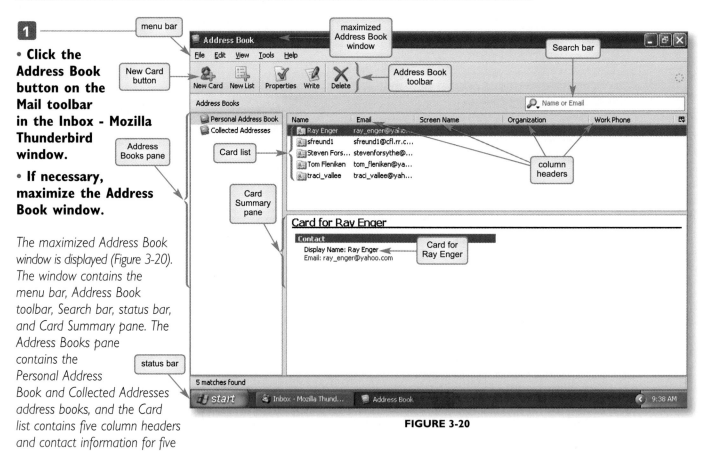

FIGURE 3-20

2

- **Click the New Card button on the Address Book toolbar.**

The New Card dialog box is displayed, where you can enter the contact information for Annie Meyer (Figure 3-21).

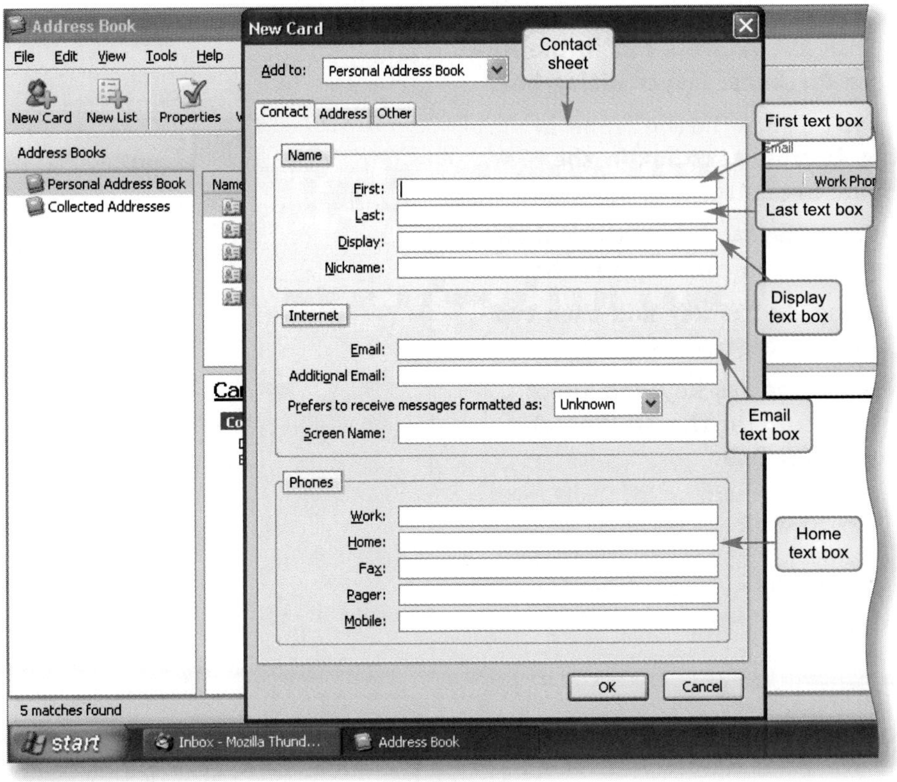

FIGURE 3-21

3

- **Type** Annie **in the First text box.**
- **Click the Last text box and then type** Meyer **in the text box.**
- **Click the Email text box and then type** agmeyer@hotmail.com **in the text box.**
- **Click the Home text box and then type** (714) 555-3292 **as the telephone number.**

As you type the first name (Annie) and last name (Meyer), the names are displayed in the Display text box and are added to the title of the window. The e-mail address (agmeyer@hotmail.com) is displayed in the Email text box. The home telephone number for Annie Meyer is displayed in the Home text box (Figure 3-22).

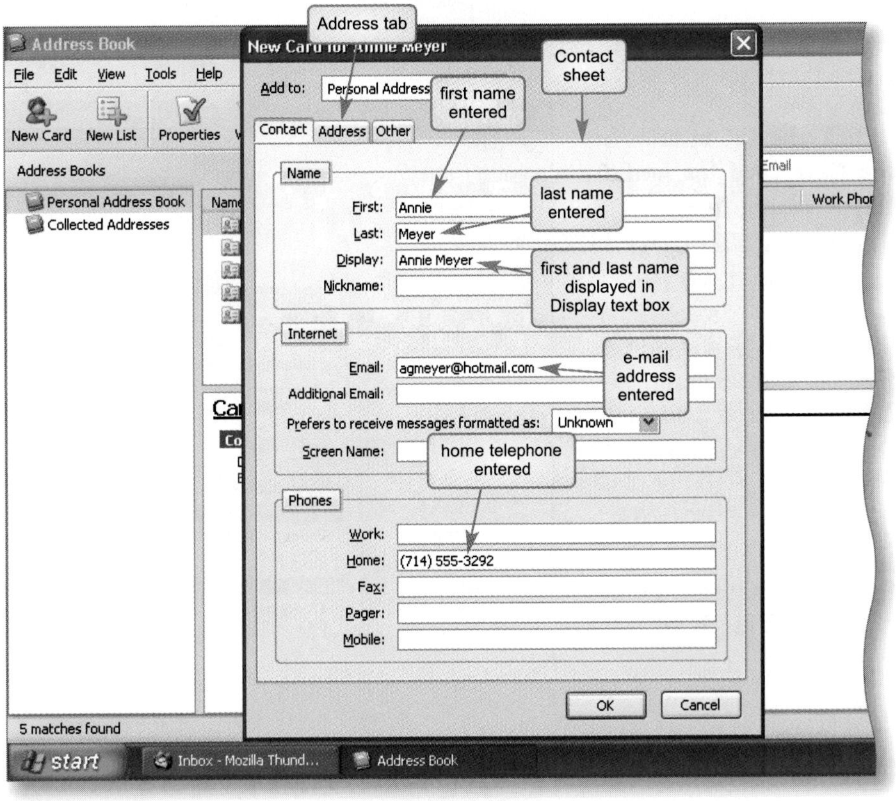

FIGURE 3-22

Mozilla
Firefox

4

• **Click the Address tab in the New Card for Annie Meyer dialog box.**

• **Type** 173 Winding Lane **in the Address text box in the Home area.**

• **Press the TAB key twice and then type** Brea **in the City text box.**

• **Press the TAB key and then type** CA **in the State/Province text box.**

• **Press the TAB key and then type** 92821 **in the ZIP/Postal Code text box.**

The Address sheet is displayed in the dialog box and the home address, city, state, and Zip code are entered in the Address sheet (Figure 3-23).

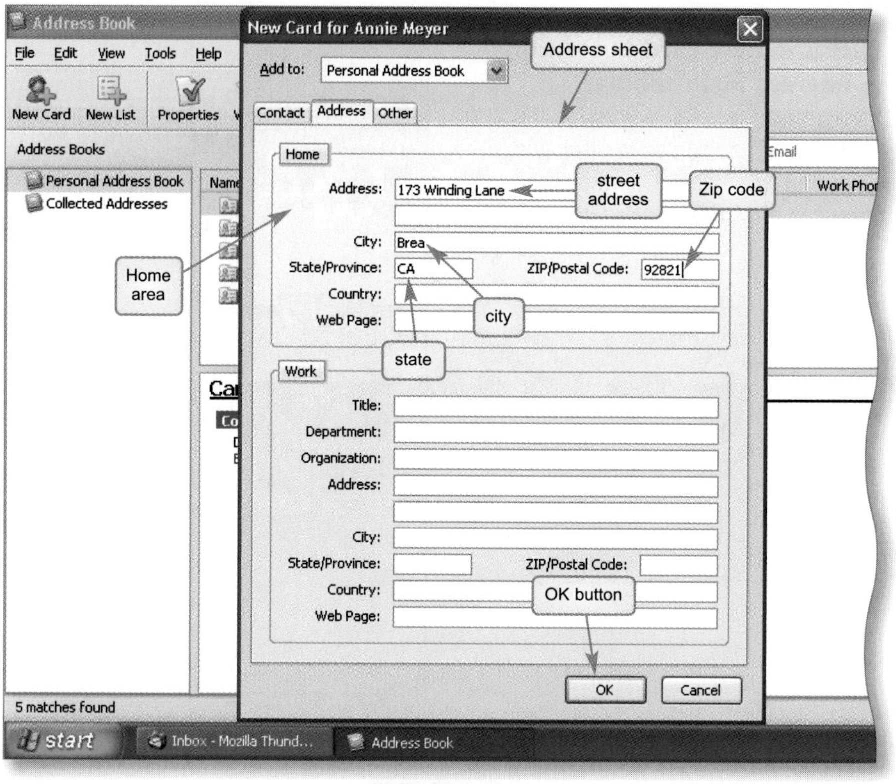

FIGURE 3-23

5

• **Click the OK button in the New Card for Annie Meyer dialog box.**

• **Click Annie Meyer's name in the Card list.**

The New Card for Annie Meyer dialog box closes and an entry for the new contact is added to the Card list in the Address Book window (Figure 3-24). The card for Annie Meyer is displayed in the Card Summary pane.

• **Click the Close button in the Address Book window.**

The Address Book window closes.

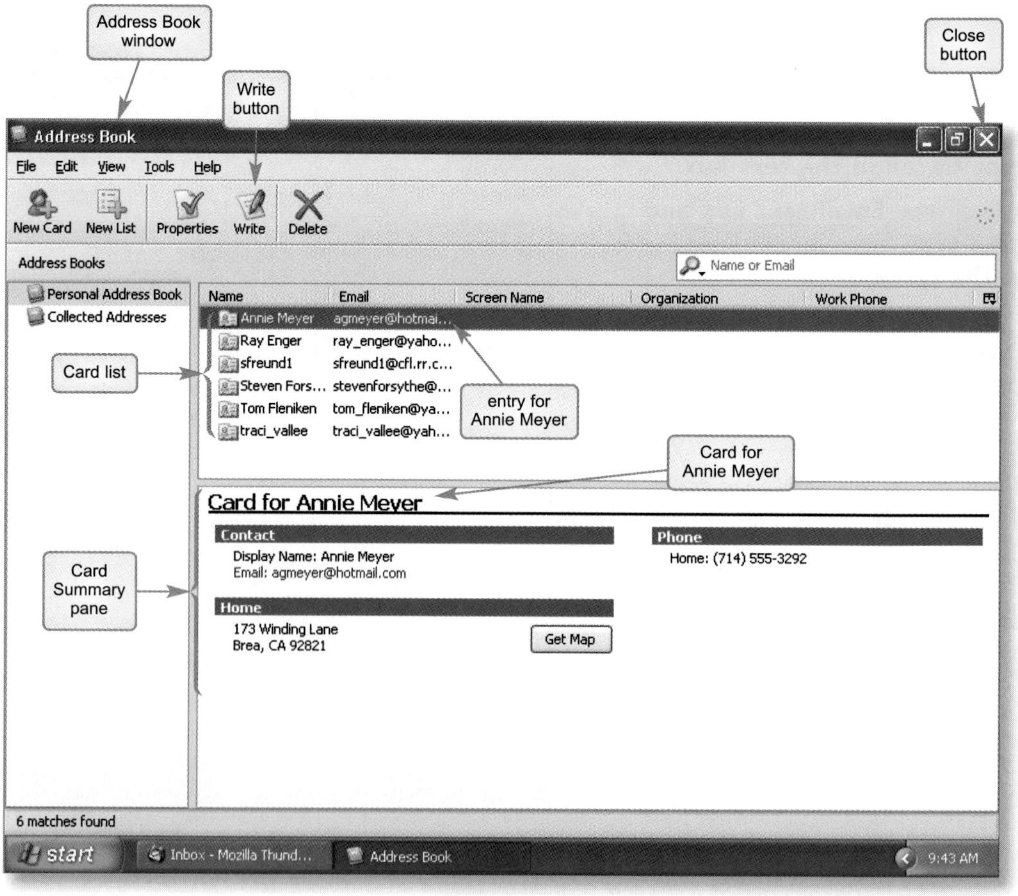

FIGURE 3-24

After entering the card information, you can update the information, copy the card to another address book, or delete the card. In addition, you can use the card information to dial a telephone number, send an e-mail message, or have an online meeting.

Clicking the Other tab in Figure 3-23 allows you to store up to four additional values of your choice, as well as notes about the contact.

Composing an E-Mail Message Using the Address Book

When you compose an e-mail message, you must know the e-mail address of the recipient of the message. Previous steps illustrated how to compose an e-mail message by typing the e-mail address in the To text box in the Compose window (see Figure 3-13 on page FX 140). In addition to entering an e-mail address by typing the e-mail address, you can enter an e-mail address using the Address Book. The following steps show how to compose an e-mail message to Annie Meyer using her e-mail address in the Address Book.

<table>
<tr><td>*Q&A*</td></tr>
<tr><td>**Q:** In the Address Book, can I sort the contacts in the Card list?</td></tr>
<tr><td>**A:** Yes. You can sort the contacts in the Card list in one of five ways: name, e-mail address, screen name, organization, or work phone. You do this by clicking the Name, Email, Screen Name, Organization, or Work Phone button at the top of the Card list.</td></tr>
</table>

To Compose an E-Mail Message Using the Address Book

1

• **Click the Write button on the Mail toolbar.**

• **If necessary, maximize the Compose: (no subject) window.**

The Compose: (no subject) window is displayed (Figure 3-25). The window contains a menu bar, Mail toolbar, text boxes, dimmed Formatting toolbar, and Message area.

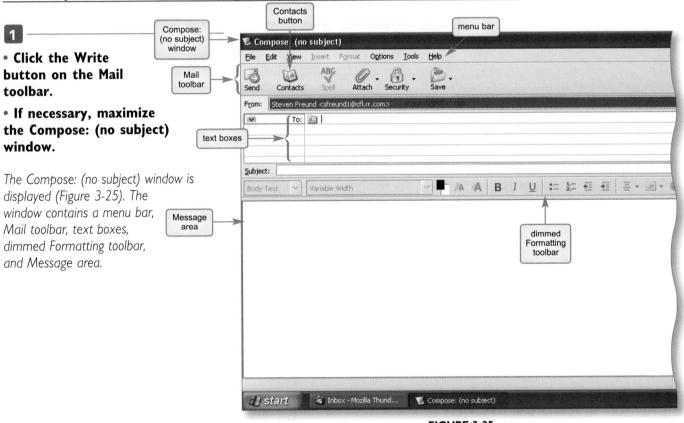

FIGURE 3-25

2

• **Click the Contacts button on the Mail toolbar.**

The Contacts sidebar is displayed (Figure 3-26). The Contacts sidebar contains the Address Book text box, Search For text box, Contacts list, Add to To button, and Add to Cc button. The Contacts list contains six contacts. The contacts in the Contacts list may be different on your computer.

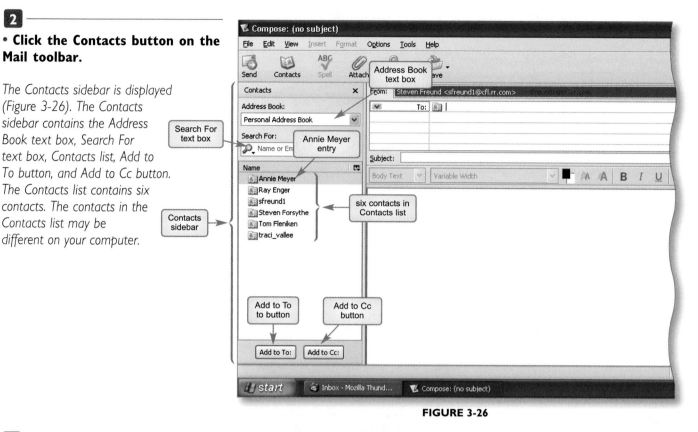

FIGURE 3-26

3

• **Double-click Annie Meyer in the Contacts list.**

Annie Meyer's name (Annie Meyer) and e-mail address (agmeyer@hotmail.com) are displayed in the first To text box (Figure 3-27).

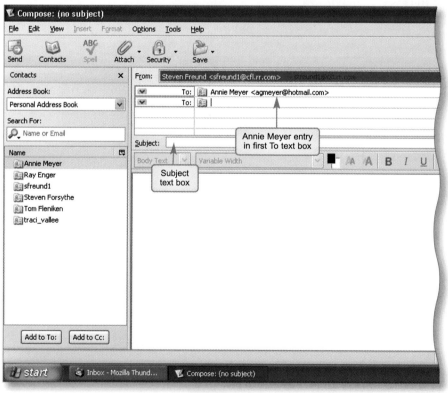

FIGURE 3-27

4

* **Click the Subject text box and then type** Great News **in the text box.**

As you type the subject in the Subject text box, the window title changes to reflect the subject of the e-mail (Figure 3-28).

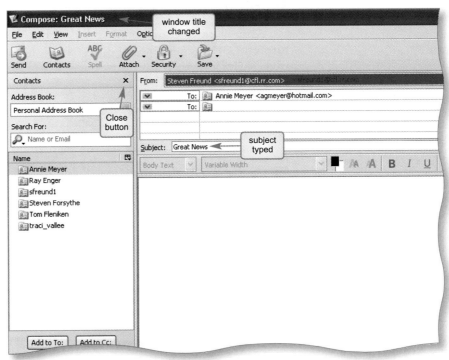

FIGURE 3-28

5

* **Press the TAB key.**

* **Type** Great News! **and then press the ENTER key twice.**

* **Type** I have learned to enter an e-mail address using the Address Book. **and then press the ENTER key twice.**

* **Type your name and then press the ENTER key.**

* **Click the Close button on the Contacts pane.**

* **Select the words, Great News!, in the Message area, click the Choose text alignment button on the Formatting toolbar, click the Center command, and then click the Larger font size button on the Formatting toolbar twice.**

* **Click the highlighted text to remove the highlight.**

The formatted e-mail message is displayed in the Message area; the words "Great News" are centered with the x-large font size (Figure 3-29).

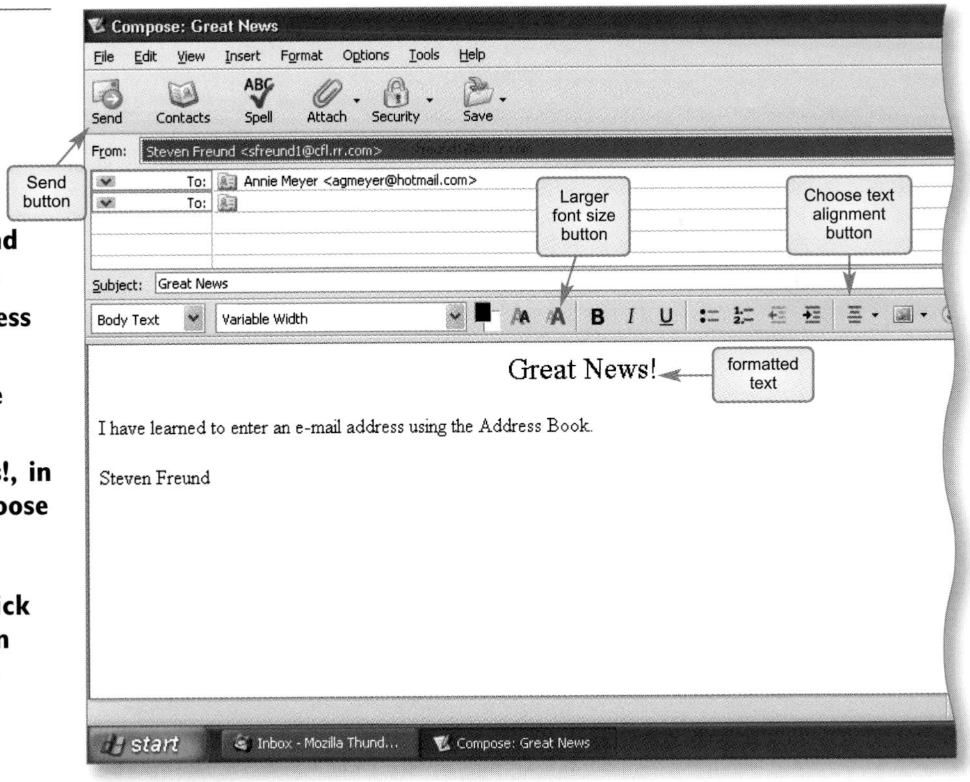

FIGURE 3-29

Sending an E-Mail Message

After retrieving an e-mail address from the Address Book and composing and formatting the e-mail message, you are ready to send the message. The following steps show how to send the message.

To Send an E-Mail Message

 Click the Send button on the Mail toolbar.

2 **If the HTML Mail Question dialog box is displayed, click the Send button.**

The Great News window closes, Thunderbird stores the e-mail message in the Unsent Messages folder temporarily while it sends the message, and then moves the message to the Sent folder (Figure 3-30). The Inbox - Mozilla Thunderbird window remains on the desktop. The Sending Messages - Internet Bookstore dialog box may appear while Mozilla Thunderbird is sending the message.

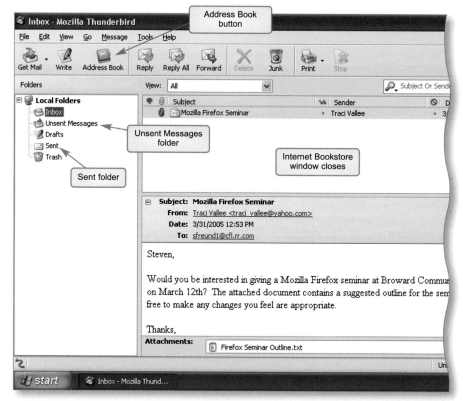

FIGURE 3-30

Deleting a Card from the Address Book

After adding many cards to the Address Book, you may want to remove one or more that you no longer need. The following steps illustrate how to remove the Annie Meyer card from the Address Book.

To Delete a Card from the Address Book

1

- **Click the Address Book button on the Mail toolbar.**

- **If necessary, maximize the Address Book window.**

- **If the Annie Meyer entry in the Card list is not selected, click the Annie Meyer entry to select it.**

The Address Book window is displayed and the Annie Meyer entry is highlighted in the Card list (Figure 3-31).

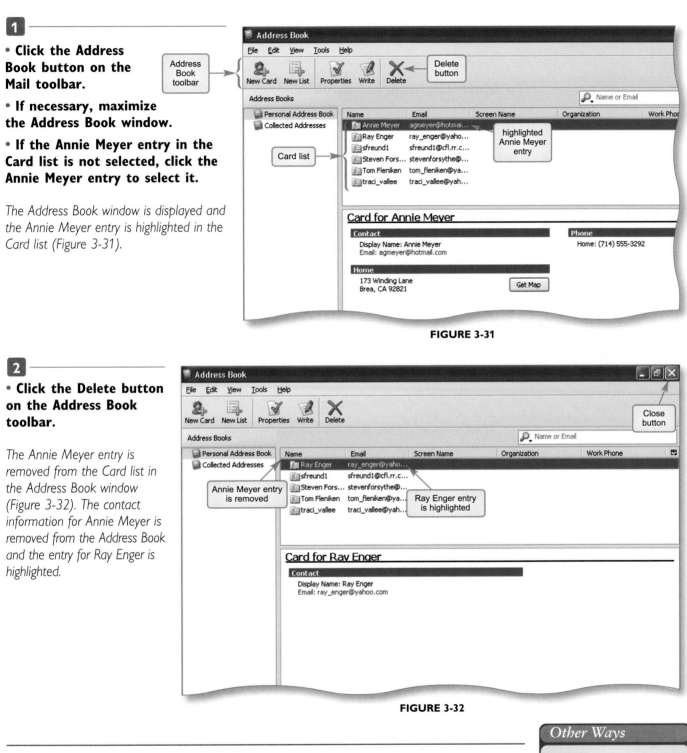

FIGURE 3-31

2

- **Click the Delete button on the Address Book toolbar.**

The Annie Meyer entry is removed from the Card list in the Address Book window (Figure 3-32). The contact information for Annie Meyer is removed from the Address Book and the entry for Ray Enger is highlighted.

FIGURE 3-32

Other Ways

1. Right-click contact entry, click Delete on shortcut menu
2. Click contact entry, on Edit menu click Delete
3. Click entry, press DELETE

Closing the Address Book

When you have finished adding a card to the Address Book, composing and sending an e-mail message, and deleting an Address Book card, you should close the Address Book. The following step shows how to close the Address Book.

To Close the Address Book

1 **Click the Close button on the Address Book window.**

The Address Book window closes.

Internet Newsgroups

Besides exchanging e-mail messages, another popular method of communicating over the Internet is to read and place messages on a newsgroup. A **newsgroup** is a news and discussion group that you can access via the Internet. Each newsgroup is devoted to a particular subject. A special computer, called a **news server**, contains related groups of newsgroups.

To participate in a newsgroup, you must use a program called a **newsreader**. The newsreader enables you to access a newsgroup and interact with it. Using a newsreader, you can read a previously entered message, called an **article**, or send an article, a process called **posting**. A newsreader also keeps track of which articles you have and have not read. In this project, you will use Thunderbird, a newsreader, to read and post articles.

Newsgroup members often post articles in reply to other articles—either to answer questions or to comment on material in the original articles. These replies often cause the author of the original article, or others, to post additional articles related to the original article. This process can be short-lived or it can go on indefinitely, depending on the nature of the topic and the interest of the participants. The original article and all subsequent related replies are called a **thread**, or **thread discussion**. Figure 3-33 shows some articles and threads from a newsgroup called microsoft.public.games.ageofkings.

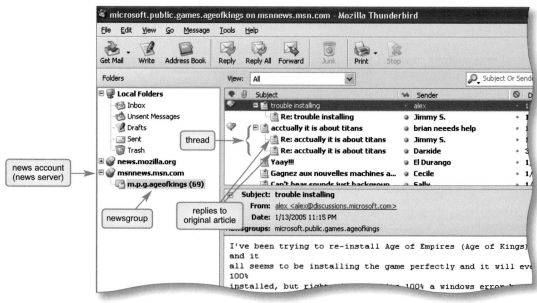

FIGURE 3-33

Newsgroup topics include products from vendors such as Mozilla and IBM; or subjects such as recipes, gardening, and music; or on just about any other topic you can imagine. A **newsgroup name** consists of a **prefix** and one or more subgroup names. For example, the comp.software newsgroup name consists of a prefix (comp), which indicates that the subject of the newsgroup is computers, a period (.), and a **subgroup name** (software), which indicates that the subject is further narrowed down to a discussion of software. A list of some prefix names and their descriptions are shown in Table 3-4.

Table 3-4 Prefix Names and Descriptions	
PREFIX	**DESCRIPTION**
alt	Groups on alternative topics
biz	Business topics
comp	Computer topics
gnu	GNU Software Foundation topics
Ieee	Electrical engineering topics
info	Information about various topics
misc	Miscellaneous topics
news	Groups pertaining to newsgroups
rec	Recreational topics
sci	Science topics
talk	Various conversation groups

The newsgroup prefixes found in Table 3-4 are not the only ones used. Innovative newsgroups are being created everyday. Many colleges and universities have their own newsgroups on topics such as administrative information, tutoring, campus organizations, and distance learning.

In addition, some newsgroups are supervised by a **moderator**, who reads each article before it is posted to the newsgroup. If the moderator thinks an article is appropriate for the newsgroup, then the moderator posts the article for all members to read.

Accessing Newsgroups Using Thunderbird

Before accessing the articles in a newsgroup or posting an article to a newsgroup, you must establish a news account on your computer. A **news account** allows access to the news server. For this project, we will use the news.mozilla.org news server to read and post information about the Mozilla Firefox Web browser.

The following steps illustrate how to add the news.mozilla.org news server to Mozilla Thunderbird.

More About

Local Newsgroups

Many schools maintain a local newsgroup to disseminate information about school events and answer technical questions asked by students. To locate your local newsgroup, search for the school's name in the list of newsgroup names.

To Add a News Server

1

• **Click File on the menu bar and then point to New on the File menu.**

Mozilla Thunderbird displays the File menu and the New submenu (Figure 3-34).

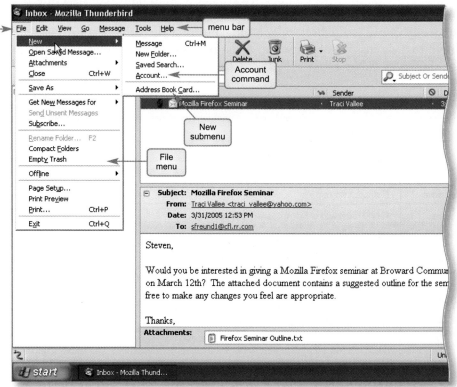

FIGURE 3-34

2

• **Click Account on the New submenu.**

The File menu and New submenu close, and the Account Wizard dialog box is displayed (Figure 3-35). The dialog box contains option buttons for the three types of accounts you can set up in Mozilla Thunderbird (Email account, RSS News & Blogs, and Newsgroup account), as well as the dimmed Back button, Next, and Cancel buttons.

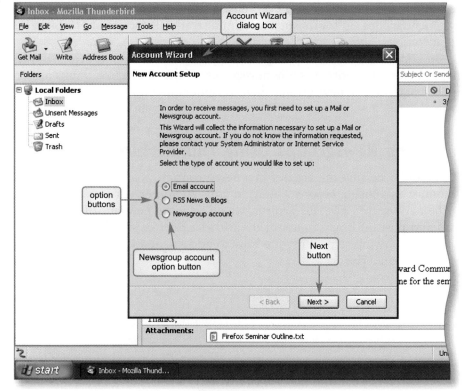

FIGURE 3-35

3

• **Click the Newsgroup account option button in the Account Wizard dialog box.**

• **Click the Next button.**

The contents of the Account Wizard dialog box change, allowing you to enter information about your identity. The Account Wizard dialog box contains the Your Name text box and the Email Address text box (Figure 3-36).

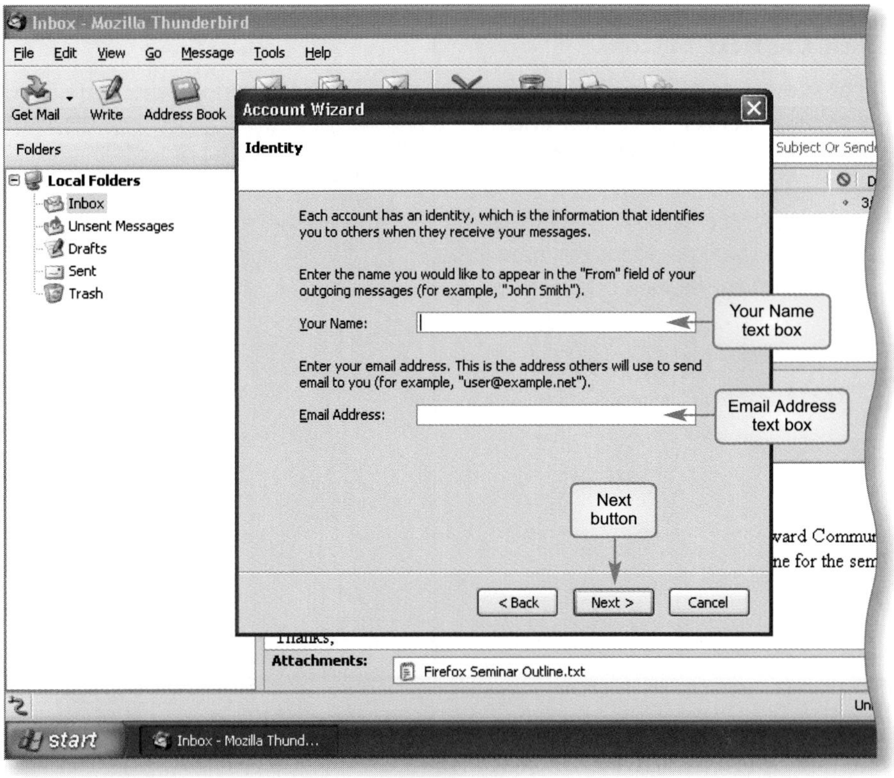

FIGURE 3-36

4

• **Enter your name in the Your Name text box.**

• **Enter your e-mail address in the Email Address text box and then point to the Next button.**

The Your Name text box is displayed with your name and the Email Address text box is displayed your e-mail address (Figure 3-37).

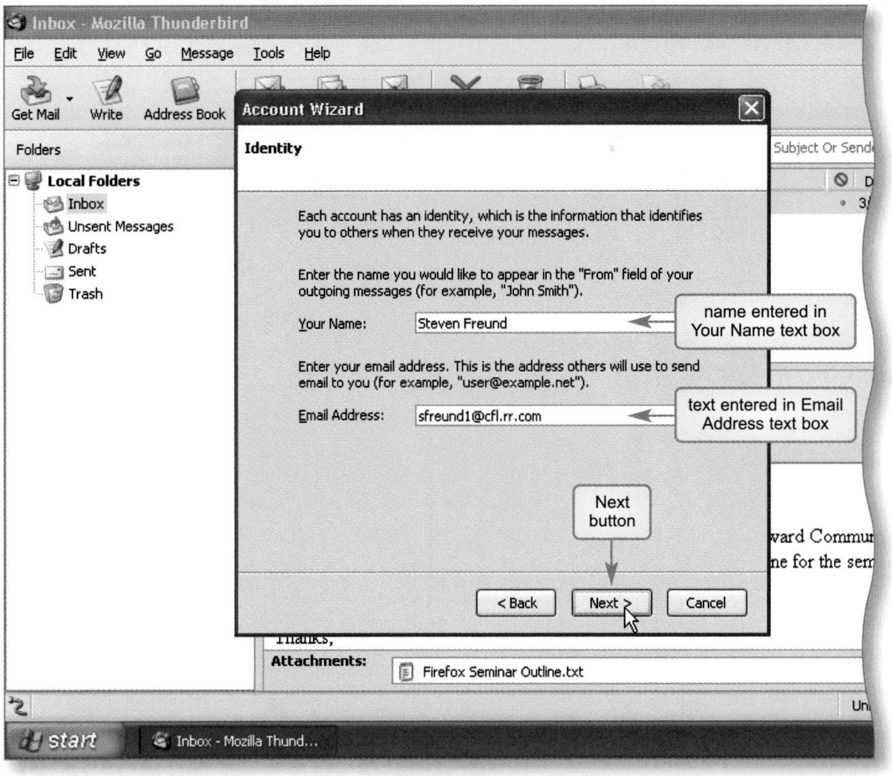

FIGURE 3-37

5

• **Click the Next button.**

• **Type** `news.mozilla.org` **in the Newsgroup Server text box and then point to the Next button.**

The contents of the Account Wizard dialog box change, allowing you to enter the server information. The newsgroup server, news.mozilla.org, is displayed in the Newsgroup Server text box (Figure 3-38).

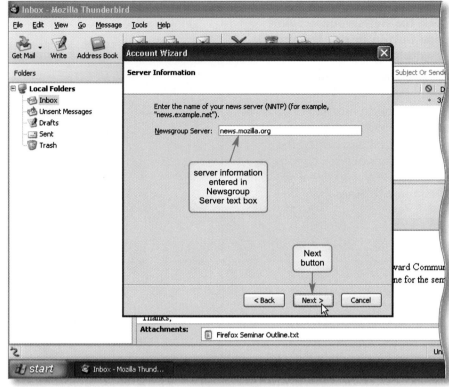

FIGURE 3-38

6

• **Click the Next button.**

The Account Wizard dialog box displays the Account Name text box containing the news.mozilla.org account name (Figure 3-39).

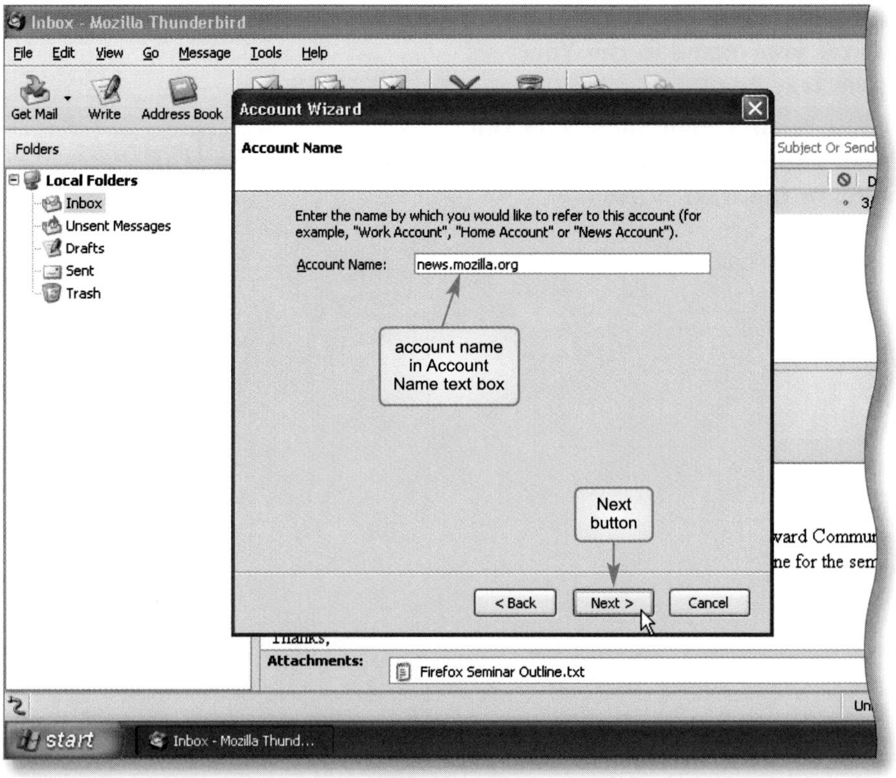

FIGURE 3-39

7

• **Click the Next button.**

The Account Wizard dialog box is displayed with the information you entered (Figure 3-40). This information includes the account name, e-mail address, news server name, and outgoing user name.

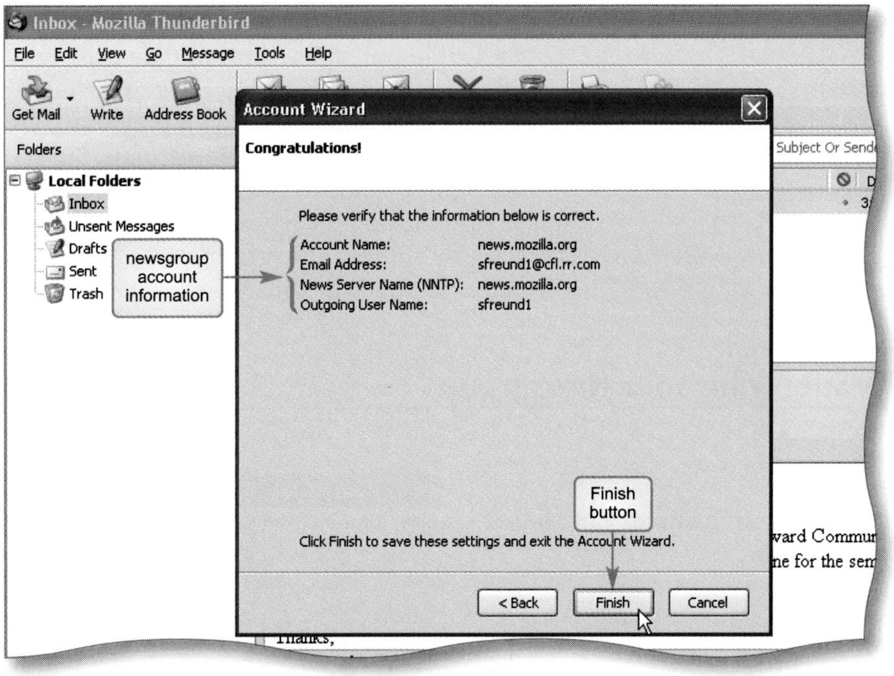

FIGURE 3-40

8

• **Click the Finish button.**

Mozilla Thunderbird adds the newsgroup account and displays the news.mozilla.org account name in the Folders pane on the left side of the Inbox - Mozilla Thunderbird window (Figure 3-41).

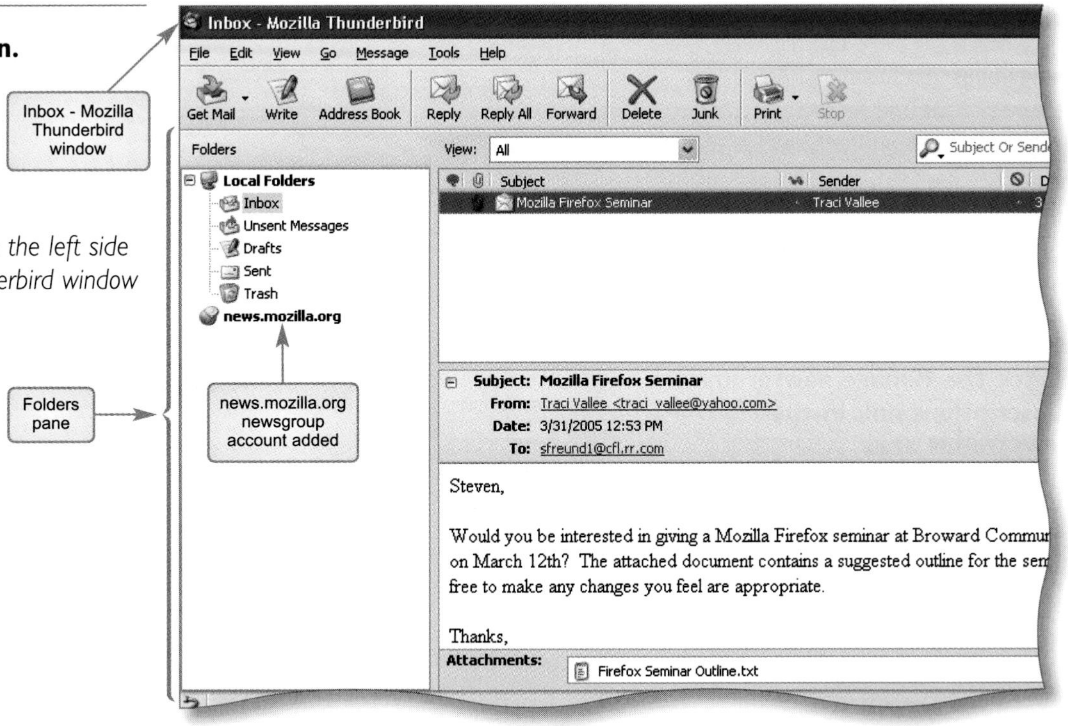

FIGURE 3-41

Now that you added the news.mozilla.org newsgroup account, you are ready to subscribe to a newsgroup on the news.mozilla.org news server.

Other Ways

1. On Tools menu click Account Settings, click Add Account button
2. Press ALT+T, press C, click Add Account button
3. Press ALT+F, press N, press A

Subscribing to a Newsgroup

Several hundred newsgroups may exist on a news server. Searching for a previously visited newsgroup or scrolling the newsgroup list to find a previously visited newsgroup can be time-consuming. To find a previously visited newsgroup quickly, Thunderbird allows you to subscribe to a newsgroup. **Subscribing to a newsgroup** permanently adds the newsgroup name to the Folders pane and allows you to return to the newsgroup quickly by clicking the newsgroup name in the Folders pane instead of searching or scrolling to find the newsgroup name. The following steps show how to subscribe to the netscape.public.mozilla.browser newsgroup.

To Subscribe to a Newsgroup

1

• **Click news.mozilla.org in the Folders pane.**

The news.mozilla.org account name is selected and the Mozilla Thunderbird News - news.mozilla.org page is displayed on the right side of the window (Figure 3-42). The Mozilla Thunderbird News - news.mozilla.org page contains the Newsgroups, Accounts, and Advanced Features areas. The Advanced Features area is not visible in the Newsgroup area.

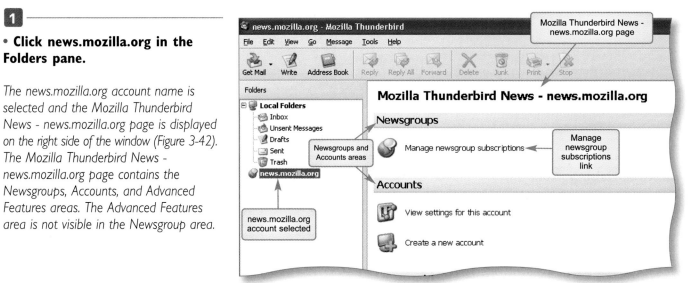

FIGURE 3-42

2

• **Click the Manage newsgroup subscriptions link in the Newsgroups area.**

The Subscribe dialog box is displayed, which contains the Account box, Show items that contain text box, newsgroups list, and the Subscribe, Unsubscribe, Refresh, dimmed Stop, OK, and Cancel buttons (Figure 3-43).

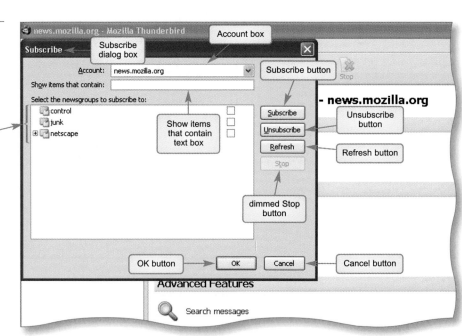

FIGURE 3-43

3

• **Type** netscape.public. mozilla.browser **in the Show items that contain text box.**

As you type the text in the Show items that contain text box, Mozilla Thunderbird searches the news.mozilla.org news server for the netscape. public.mozilla.browser newsgroup (Figure 3-44). The newsgroup name also is displayed in the newsgroup list.

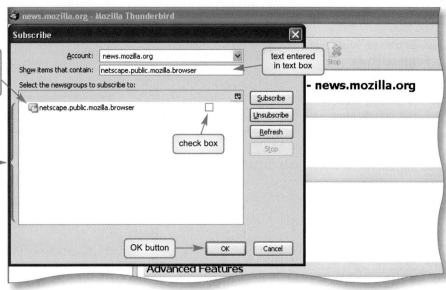

FIGURE 3-44

4

• **Click the check box to the right of the netscape.public.mozilla .browser newsgroup name in the newsgroups list.**

The netscape.public.mozilla.browser check box contains a check mark and the netscape.public.mozilla.browser newsgroup name in the newsgroups list is highlighted (Figure 3-45).

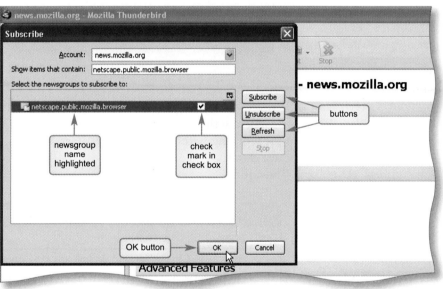

FIGURE 3-45

5

• **Click the OK button.**

The Subscribe dialog box closes as Mozilla Thunderbird subscribes to the netscape.public. mozilla.browser newsgroup on the news.mozilla.org news server. The n.p.m.browser folder is displayed under the news.mozilla.org account name in the Folders pane (Figure 3-46).

FIGURE 3-46

6

• **Click the n.p.m.browser folder in the Folders pane.**

• **When the Download Headers dialog box is displayed, click the Download button.**

Mozilla Thunderbird contacts the news server and displays the Download Headers dialog box. After clicking the Download button in the Download Headers dialog box, Mozilla Thunderbird downloads the message headers in the netscape.public.mozilla .browser newsgroup to the computer, and the Welcome to Mozilla Thunderbird! page is displayed in the Message pane. (Figure 3-47). The messages on your computer may be different.

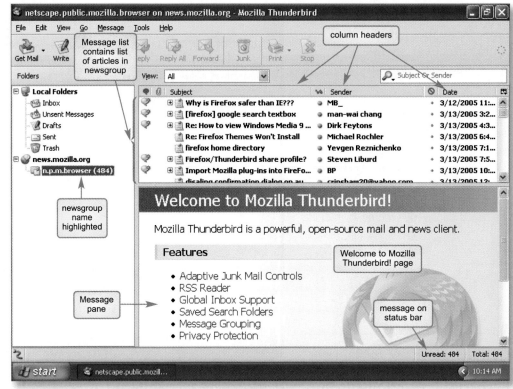

FIGURE 3-47

Below the menu bar shown in Figure 3-47 is the Mail toolbar containing buttons for working with news messages (Get Mail, Write, Address Book, Reply, Reply All, and so on). Table 3-5 contains the toolbar buttons and a brief explanation of their functions.

Table 3-5 Mail Toolbar Buttons and Functions

BUTTON	FUNCTION
Get Mail	Checks for and downloads new messages on the server.
Write	Displays a window that allows you to post a new article to the newsgroup.
Address Book	Displays the Address Book window containing a list of frequently used contacts.
Reply	Displays a window that allows you to post a reply to a newsgroup article.
Reply All	Displays a window that allows you to reply to all authors of articles in the newsgroup by e-mail.
Forward	Displays a window that allows you to forward a newsgroup article by e-mail.
Junk	This button is disabled while viewing a newsgroup article.
Print	Prints the highlighted article in the Message area.
Stop	Stops the current connection to and transfer from the news server.

In Figure 3-45 on page FX 159, the buttons to the right of the newsgroups list allow you to subscribe to a newsgroup (Subscribe), unsubscribe from a newsgroup (Unsubscribe), and redisplay the list of newsgroups (Refresh). When you **subscribe** to a newsgroup, the newsgroup name is displayed in the Folders pane, making it easy to return to the newsgroup.

The Message list in Figure 3-47 contains column headers and a list of the original articles (postings) in the netscape.public.mozilla.browser newsgroup. Each original article consists of the subject of the article, author name, and date and time the article was posted.

The plus sign in a small box to the left of some of the articles indicates the article is part of a thread. Clicking the plus sign expands the thread so you can see a list of the replies to the original article. A minus sign in a small box icon to the left of an article indicates the article is expanded. Clicking the minus sign collapses the thread so you cannot see the replies to the original article, leaving more room for the list of original articles.

When you select an article in the Message list, the text of the article is displayed in the Message pane. In Figure 3-47, the preview pane indicates no message is selected.

The status bar at the bottom of the Thunderbird window indicates that 484 articles (messages) have been retrieved and 484 articles have not been read. The numbers on the status bar may be different on your computer.

Reading Newsgroup Articles

The entries in the Subject column in the Message list allow you to look at the subject of an article before deciding to read the article. The following step illustrates how to read the Newsgroup article.

To Read a Newsgroup Article

1

- **Scroll the Message list to display the article titled Firefox Quick Launch. If you do not see the Firefox Quick Launch article, scroll to display another article.**

- **Click the Firefox Quick Launch article (or another article) in the Message list.**

The contents of the Firefox Quick Launch article are displayed in the Message pane (Figure 3-48). A header in the Message pane contains the subject, name of the person who posted the article, date the article was posted, and newsgroup name. The contents of the article are displayed below the header. A question is displayed in the Message pane.

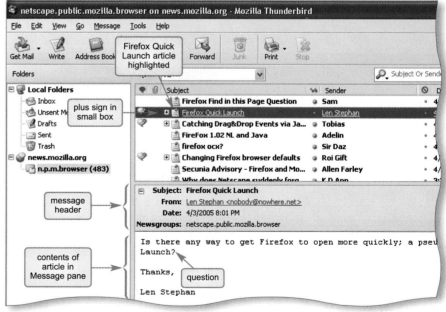

FIGURE 3-48

More About

Column Headers

You can change the width of columns in the Message list by dragging the vertical line between two column headers. Likewise, you can drag the vertical line that separates the Folders pane from the Message list and Message pane to change the size of the two areas.

More About

Newsgroups

Instructors often use newsgroups to teach courses over the Internet. An instructor posts a question and students respond by posting an article. Students can read the articles in the thread to be aware of all responses. Students usually subscribe to the newsgroup so they can easily return to it.

Other Ways

1. Press P to read previous article
2. Press F to read next article

Expanding a Thread

When a plus sign is displayed to the left of an article in the Message list, the article is part of a thread and can be expanded. **Expanding the thread** displays the replies to the original article below the original article and changes the plus sign to a minus sign. The following step illustrates how to expand the Firefox Quick Launch thread and view the replies to the article.

To Expand a Thread

1

• **Click the plus sign in the small box to the left of the Firefox Quick Launch name.**

• **Click the reply (Re: Firefox Quick Launch) below the original article.**

• **If necessary, scroll the Message pane to view an answer to the question.**

The plus sign to the left of the original article changes to a minus sign and a reply is displayed in the Message list (Figure 3-49). The Re: entry in the Message list is highlighted and the text of the reply is displayed in the Message pane. The text in the Message pane contains an answer to the question asked in the original article.

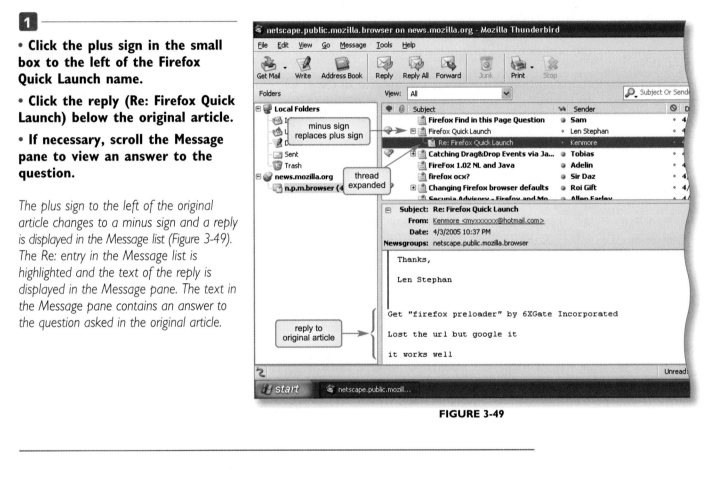

FIGURE 3-49

Collapsing a Thread

When you expand a thread, a minus sign replaces the plus sign to the left of the original article within the thread. Sometimes, after reading the reply within a thread, you will want to collapse the expansion. **Collapsing the thread** hides the replies, displays the original article in the preview pane, and changes the minus sign to the left of the original article to a plus sign. The following step shows how to collapse the Firefox Quick Launch thread.

To Collapse a Thread

1

• **Click the minus sign in the small box to the left of the original Firefox Quick Launch article.**

The minus sign to the left of the original article changes to a plus sign and the reply to the original article no longer is displayed (Figure 3-50).

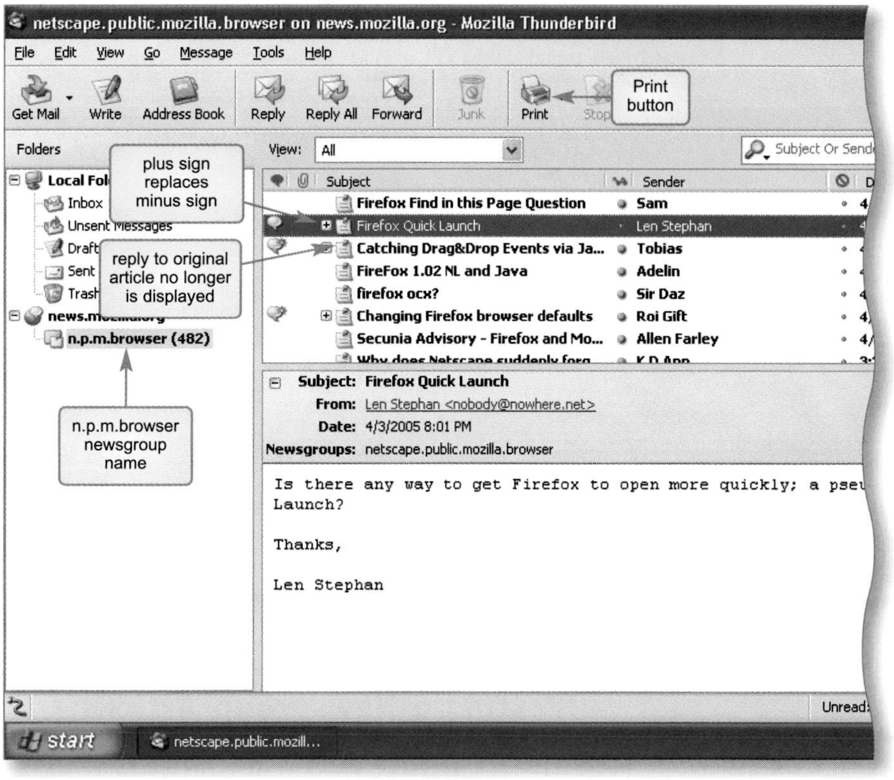

FIGURE 3-50

Printing a Newsgroup Article

After displaying and reading an article, you may want to print the article. The printout is similar to the printout that results when you print an e-mail message (see Figure 3-5 on page FX 134). The following steps illustrate how to print the contents of the Firefox Quick Launch article.

To Print a Newsgroup Article

1 Click the **Print** button on the toolbar.

2 Click the **OK** button in the Print dialog box.

The newsgroup article is printed (Figure 3-51).

In Figure 3-51 on the next page, the printed newsgroup article consists of a header at the top of the page containing the subject (Firefox Quick Launch). Below the header are the Subject, From, Date, and Newsgroups entries and the body of the Firefox Quick Launch article. The Newsgroups entry contains the newsgroup name and the Subject entry contains the article name. A footer at the bottom of the page contains the page number (1 of 1) and current date and time (4/5/2005 10:22 AM). If the article contains pictures, the pictures do not print.

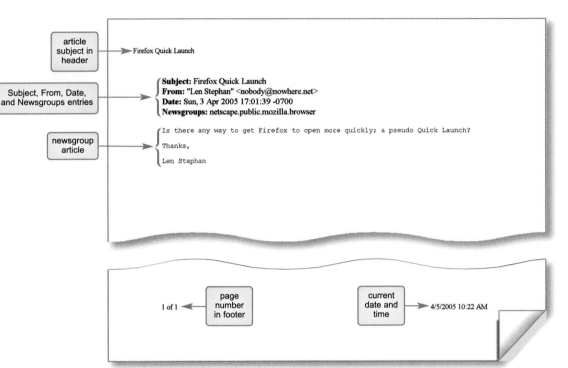

FIGURE 3-51

Posting a Newsgroup Article

At some point in time you may want to post, or send, a reply to a newsgroup article. The following steps illustrate how to post a newsgroup article to the netscape.test newsgroup. The netscape.test newsgroup is a newsgroup just for miscellaneous purposes. Posting to this newsgroup will not disturb any other newsgroup articles.

To Display the Articles in the netscape.test Newsgroup

1 Right-click news.mozilla.org in the Folders pane and then click Subscribe on the shortcut menu.

2 Type netscape.test in the Show items that contain text box.

3 Double-click the netscape.test entry in the newsgroups list.

4 Click the OK button.

5 Click the n.test newsgroup name in the Folders pane. When the Download Headers dialog box is displayed, click the Download button.

The Subscribe dialog box is displayed, the keyword, netscape.test, is displayed in the Show items that contain text box, and (after you click the OK button) the Subscribe dialog box closes (Figure 3-52). The articles in the netscape.test newsgroup are displayed in the Message list. The n.test newsgroup name is indented below the news.mozilla.org entry in the Folders pane and in the window title. A partial list of articles in the netscape.test newsgroup are displayed in the Message list.

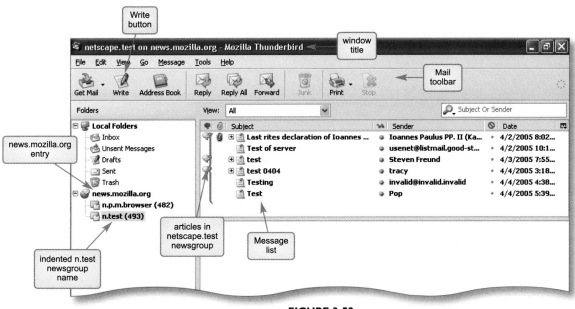

FIGURE 3-52

The following steps illustrate how to post a test article to the newsgroup using the words, Test Message, as the subject of the article to indicate that the article is a test and can be disregarded by anyone browsing the newsgroup.

To Post a Newsgroup Article

1

• **Click the Write button on the Mail toolbar.**

• **If necessary, maximize the Compose: (no subject) window.**

The maximized Compose: (no subject) window appears (Figure 3-53). The window contains a menu bar, Mail toolbar, text boxes, and Message pane. The Newsgroups text box contains the newsgroup name (netscape.test) and the Subject text box contains the insertion point.

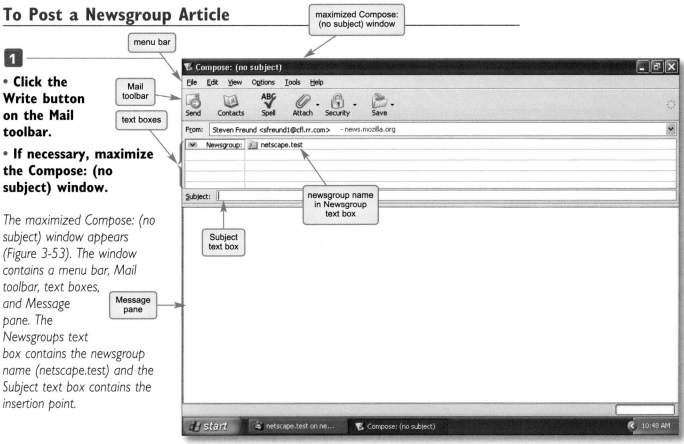

FIGURE 3-53

2

• **Type** Test Message **in the Subject text box and then press the TAB key.**

• **Type** Please ignore this message. I am learning to post a message to a newsgroup. **as the message.**

The subject (Test Message) is displayed in the window title and Subject text box and the message is displayed in the Message pane (Figure 3-54). The subject indicates that this is a test message and can be disregarded.

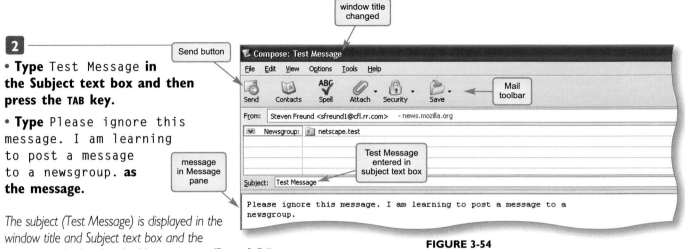

FIGURE 3-54

3

• **Click the Send button on the Mail toolbar.**

The Compose: Test Message window closes and the Sending Messages dialog box is displayed while the message is being posted to the netscape.test newsgroup. The Sending Messages dialog box closes and the netscape.test on news.mozilla.org - Mozilla Thunderbird window is displayed (Figure 3-55). You may have to wait several minutes for the article to be posted to the netscape.test newsgroup.

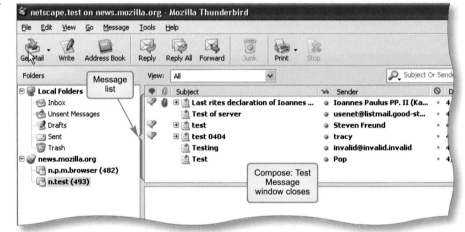

FIGURE 3-55

4

• **When the message is displayed in the Message list, scroll the Message list to view the test message and then click the Test Message.**

The Test Message article is displayed in the Message list and the contents of the message are displayed in the Message pane (Figure 3-56).

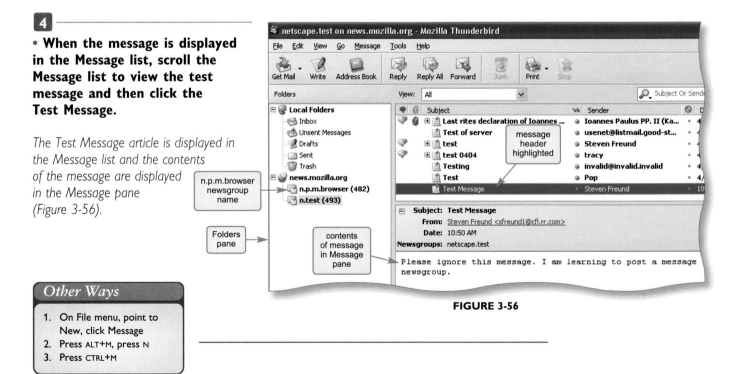

FIGURE 3-56

Other Ways

1. On File menu, point to New, click Message
2. Press ALT+M, press N
3. Press CTRL+M

The buttons on the toolbar illustrated in Figure 3-54 (Send, Spell, Attach, and so on) are useful when posting a new article. Table 3-6 shows the buttons on the toolbar and their functions.

Table 3-6 Toolbar Buttons and Functions	
BUTTON	**FUNCTION**
Send	Sends the article in the Compose window to a news server.
Contacts	Displays the Contacts sidebar, allowing you to select recipients from the Address Book.
ABC Spell	Spell checks the article.
Attach	Attaches a file to the article.
Security	Allows you to digitally sign an e-mail message (allowing the recipient to verify the sender's identity), and/or encrypt an e-mail message (preventing someone other than the recipient from reading the message).
Save	Saves the article as a file, draft, or template.

Displaying the Articles in a Newsgroup after Subscribing to the Newsgroup

Earlier in this project you learned how to subscribe to the netscape.public. mozilla.browser newsgroup. After subscribing to a newsgroup, you can view the articles in the newsgroup by clicking the newsgroup name in the Folders pane without having to search or scroll to find the articles in the newsgroup. The following step illustrates how to view the articles in the netscape.public.mozilla.browser newsgroup.

To Display the Articles in a Newsgroup

1

• **Click n.p.m.browser in the Folders pane.**

The n.p.m.browser newsgroup name is highlighted in the Folders pane and the articles in the newsgroup are displayed in the Message list (Figure 3-57).

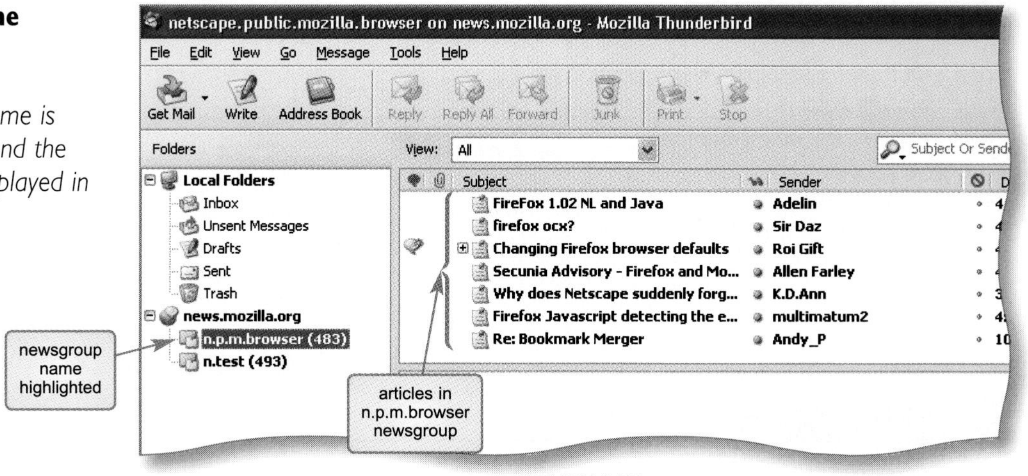

FIGURE 3-57

Unsubscribing from a Newsgroup

When you no longer need access to a newsgroup, you can **unsubscribe** from it, which removes you from the newsgroup and also removes the newsgroup name from the Folders pane. The next steps show how to unsubscribe from the netscape.public.mozilla.browser newsgroup.

To Unsubscribe from a Newsgroup

1

• **Right-click the n.p.m.browser newsgroup name in the Folders pane and then point to Unsubscribe on the shortcut menu.**

A shortcut menu, containing the Unsubscribe command, is displayed (Figure 3-58). The Unsubscribe command is highlighted.

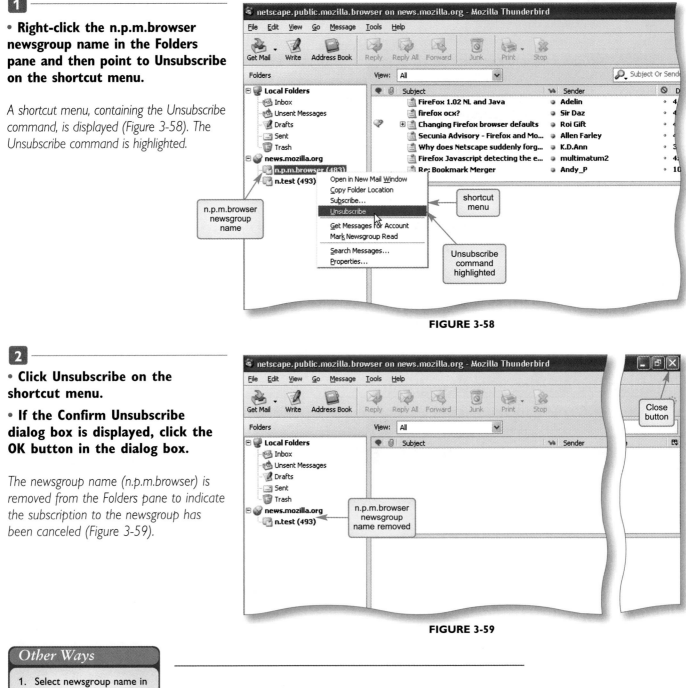

FIGURE 3-58

2

• **Click Unsubscribe on the shortcut menu.**

• **If the Confirm Unsubscribe dialog box is displayed, click the OK button in the dialog box.**

The newsgroup name (n.p.m.browser) is removed from the Folders pane to indicate the subscription to the newsgroup has been canceled (Figure 3-59).

FIGURE 3-59

Other Ways

1. Select newsgroup name in Subscribe dialog box, click Unsubscribe button

Quitting Thunderbird

When you have finished working with newsgroups, you should quit Thunderbird, as the following step illustrates.

To Quit Thunderbird

1 **Click the Close button in the Mozilla Thunderbird window.**

The Mozilla Thunderbird window closes.

Yahoo! Messenger and Instant Messaging

One of the more useful communication tools available today is Yahoo! Messenger. **Yahoo! Messenger** allows you to communicate instantly with your online contacts. Yahoo! Messenger is available free of charge from Yahoo's Web site (http://www.yahoo.com). For more information about downloading and installing Yahoo! Messenger, see your instructor. The advantage of using Yahoo! Messenger instead of e-mail is that the message you send is displayed immediately on the computer of the person with whom you are communicating, provided that person has signed in to Yahoo! Messenger. That person can respond immediately by sending a reply to you.

Yahoo! Messenger maintains a **Messenger List** of individuals with whom you can communicate. You can use Yahoo! Messenger for a multitude of communication tasks. You can add a contact to the Messenger List, view a list of online and offline contacts, talk to a single contact or a group of contacts, place an Internet call from the computer and talk using a microphone and headset, send files to another computer, send a text message, and invite someone to an online conference, and even play an Internet game.

Before using Yahoo! Messenger, both you and the person you wish to contact must have a Yahoo! account and have the Yahoo! Messenger software installed on your computers. **Yahoo!** is a service that provides free e-mail accounts. With a Yahoo! account you use a sign-in name and password to access your e-mail from any computer on the Internet. As a Yahoo! Messenger user, your Yahoo! Messenger ID and password also are your Yahoo! Mail ID and password. For more information about signing up for a free Yahoo! account, visit http://www.yahoo.com or see your instructor.

Before using Yahoo! Messenger, you must start Yahoo! Messenger and sign in using your Yahoo! ID and password. The steps on the next page illustrate how to sign in and enter the password for your Yahoo! account. They show how to start Yahoo! Messenger and sign in to the Yahoo! Messenger Service using a Yahoo! ID and password.

To Start Yahoo! Messenger and Sign In

1

• **Click the Start button on the Windows taskbar, point to All Programs on the Start menu, and then point to Yahoo! Messenger on the All Programs submenu.**

Windows displays the Start menu and the All Programs submenu (Figure 3-60).

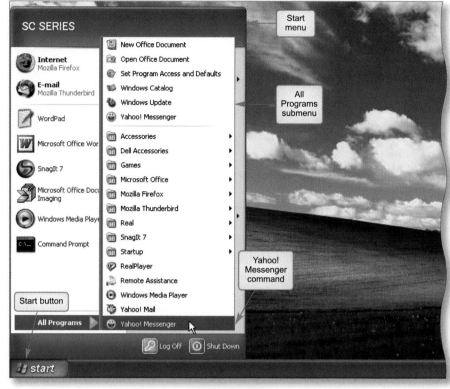

FIGURE 3-60

2

• **Click Yahoo! Messenger.**

The Yahoo! Messenger window is displayed along with the Sign In dialog box (Figure 3-61). The Sign In dialog box contains the Get a Yahoo! ID button, Yahoo! ID text box, Password text box, three check boxes, and the Sign In, Cancel, and Help buttons.

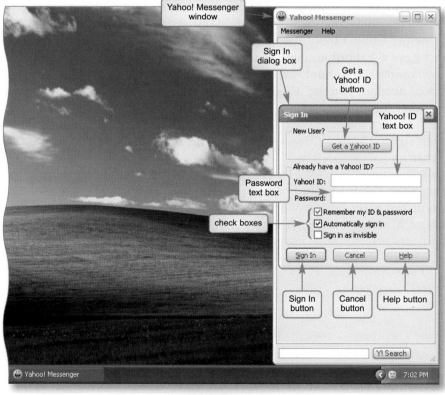

FIGURE 3-61

3

• **Type your Yahoo! ID in the Yahoo! ID text box.**

• **Type your Yahoo! password in the Password text box.**

• **Click the Sign In button in the Yahoo! Messenger window.**

• **If the Yahoo! Insider window is displayed, click the Close button on the title bar to close the window.**

• **If the Yahoo! Mail Alert window is displayed, click the OK button in the Yahoo! Mail Alert window, or wait for the Yahoo! Mail Alert window to close automatically.**

Yahoo! Messenger signs you in to the Yahoo! Messenger service and the contents of the Yahoo! Messenger window change (Figure 3-62). The Yahoo! Messenger window contains a menu bar, status chooser, toolbar, Messenger list, LAUNCHcast Radio area, content tabs, and Yahoo! Search bar.

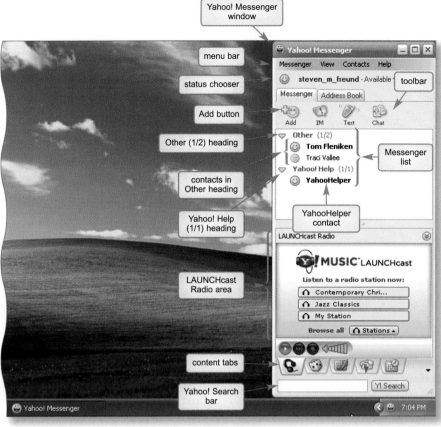

FIGURE 3-62

The Messenger list in Figure 3-62 contains the Other heading and the Yahoo! Help (1/1) heading. The contacts in the Other heading include Tom Fleniken and Traci Vallee and the YahooHelper contact is displayed below the Yahoo! Help heading. A gray face icon is displayed next to contacts who are not currently online, while a yellow happy face icon is used for contacts who are currently online. A down arrow button precedes the Other heading and Yahoo! Help heading. The (1/2) entry next to the Other heading indicates one contact is currently online out of the two total contacts under the Other heading. The (1/1) entry next to the Yahoo! Help heading indicates that the one contact under the Yahoo! Help heading is currently online. These entries change as contacts sign on and off. Clicking the down arrow button preceding either of these headings collapses the appropriate corresponding list.

The toolbar containing the Add button is displayed immediately above the Messenger list. The Add button, which allows you to add a contact to the Messenger list, is identified by a yellow plus sign next to a yellow happy face.

Five tabs are displayed along the bottom of the Yahoo! Messenger window. Table 3-7 on the next page shows the tabs and a brief explanation of their functions.

More About

Yahoo! Messenger Alerts and Sounds

Various Yahoo! Messenger alerts are displayed near the Yahoo! Messenger icon in the notification area on the Windows taskbar as various Messenger events occur. When a Messenger contact comes online, a Sign-in alert displays the person's name and plays a sound. When you receive an Instant Message, you receive an alert, which you can click to open and carry on a conversation. In addition, you can receive stock alerts, Yahoo! Calendar reminder alerts, as well as alerts when you receive an e-mail in Yahoo! Mail.

Table 3-7 Yahoo! Messenger Window Tabs and Functions	
TAB	FUNCTION
	Displays the LAUNCHcast Radio tab, allowing you to listen to radio stations online.
	Displays the Yahoo! Games tab, allowing you to access a list of free single- and multi-player Yahoo! Games.
	Displays the Stocks tab, allowing you to view your stock portfolios in the Yahoo! Messenger window.
	Displays the Weather tab, allowing you to view the current weather conditions around the world.
	Displays the Calendar tab, allowing you to add and view events and tasks on your Yahoo! Calendar.

Adding a Contact to the Messenger List

After starting Yahoo! Messenger, you can add a person to the contact list. You need the person's e-mail address or Yahoo! ID, and he or she needs to have the Yahoo! Messenger software. If you try to add someone who does not meet these requirements, Yahoo! Messenger will display an error message indicating the Yahoo! ID does not exist. Note that someone with a Yahoo! ID does not necessarily have a Yahoo! Mail account—you can use the ID *or* an e-mail address.

The following steps illustrate how to add a contact to the Messenger list using the e-mail address of someone you know who has signed in to Yahoo! Messenger.

To Add a Contact to the Messenger List

1

• **Click the Add button on the Yahoo! Messenger toolbar.**

The Add to Messenger List dialog box is displayed, containing the Yahoo! ID or Email Address text box, First Name text box, Last Name text box, and the Back, Next, Finish, and Cancel buttons (Figure 3-63).

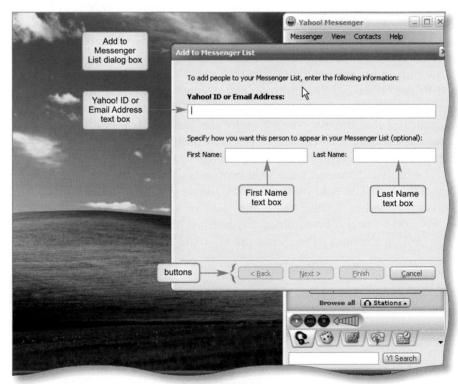

FIGURE 3-63

2

- **Type** ray_enger@yahoo.com **in the Yahoo! ID or Email Address text box.**
- **Type** Ray **in the First Name text box.**
- **Type** Enger **in the Last Name text box.**
- **Point to the Next button.**

The Yahoo! E-mail address for Ray Enger (ray_enger@yahoo.com) is displayed in the Yahoo! ID or Email Address text box, Ray is entered in the First Name text box, and Enger is entered in the Last Name text box (Figure 3-64).

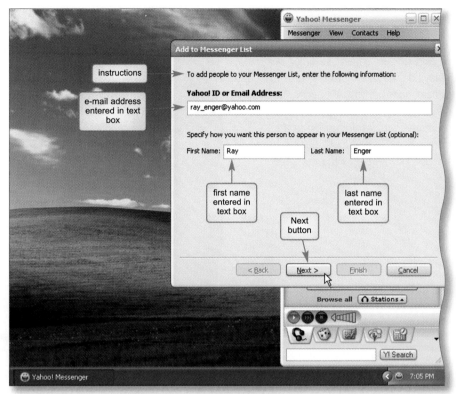

FIGURE 3-64

3

- **Click the Next button.**
- **Type** I would like to add you to my Yahoo! Messenger List. **in the Enter a brief introduction to this person (optional) box.**

The Add to Messenger List dialog box contains the Choose or enter a group for this person box and the Enter a brief introduction to this person (optional) box. A message is displayed in the Enter a brief introduction to this person (optional) box (Figure 3-65).

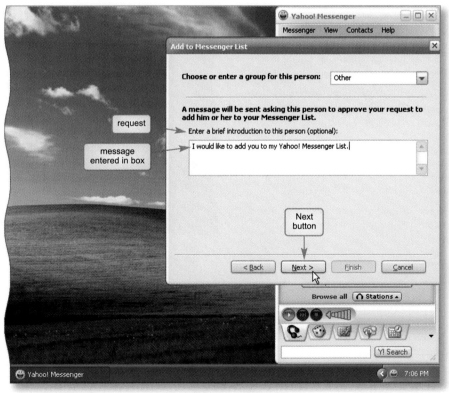

FIGURE 3-65

4

• **Click the Next button.**

The Add to Messenger List dialog box displays a message indicating that ray_enger has been added to your Messenger list and Address Book (Figure 3-66). Instructions to add more contact information in the Address Book or add more people to the Message list are below the message.

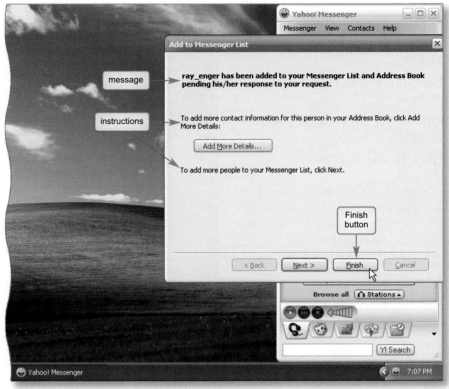

FIGURE 3-66

5

• **Click the Finish button.**

The Add to Messenger List dialog box closes and the new contact (Ray Enger) is added to the Messenger list (Figure 3-67).

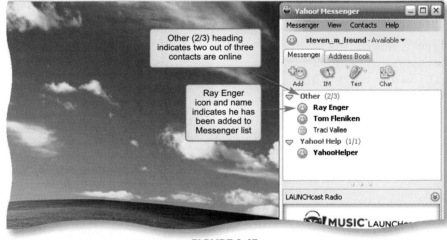

FIGURE 3-67

After adding a contact, you can use Yahoo! Messenger to send an instant message to the new contact (Ray Enger).

Communicating Using Yahoo! Messenger

To use Yahoo! Messenger, the person with whom you want to communicate must be online. The Online list shown in Figure 3-67 indicates Ray Enger is online. The following steps illustrate how to send an instant message to someone you know is online.

To Send an Instant Message

1

• **Double-click the Ray Enger icon (or another contact currently online) in the Messenger list.**

• **Maximize the Ray Enger (ray_enger) - Instant Message window.**

• **Type** Do you still need me to cover your Web Publishing class when you attend your Program Director's dinner? **in the Send text box.**

The Ray Enger (ray_enger) - Instant Message window is displayed and maximized (Figure 3-68). The window contains a toolbar containing seven buttons, conversation area, and Message area. The conversation area contains the To entry and a blank area to view typed messages. The Message area contains a toolbar containing five buttons, a message to Ray Enger, and the Send button.

Ray Enger (ray_enger) - Instant Message window

Ray Enger (ray_enger) - Instant Message

Conversation   Edit   View   Contact   Help

Webcam   Games   Voice   Send File   Photos   Conference   Search — toolbar

To: ray_enger   Send As: steven_m_freund

To entry

conversation area

Message area

toolbar

Send button

IMVironment

Do you still need me to cover your Web Publishing class when you attend your Program Director's dinner?   Send

start   Yahoo! Messenger   Ray Enger (ray_enge...

FIGURE 3-68

2

• **Click the Send button in the Ray Enger (ray_enger) - Instant Message window.**

Yahoo! Messenger removes the message from the Message area, the sender's name and message are displayed in the conversation area, and the status of the receiver (writing a message) is displayed at the bottom of the conversation area (Figure 3-69).

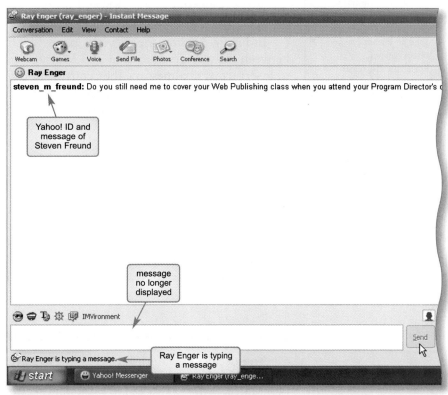

Ray Enger (ray_enger) - Instant Message

Conversation   Edit   View   Contact   Help

Webcam   Games   Voice   Send File   Photos   Conference   Search

Ray Enger

steven_m_freund: Do you still need me to cover your Web Publishing class when you attend your Program Director's d

Yahoo! ID and message of Steven Freund

message no longer displayed

IMVironment   Send

Ray Enger is typing a message.   Ray Enger is typing a message

start   Yahoo! Messenger   Ray Enger (ray_enge...

FIGURE 3-69

3

• **The receiver of the message (Ray Enger) types and then sends a response.**

Yahoo! Messenger displays the receiver's name (Ray Enger) and message in the conversation area and changes the message at the bottom of the Conversation window to indicate the date and time the message was sent (Figure 3-70).

4

• **Click the Close button on the Ray Enger (ray_enger) - Instant Message window to close the window.**

The Ray Enger (ray_enger) - Instant Message window closes.

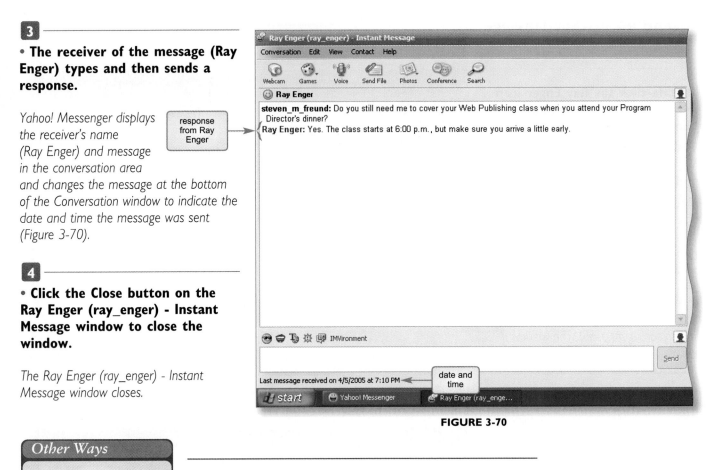

response from Ray Enger

date and time

FIGURE 3-70

You can continue conversing in this manner, reading what the other user has to say and then typing your response.

In Figure 3-68 on the previous page, five buttons are displayed on the toolbar between the conversation area and Message area. The **Emoticons button** allows you to insert icons in a message that convey an emotion or feeling. The **Audibles button** allows you to send a graphic, message, and sound to a contact. Yahoo! updates the audibles throughout the year, corresponding to holidays and special events. For example, Valentine's Day audibles may be available during the month of February. The **Format button** displays a toolbar that allows you to change the style, color, font, and font size of text. The Format button is a **toggle button**, which means the toolbar will alternate between displayed and hidden each time it is clicked. The **Buzz! button** will play a doorbell sound, vibrate the Instant Message window, and display the word "BUZZ!!!" in red text on your contact's computer. The **IMVironment button** allows you to change the theme and style of the conversation area on your computer and your contact's computer. For example, the Fishtank IMVironment displays swimming fish in the background of the conversation area.

The items in the toolbar shown in Figure 3-62 on page FX 171 allow you to add a contact, send an instant message, send a text message, or join a chat room.

Deleting a Contact on the Messenger List

You decide it is no longer necessary to have Traci Vallee on your Messenger list. Removing old contacts from your Messenger list is a good way to keep your list organized, which is important if you have more than a few. The following steps illustrate how to delete the Traci Vallee contact and remove her entry from the Messenger list.

To Delete a Contact on the Messenger List

1

• **Right-click the Traci Vallee contact in the Messenger list and then point to the Delete command on the shortcut menu.**

The Delete command is displayed on the shortcut menu (Figure 3-71).

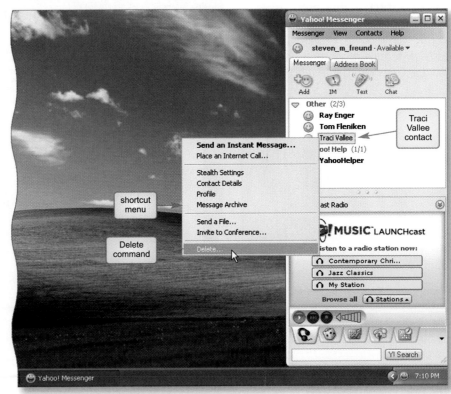

FIGURE 3-71

2

• **Click Delete on the shortcut menu.**

The shortcut menu closes and the Delete Contact dialog box is displayed (Figure 3-72). The dialog box contains a question, contact name, check box, and Yes button.

FIGURE 3-72

3

• **Click the Yes button in the Delete Contact dialog box.**

The Traci Vallee name is removed from the Messenger list and no longer is displayed below the Other heading (Figure 3-73).

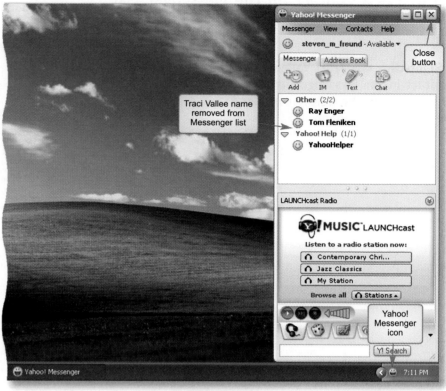

FIGURE 3-73

Other Ways

1. Select contact, on Contacts menu click Delete, click Yes button
2. Select contact, press DELETE

Closing the Yahoo! Messenger Window

When you have finished using Yahoo! Messenger, close the Yahoo! Messenger window. The following steps show how to close the Yahoo! Messenger window.

To Close the Yahoo! Messenger Window

1 Click the Close button in the Yahoo! Messenger window.

2 If the Yahoo! Messenger dialog box is displayed, click the OK button.

The Yahoo! Messenger window closes.

Although the Yahoo! Messenger window closes, the Yahoo! Messenger program continues to run and the Yahoo! Messenger icon is displayed in the notification area on the Windows taskbar to allow you to continue receiving Yahoo! alerts and instant messages.

Signing Out from the Yahoo! Messenger Service and Exiting Yahoo! Messenger

After closing the Yahoo! Messenger window, you may want to quit the Yahoo! Messenger program and then sign out from the Yahoo! Messenger Service. The following steps show how to sign out from the Yahoo! Messenger Service.

To Sign Out from the Yahoo! Messenger Service and Exit Yahoo! Messenger

1 Right-click the Yahoo! Messenger icon in the notification area on the Windows taskbar.

2 Click the Exit command on the shortcut menu.

3 If the Exit Yahoo! Messenger? dialog box is displayed, click the OK button.

You are signed out from the Yahoo! Messenger Service. The Yahoo! Messenger icon in the notification area is removed.

Project Summary

In this project, you learned how to use Mozilla Thunderbird to open, read, print, reply to, delete, compose, format, and send e-mail messages, and to view file attachments. You added and deleted contacts in an Address Book. You also used Mozilla Thunderbird to search for and display newsgroups, read and post newsgroup articles, print newsgroup articles, expand and collapse a thread, and subscribe and unsubscribe to a newsgroup. You started Yahoo! Messenger, signed in to Yahoo! Messenger, added and removed a contact on the Messenger list, and sent an instant message. Finally, you learned how to sign out of Yahoo! Messenger and close the Yahoo! Messenger window.

What You Should Know

Having completed the project, you now should be able to perform the tasks below. The tasks are listed in the same order they were presented in this project. For a list of the buttons, menus, toolbars, and commands introduced in this project, see the Quick Reference Summary at the back of this book and refer to the Page Number column.

1. Start Mozilla Thunderbird (FX 129)
2. Open (Read) an E-Mail Message (FX 132)
3. Print an Opened E-Mail Message (FX 133)
4. Close an E-Mail Message (FX 134)
5. Reply to an E-Mail Message (FX 135)
6. Delete an E-Mail Message (FX 137)
7. View a File Attachment (FX 138)
8. Compose a New E-Mail Message (FX 139)
9. Format an E-Mail Message (FX 141)
10. Send an E-Mail Message (FX 143)
11. Add a Card to the Address Book (FX 144)
12. Compose an E-Mail Message Using the Address Book (FX 147)
13. Delete a Card from the Address Book (FX 151)
14. Close the Address Book (FX 152)
15. Add a News Server (FX 154)
16. Subscribe to a Newsgroup (FX 158)
17. Read a Newsgroup Article (FX 161)
18. Expand a Thread (FX 162)
19. Collapse a Thread (FX 163)
20. Print a Newsgroup Article (FX 163)
21. Display the Articles on the netscape.test Newsgroup (FX 164)
22. Post a Newsgroup Article (FX 165)
23. Display the Articles in a Newsgroup (FX 167)
24. Unsubscribe from a Newsgroup (FX 168)
25. Quit Thunderbird (FX 169)
26. Start Yahoo! Messenger and Sign In (FX 170)
27. Add a Contact to the Contact List (FX 172)
28. Send an Instant Message (FX 175)
29. Delete a Contact on the Contact List (FX 177)
30. Close the Yahoo! Messenger Window (FX 178)
31. Sign Out from the Yahoo! Messenger Service and Exit Yahoo! Messenger (FX 179)

Learn It Online

Instructions: To complete the Learn It Online exercises, start your browser, click the Address box, enter scsite.com/firefox/learn, and then click the Go button. When the Firefox Learn It Online page is displayed, follow the instructions in the exercises below. Each exercise has instructions for printing your results, either for your own records or for submission to your instructor.

1 Project Reinforcement TF, MC, and SA

Below Firefox Project 3, click the Project Reinforcement link. Print the quiz by clicking Print on the File menu for each page. Answer each question.

2 Flash Cards

Below Firefox Project 3, click the Flash Cards link and read the instructions. Type 20 (or a number specified by your instructor) in the Number of Playing Cards text box, type your name in the Enter your name text box, and then click the Flip Card button. When the flash card is displayed, read the question and then click the ANSWER box arrow to select an answer. Flip through Flash Cards. If your score is 15 (75%) correct or greater, click Print on the File menu to print your results. If your score is less than 15 (75%) correct, then redo this exercise by clicking the Replay button.

3 Practice Test

Below Firefox Project 3, click the Practice Test link. Answer each question, enter your first and last name at the bottom of the page, and then click the Grade Test button. When the graded practice test is displayed on your screen, click Print on the File menu to print a hard copy. Continue to take practice tests until you score 80% or better.

4 Who Wants To Be a Computer Genius?

Below Firefox Project 3, click the Computer Genius link. Read the instructions, enter your first and last name at the bottom of the page, and then click the PLAY button. When your score is displayed, click the PRINT RESULTS link to print a hard copy.

5 Wheel of Terms

Below Firefox Project 3, click the Wheel of Terms link. Read the instructions, and then enter your first and last name and your school name. Click the PLAY button. When your score is displayed, right-click the scores and then click Print on the shortcut menu to print a hard copy.

6 Crossword Puzzle Challenge

Below Firefox Project 3, click the Crossword Puzzle Challenge link. Read the instructions, and then enter your first and last name. Click the SUBMIT button. Work the crossword puzzle. When you are finished, click the Submit button. When the crossword puzzle is displayed, click the Print Puzzle button to print a hard copy.

7 Tips and Tricks

Below Firefox Project 3, click the Tips and Tricks link. Click a topic that pertains to Project 3. Right-click the information and then click Print on the shortcut menu. Construct a brief example of what the information relates to in Thunderbird to confirm you understand how to use the tip or trick.

8 Newsgroups

Below Firefox Project 3, click the Newsgroups link. Click a topic that pertains to Project 3. Print three comments.

9 Expanding Your Horizons

Below Firefox Project 3, click the Expanding Your Horizons link. Click a topic that pertains to Project 3. Print the information. Construct a brief example of what the information relates to in Thunderbird to confirm you understand the contents of the article.

10 Search Sleuth

Below Firefox Project 3, click the Search Sleuth link. To search for a term that pertains to this project, select a term below the Project 3 title and then use the Google search engine at google.com (or any major search engine) to display and print two Web pages that present information on the term.

11 Firefox How-To Article

Below Firefox Project 3, click the Firefox How-To Articles link. When your browser displays the Firefox How-To Articles Web page, scroll down and click one of the links that covers one or more of the objectives listed at the beginning of the project on page FX 128. Print the first page of the How-To article before stepping through it.

12 Getting More from the Web

Below Firefox Project 3, click the Getting More from the Web link. When your browser displays the Getting More from the Web with Firefox Web page, click one of the Top Stories or Featured Contents links. Print the first page.

In the Lab

1 Sending E-Mail Messages

Problem: You are enrolled in two courses at the local college. You want to send the same e-mail to the instructor of each course stating what you like best about his or her class. You decide to use Thunderbird and the carbon copy feature to send the e-mails.

Instructions: Use Firefox, Thunderbird, and a computer to perform the following tasks.

1. If necessary, connect to the Internet and then start Firefox.
2. Search for the home page for your school. Figure 3-74 shows the home page for Valencia Community College located in Orlando, Florida.

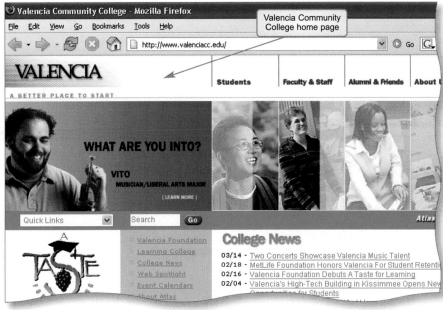

FIGURE 3-74

3. Find and write down the e-mail address of your instructor.
4. Find and write down the e-mail address of an instructor from your school that teaches another course that you are enrolled in.
5. If necessary, start Thunderbird. If the Enter your password dialog box is displayed, enter your e-mail account password and then click the OK Button.
6. Click the Write button on the Mail toolbar to open the Compose: (no subject) window.
7. Using the e-mail address of the instructor you obtained in Step 4, compose a mail message to this instructor stating what you like best about his or her class.
8. Using the e-mail address of your instructor obtained in Step 3, send a carbon copy of the message to your instructor.
9. Print a copy of the e-mail message, write your name on the printout, and then hand it in to the instructor.
10. Close all open windows.

2 Adding Cards to the Address Book

Problem: You want to use the Address Book to keep track of the names, e-mail addresses, home addresses, and home telephone numbers of your favorite school friends. You use Thunderbird's Address Book to create a card for each of your friends.

Instructions: Use Thunderbird and a computer to perform the following tasks.

Part 1: *Display the Address Book*

1. If necessary, connect to the Internet and then start Thunderbird.
2. Click the Address Book button on the Mail toolbar to open the Address Book window. If necessary, maximize the window (Figure 3-75).

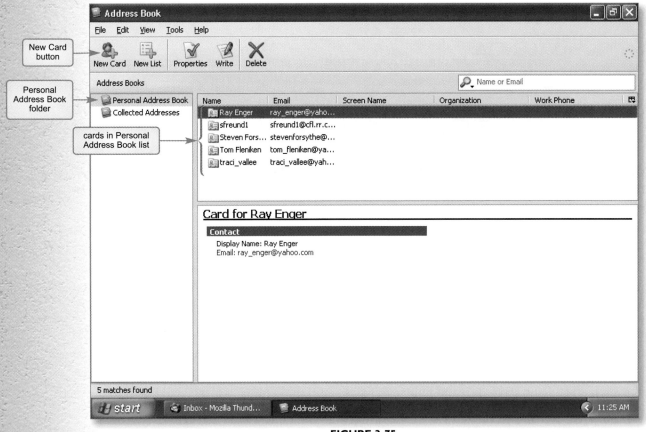

FIGURE 3-75

Part 2: *Add New Cards to the Address Book*

1. Use the New Card button on the Address Book toolbar to add the contacts listed in Table 3-8 to the Address Book.

Table 3-8 Contact List for Address Book

NAME	E-MAIL ADDRESS	ADDRESS	HOME PHONE
Barbara Clark	bclark@isp.com	8451 Colony Dr., Brea, CA 92821	(714) 555-7384
Javier Cortez	jcortez@isp.com	3581 Clayton Rd., Placentia, CA 92871	(714) 555-2982
Allen Goldberg	agoldberg@isp.com	5689 State St., Fullerton, CA 92834	(714) 555-3938
Frank Springer	fspringer@isp.com	7812 Bennington Dr., Atwood, CA 92811	(714) 555-9832
Carol Thomas	cthomas@isp.com	257 W. Wilson St., Yorba Linda, CA 92885	(714) 555-0393
Julie Price	jprice@isp.com	648 Flower Rd., Brea, CA 92821	(714) 555-3730

2. Print a Card for each contact by selecting a contact name, clicking the Print Card command on the File menu, and then clicking the OK button in the Print dialog box. Write your name on each printout.

Part 3: *Delete the Cards*

1. Delete each card by selecting the contact name and then clicking the Delete button on the toolbar.
2. Close all open windows.

3 Reading Newsgroup Articles

Problem: You want to display the list of all newsgroups on the default news server, search for a newsgroup of interest to you, select a thread that contains at least three replies, and then print each article in the thread.

Instructions: Use Thunderbird and a computer to perform the following tasks.

1. If necessary, connect to the Internet and then start Thunderbird.
2. Right-click the news.mozilla.org news server name in the Folders pane, and then click Subscribe on the shortcut menu (Figure 3-76). If necessary, expand the netscape entries in the newsgroup list by clicking the plus sign to the left of the netscape entry.

FIGURE 3-76

(continued)

Reading Newsgroup Articles *(continued)*

3. Search for or scroll to find a newsgroup of interest to you, click the newsgroup, and then click the Subscribe button. Click the OK button to close the dialog box.
4. Find a thread that contains the original article and at least three replies.
5. Read and then print each article in the thread. Write your name on each printout and then hand them in to your instructor.
6. Close all open windows.

4 Posting Newsgroup Articles

Problem: You want to display the list of all newsgroups on the netscape.public.mozilla.browser news server, search for and display a newsgroup of interest to you, use the Write button to compose and send a message to the newsgroup, find your message in the message pane, and then print the message.

Instructions: Use Thunderbird and a computer to perform the following tasks.

1. If necessary, connect to the Internet and then start Thunderbird.
2. Right-click the news.mozilla.org news server name in the Folders pane, and then click Subscribe on the short-cut menu. If necessary, expand the netscape entries in the newsgroup list by clicking the plus sign to the left of the netscape entry.
3. Search for or scroll to find a newsgroup of interest to you, click the newsgroup, and then click the Subscribe button.
4. Click the OK button in the Subscribe dialog box.
5. Locate and click the newsgroup name in the Folders pane. If the Download Headers dialog box displays, click the Download button.
6. Click the Write button to display the Compose: (no subject) window (Figure 3-77).

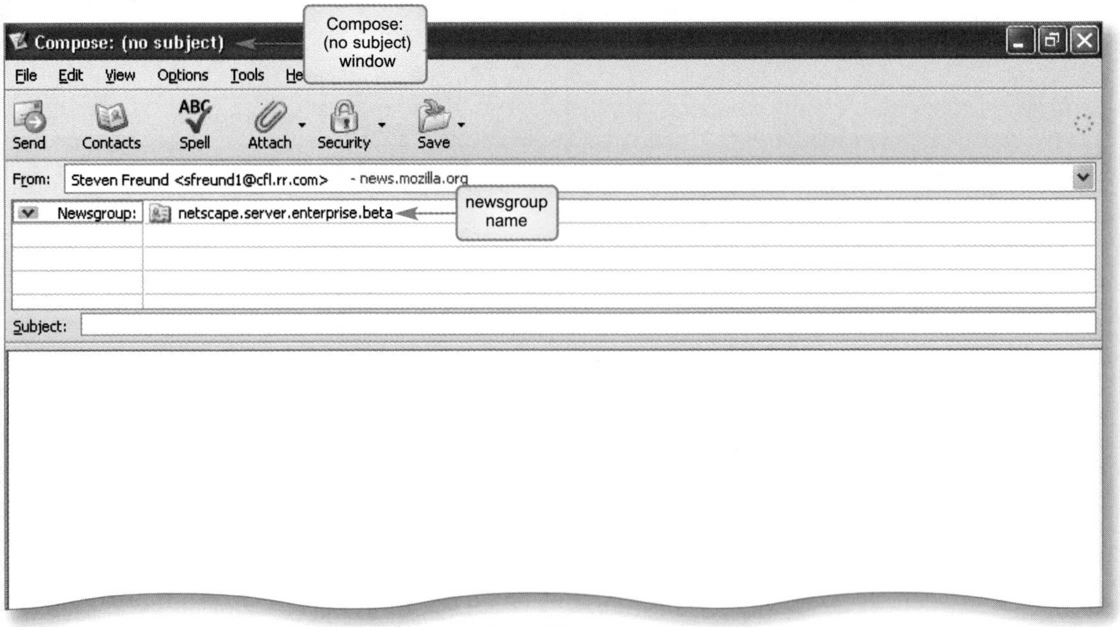

FIGURE 3-77

7. Compose and then send a message to the newsgroup.
8. Find your message in the Message list. Print the message, write your name on the printout, and then hand it in to your instructor.
9. Close all open windows.

5 Finding E-Mail Addresses

Problem: You want to use the White Pages Web site (http://www.whitepages.com) to search for and print information about yourself, a friend, and a famous person whom you admire.

Instructions: Use Firefox and a computer to perform the following tasks.

1. If necessary, connect to the Internet and then start Firefox.
2. Click the Location bar in the Mozilla Firefox window, type `www.whitepages.com` as the entry, and then click the Go button. The White Pages Phone Directory with Free People Search Web page is displayed (Figure 3-78).

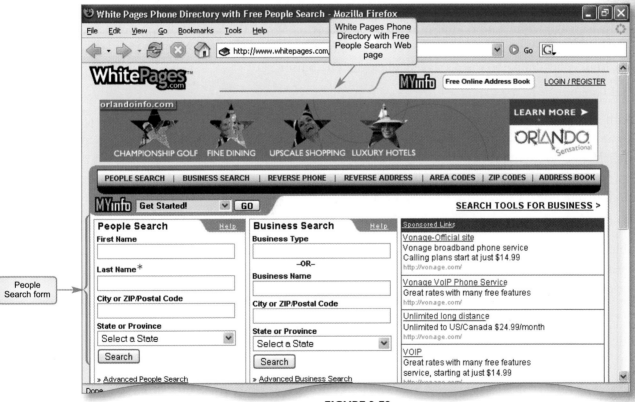

FIGURE 3-78

3. Use the People Search form on the White Pages Phone Directory with Free People Search Web page to search for your name. Print the resulting page and then write your name on the printout.
4. Use the People Search form to search for one of your friends. Print the resulting page and then write your name on the printout.

(continued)

Finding E-Mail Addresses *(continued)*

5. Use the People Search form to search for someone famous or someone whom you admire. Print the resulting page and then write your name on the printout.
6. Hand in all printouts to your instructor.
7. Close all open windows.

6 Using Yahoo! Messenger

Problem: You want to add a new person to your Yahoo! Messenger contacts. After adding the contact, you want to send instant messages to each other, and then save and print the entire conversation.

Instructions: Use Yahoo! Messenger and a computer to perform the following tasks.

Part 1: *Start Yahoo! Messenger and Sign In*

1. If necessary, connect to the Internet.
2. Click the Start menu on the Windows taskbar, point to All Programs on the Start menu, and then click the Yahoo! Messenger command on the All Programs submenu. When the Sign In dialog box is displayed, enter your Yahoo! ID and password and then click the Sign In button to sign into Yahoo! Messenger. If the Yahoo Mail Alert dialog box is displayed, click the OK button.

Part 2: *Add a Contact to the Contact List*

1. Click the Add button on the toolbar in the Yahoo! Messenger window.
2. Type the Yahoo! ID or Yahoo! e-mail address of a friend in the Yahoo! ID or Email Address text box, and then click the Next button.
3. When the message indicating your contact has been added to your Messenger List is displayed, click the Finish button.

Part 3: *Send an Instant Message*

1. Double-click the icon of the contact you added in the Messenger list.
2. Type each message below in the Message area, click the Send button, wait for the response, and then write the response in the space provided. A sample conversation is shown in Figure 3-79.

sample conversation →

FIGURE 3-79

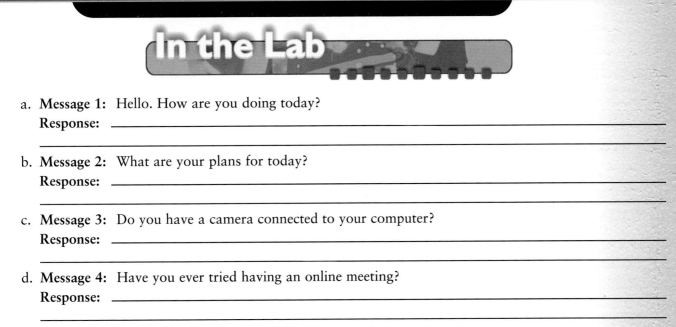

In the Lab

a. **Message 1:** Hello. How are you doing today?

Response: _____

_____

b. **Message 2:** What are your plans for today?

Response: _____

_____

c. **Message 3:** Do you have a camera connected to your computer?

Response: _____

_____

d. **Message 4:** Have you ever tried having an online meeting?

Response: _____

_____

3. Continue conversing in this manner until you want to end the conversation.

Part 4: *Save and Print the Conversation*

1. Click File on the menu bar in the Instant Message window and then click Save As on the File menu.
2. In the Save Conversation History As dialog box, type My Conversation in the File name text box.
3. Click the Save in box arrow and then click Desktop in the Save in list.
4. Click the Save button in the Save Conversation History As dialog box to save the file on your desktop.
5. Move the Conversation window and/or Yahoo! Messenger window to make the My Conversation icon visible on the desktop.
6. Double-click the My Conversation icon on the desktop to open the file in Notepad.
7. Click Conversation on the menu bar and then click Print on the Conversation menu, and then click the Print button in the Print dialog box. Write your name on the printout.
8. Click the Close button in the My Conversation - Notepad window.
9. Right-click the My Conversation icon on the desktop, click Delete on the shortcut menu, and then click Yes in the Confirm File Delete dialog box.
10. Click the Close button in the Instant Message window.

Part 5: *Delete a Contact on the Contact List*

1. In the Yahoo! Messenger window, right-click the contact you want to delete.
2. Click Delete on the shortcut menu.
3. Click the Yes button in the Delete Contact dialog box.

Part 6: *Close the Yahoo! Messenger Window and Sign Out from the Yahoo! Messenger Service*

1. Click the Close button in the Yahoo! Messenger window. If the Yahoo! Messenger dialog box is displayed, click the OK button.
2. Right-click the Yahoo! Messenger icon in the notification area on the Windows taskbar.
3. Click Exit on the shortcut menu.
4. If necessary, click the OK button in the Exit Yahoo! Messenger? dialog box.
5. Hand in all printouts to your instructor.

In the Lab

7 Using Yahoo! Messenger to Have an Online Meeting

Problem: You want to use Yahoo! Messenger to have an online meeting with a friend. After having the conversation, you want to print a copy of the conversation.

Instructions: Use Yahoo! Messenger and a computer to perform the following tasks.

Part 1: Start Yahoo! Messenger and Sign In

1. If necessary, connect to the Internet.
2. Click the Start menu on the Windows taskbar, point to All Programs on the Start menu, and then click the Yahoo! Messenger command on the All Programs submenu. When the Sign In dialog box is displayed, enter your Yahoo! ID and password and then click the Sign In button to sign into Yahoo! Messenger. If the Yahoo Mail Alert dialog box is displayed, click the OK button.

Part 2: Start an Online Meeting

1. Double-click the icon of a contact in the Messenger List.
2. Type the following messages in the Message area, click the Send button, wait for the response, and then write the response in the space provided (Figure 3-80).

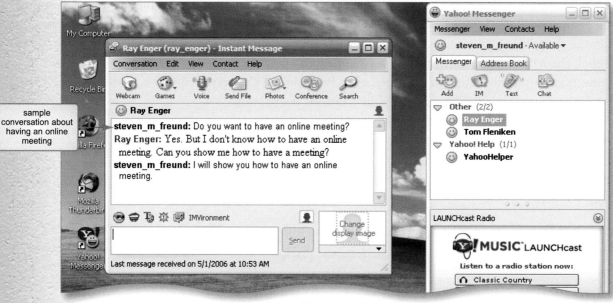

FIGURE 3-80

a. **Message 1:** Do you want to have an online meeting?

   Response: _____

   _____

b. **Message 2:** I will show you how to have an online meeting.

   Response: _____

   _____

In the Lab

Part 3: *Printing a Copy of the Desktop*

1. Press the PRINT SCREEN key on the keyboard to place an image of the desktop on the Clipboard. The Clipboard is a temporary Windows storage area.
2. Click the Start button on the Windows taskbar, point to All Programs on the Start menu, point to Accessories on the All Programs submenu, and then click Paint on the Accessories submenu to start the Paint program.
3. Click Edit on the menu bar and then click Paste to copy the image of the desktop from the Clipboard to the Paint window.
4. Click File on the menu bar, click Print on the File menu, and then click the Print button in the Print dialog box to print the image of the desktop.
5. Write your name on the printout.
6. Click the Close button in the Paint window and then click the No button in the Paint dialog box to close the Paint window.

Part 4: *Close All Open Windows, Sign Out from the Yahoo! Messenger Service, and exit Yahoo! Messenger*

1. Click the Close button in the Yahoo! Messenger window. If the Yahoo! Messenger dialog box is displayed, click the OK button.
2. Right-click the Yahoo! Messenger icon in the notification area on the Windows taskbar.
3. Click Exit on the shortcut menu.
4. If necessary, click the OK button in the Exit Yahoo! Messenger? dialog box.
5. Hand in all printouts to your instructor.

Cases and Places

The difficulty of these case studies varies:
■ are the least difficult and ■■ are more difficult. The last exercise is a group exercise.

1 ■ Several Web sites are available that allow you to enter a person's name and search for information about the individual. Using a search engine, locate three of these sites. Use your name, a friend's name, and a relative's name to search for information using all three sites you find. Print the information you find, write your name on the printouts, and then hand them in to your instructor.

2 ■ Many software products such as Microsoft Word contain a library of images, graphics, pictures, and other clip art. Libraries of clip art also are available for you to download on the Web. Using the Web search engine of your choice, search for five sites that offer clip art for use on Web pages. Print a few of the images from each site.

3 ■■ Using computer magazines, advertising brochures, the Internet, or other resources, compile information about the latest version of Mozilla Thunderbird and Microsoft Outlook. In a brief report, compare the two programs. Include the differences and similarities, how to obtain the software, the function and features of each program, and so forth. If possible, test Microsoft Outlook and add your personal comments.

4 ■■ Using Address Book, add new cards for your family, friends, and colleagues. Include their names, addresses, telephone numbers, and e-mail addresses, if any. Enter the name of the organization each one works for, if appropriate. For family members, list their birthdays and wedding anniversaries using the Other tab. Submit a printout of each card to your instructor.

5 ■■ Mozilla owns and operates the news.mozilla.org news server. Conservative users have expressed concerns that some users try to disguise their identities by displaying false information when signing up for a Yahoo! account. In a brief report, summarize the reasons for correctly identifying yourself on the Internet, problems that result when users disguise their identities, who you think is responsible, and how to prevent this problem.

Cases and Places

6 ■■ Using computer magazines, advertising brochures, the Internet, or other resources, compile information about two e-mail programs other than Mozilla Thunderbird. In a brief report, compare the two programs and the Mozilla Thunderbird e-mail program. Include the differences and similarities, how to obtain the software, the functions and features of each program, and so forth. Submit the report to your instructor.

7 ■■ **Working Together** Many colleges and universities maintain their own news servers containing school-related newsgroups. Have each member of your group locate a school that has a news server. Each member should explore the news server, determine how many newsgroups are on the server, locate at least two newsgroups of interest, determine the number of articles in each newsgroup, and then read several articles in each newsgroup. Write a brief report summarizing your findings and then present the findings to your class.

MOZILLA
Firefox

Open Source Concepts and Firefox Customization

CASE PERSPECTIVE

In Projects 1, 2, and 3 you learned how to navigate and search the World Wide Web using Mozilla Firefox, and you learned how to communicate with others on the Internet with Mozilla Thunderbird and Yahoo! Messenger. You decide it is time to learn more about open source, a concept you were introduced to in Project 1. In addition, you now know that because Mozilla Firefox is open source software, various developers can create extensions and themes, which are used to customize the Firefox browser.

Upon navigating the Web, you also learn that the basic Firefox installation does not display the content on some Web pages. You e-mail the instructor who taught your Introduction to the Internet class, and she informs you that some Web pages require special software to display the contents. You begin to research how to obtain and install this software, called **plugins**, which allow more Web content to be displayed.

After researching how extensions, themes, and plugins can enhance your Web browsing experience, you decide to take this opportunity to locate an extension that will display the current weather conditions from within the Mozilla Firefox window, install a theme to enhance the Firefox interface, and install the Macromedia Flash plugin to display Flash content, a very common technology in various Web sites.

As you read through this special feature, you will learn about open source software, the Open Source Definition, and how to customize Mozilla Firefox by installing extensions, themes, and plugins. If you are stepping through this special feature on a computer, you must have sufficient access privileges to install and modify software.

Objectives

You will have mastered the material in this special feature when you can:

- Describe open source and source code
- List the advantages of open source software
- Explain the Open Source Definition
- Install and uninstall an extension
- Install and uninstall a theme
- Install a plugin

Introduction

Mozilla Firefox and Mozilla Thunderbird are examples of open source software. **Open source** is a philosophy for software licensing and distribution designed to encourage the use and improvement of the software by allowing anyone to use and modify the source code. With conventional software, such as Microsoft Windows or Adobe Photoshop, individuals are allowed to use the software, but cannot view the source code or make modifications. **Source code** is code written in a particular programming language such as Java. When source code is translated into machine language, the computer becomes capable of understanding the source code and running the program. The **Open Source Initiative OSI - Welcome Web page** shown in Figure 1 (on the next page) contains guidelines for developing open source software, sample license agreements for open source software, current Open Source Initiative news, and trademarks and graphics related to the Open Source Initiative. You can visit the Open Source Initiative OSI - Welcome Web page at www.opensource.org.

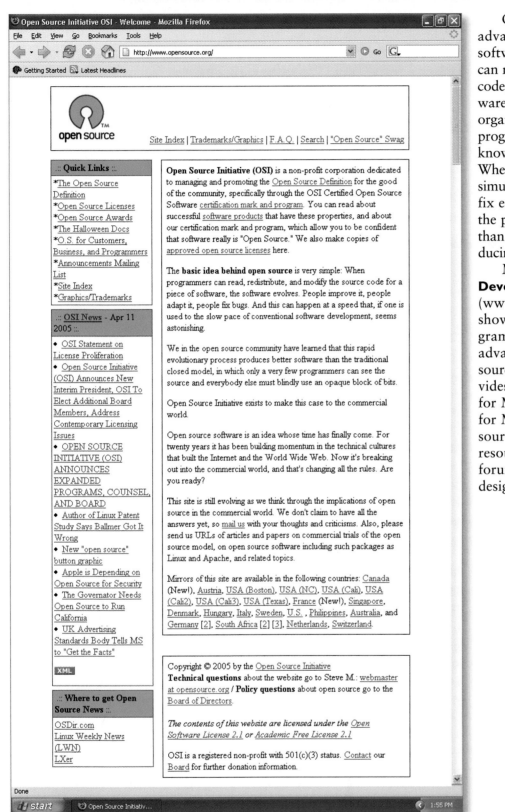

FIGURE 1

Open source software has many advantages over conventional software. Because programmers can read and modify the source code, they can customize the software to meet their personal or organization needs. In addition, programmers are able to fix errors, known as **bugs**, in the programs. When multiple programmers work simultaneously to enhance and/or fix errors in a software program, the program evolves more rapidly than conventional software, producing better software.

Mozilla hosts the **Mozilla - Developer Central Web page** (www.mozilla. org/developer), shown in Figure 2, to assist programmers who want to take advantage of Mozilla's open source nature. The Web page provides information on writing code for Mozilla, contact information for Mozilla developers, links to source code, and tools and resources such as developer forums and Bugzilla (a system designed to track software bugs).

In addition to Mozilla Firefox and Thunderbird, you can find open source operating systems, Internet software, and programming tools. **Open source operating systems** include Linux (www.linux.org), FreeBSD (www. freebsd.org), Open BSD (www. openbsd.org), and NetBSD (www.netbsd.org). Apple Computer, Inc. started the Darwin project, which relies on the expertise and experience of the open source software development community to improve the core operating system of Mac OS X.

Open source Internet software includes the Apache Web server (www.apache. org), OpenSSL (www.openssl.org), and BIND (www.isc.org/bind. html). **Open source programming tools** include Perl (www.perl.org), PHP (www.php.net), and Python (www.python.org). Companies such as IBM (www.ibm.com), Sun (www.sun.com), and Novell (www.novell.com) also have realized the benefits available from participating in the open source community by providing open source solutions for their customers.

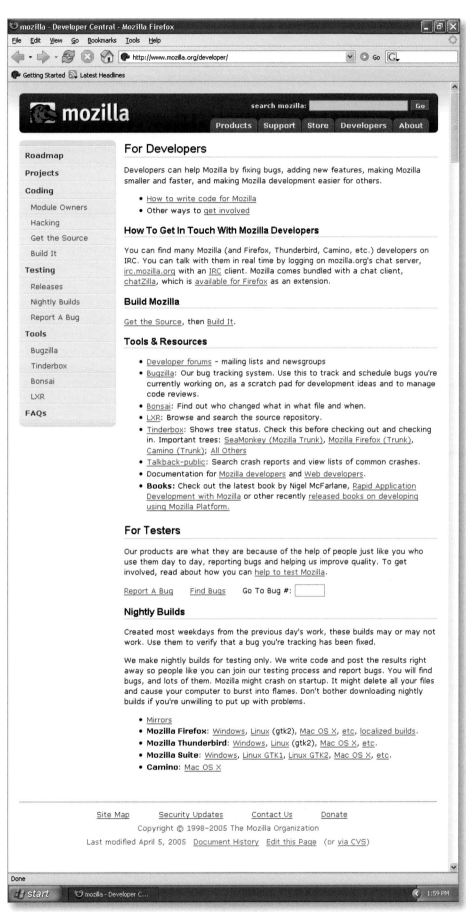

FIGURE 2

The Open Source Definition

The **Open Source Definition (OSD)** was developed to identify the criteria for distributing a program designated as open source. Table 1 contains information regarding the guidelines for distribution of open source software. The Open Source Definition is periodically updated to clarify the guidelines for identifying software as open source. Table 1 contains the most current version of the Open Source Definition (version 1.9) at the time of this writing. The most current version of the Open Source Definition is available at http://www.opensource.org.

Table 1 The Open Source Definition version 1.9	
CRITERIA	**EXPLANATION**
Free Redistribution	The license shall not restrict any party from selling or giving away the software as a component of an aggregate software distribution containing programs from several different sources. The license shall not require a royalty or other fee for such sale.
Source Code	The program must include source code and must allow distribution in source code as well as compiled form. Where some form of a product is not distributed with source code, there must be a well-publicized means of obtaining the source code for no more than a reasonable reproduction cost preferably, downloading via the Internet without charge. The source code must be the preferred form in which a programmer would modify the program. Deliberately confusing source code is not allowed. Intermediate forms such as the output of a preprocessor or translator are not allowed.
Derived Works	The license must allow modifications and derived works, and must allow them to be distributed under the same terms as the license of the original software.
Integrity of The Author's Source Code	The license may restrict source code from being distributed in modified form only if the license allows the distribution of "patch files" with the source code for the purpose of modifying the program at build time. The license must explicitly permit distribution of software built from modified source code. The license may require derived works to carry a different name or version number from the original software.
No Discrimination Against Persons or Groups	The license must not discriminate against any person or group of persons.
No Discrimination Against Fields of Endeavor	The license must not restrict anyone from making use of the program in a specific field of endeavor. For example, it may not restrict the program from being used in a business or from being used for genetic research.
Distribution of License	The rights attached to the program must apply to all to whom the program is redistributed without the need for execution of an additional license by those parties.
License Must Not Be Specific to a Product	The rights attached to the program must not depend on the program's being part of a particular software distribution. If the program is extracted from that distribution and used or distributed within the terms of the program's license, all parties to whom the program is redistributed should have the same rights as those that are granted in conjunction with the original software distribution.
License Must Not Restrict Other Software	The license must not place restrictions on other software that is distributed along with the licensed software. For example, the license must not require that all other programs distributed on the same medium must be open-source software.
License Must Be Technology-Neutral	No provision of the license may be predicated on any individual technology or style of interface.

The Open Source Definition enables developers to create modifications to the Firefox browser in an effort to enhance the browsing experience. These special features allow you to customize Firefox by installing an extension, theme, and plugin.

Installing an Extension

Hundreds of **extensions**, software that adds one or more features, are available to customize the Mozilla Firefox browser. You can download them free of charge from the Mozilla Web site. Extensions are available to test the speed of your Internet connection, increase customization of Firefox's tabbed browsing feature, enhance the Download Manager, and much more. The following steps illustrate how to install the **Forecastfox extension** that is designed to display current and future weather conditions in the Firefox window.

> **More About**
>
> ## Extensions
>
> Extensions are frequently updated to fix bugs and enhance performance. To check whether an update exists for any extension you have installed, open the Extensions dialog box, select the extension you wish to update, and then click the Update button.

To Install an Extension

1

• **Click the Start button on the Windows taskbar, point to All Programs on the Start menu, point to Mozilla Firefox on the All Programs submenu, and then click Mozilla Firefox on the Mozilla Firefox submenu. If necessary, maximize the Mozilla Firefox Start Page - Mozilla Firefox window.**

Mozilla Firefox starts and the Mozilla Firefox Start page is displayed in the maximized Mozilla Firefox window (Figure 3).

FIGURE 3

2

• **Click the Firefox Help & Add-ons link on the Mozilla Firefox Start Page.**

The Firefox Central page is displayed in the Mozilla Firefox window (Figure 4).

FIGURE 4

3

• **Click the extensions link in the Enhancing Firefox list on the Firefox Central Web page. If the Security Warning dialog box is displayed, click the OK button to close the dialog box.**

The Mozilla Update :: Extensions - Add Features to Mozilla Software Web page is displayed (Figure 5). The Most Popular Firefox Extensions list contains the FlashGot extension.

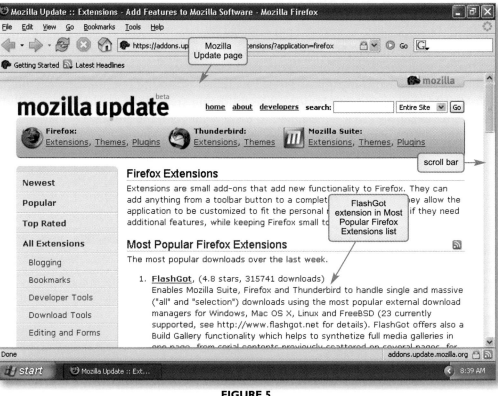

FIGURE 5

4

• **Scroll to view the Forecastfox link. If the Forecastfox link is not available, select another extension.**

The Web page scrolls and the Forecastfox extension is displayed on the Web page (Figure 6).

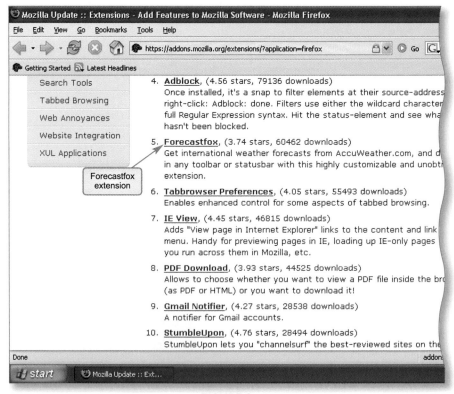

FIGURE 6

5

• **Click the Forecastfox link.**

• **If necessary, scroll to view the Install Now link.**

The Forecastfox - Firefox Extension page is displayed, containing a quick description, an image of the Forecastfox extension, and the Install Now link (Figure 7).

FIGURE 7

6

• **Click the Install Now link.**

The Software Installation dialog box is displayed with the Install Now and Cancel buttons (Figure 8).

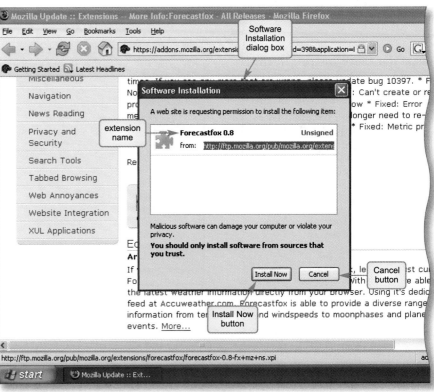

FIGURE 8

7

• **Click the Install Now button.**

The Software Installation dialog box closes and in a moment, the Extensions dialog box is displayed (Figure 9). A message in the dialog box indicates that the Forecastfox extension will be installed after restarting Firefox.

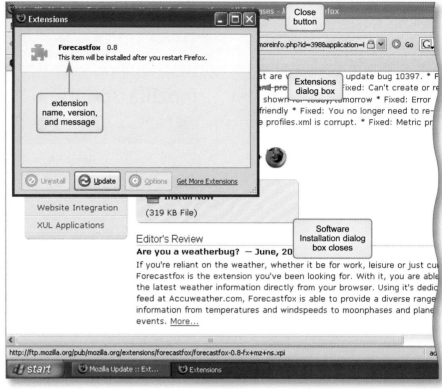

FIGURE 9

8

• **Click the Close button in the Extensions dialog box.**

• **Click the Close button in the Mozilla Update :: Extensions -- More Info:Forecastfox - All Releases - Mozilla Firefox window.**

• **Start Mozilla Firefox.**

The Extensions dialog box closes, the Mozilla Update :: Extensions -- More Info:Forecastfox - All Releases - Mozilla Firefox window closes, and Firefox starts. The Forecastfox Options dialog box is displayed and contains the Forecast Location area, Unit of Measure area, Display Placement area, and the OK, Cancel, and dimmed Apply buttons (Figure 10).

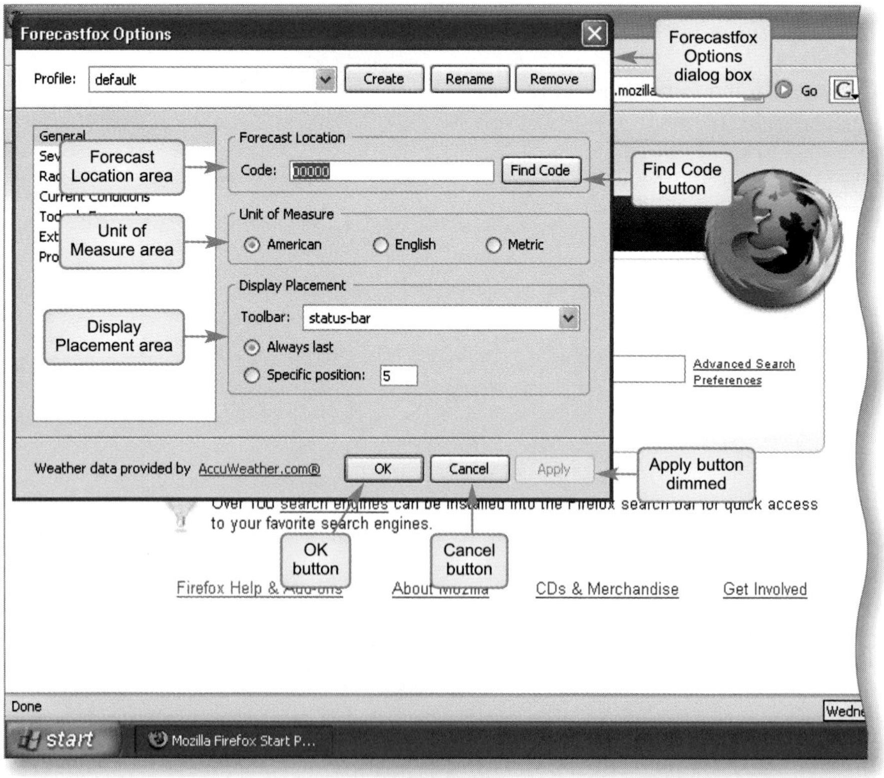

FIGURE 10

9

• **Click the Find Code button in the Forecast Location area in the Forecastfox Options dialog box.**

The Forecastfox Location Search dialog box is displayed and contains the Search text box, Location list, and Search, OK, and Cancel buttons (Figure 11).

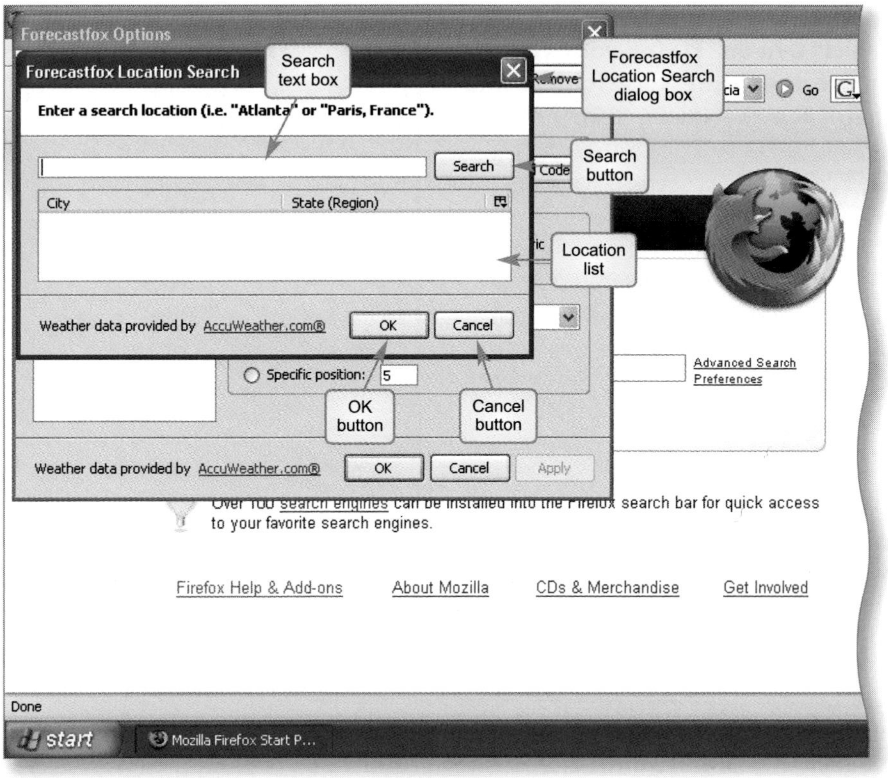

FIGURE 11

10

• **Type** Oviedo, FL **(or your city and state) in the Search text box and then click the Search button.**

Forecastfox searches for the location entered in the Search text box and displays matching items in the Location list (Figure 12).

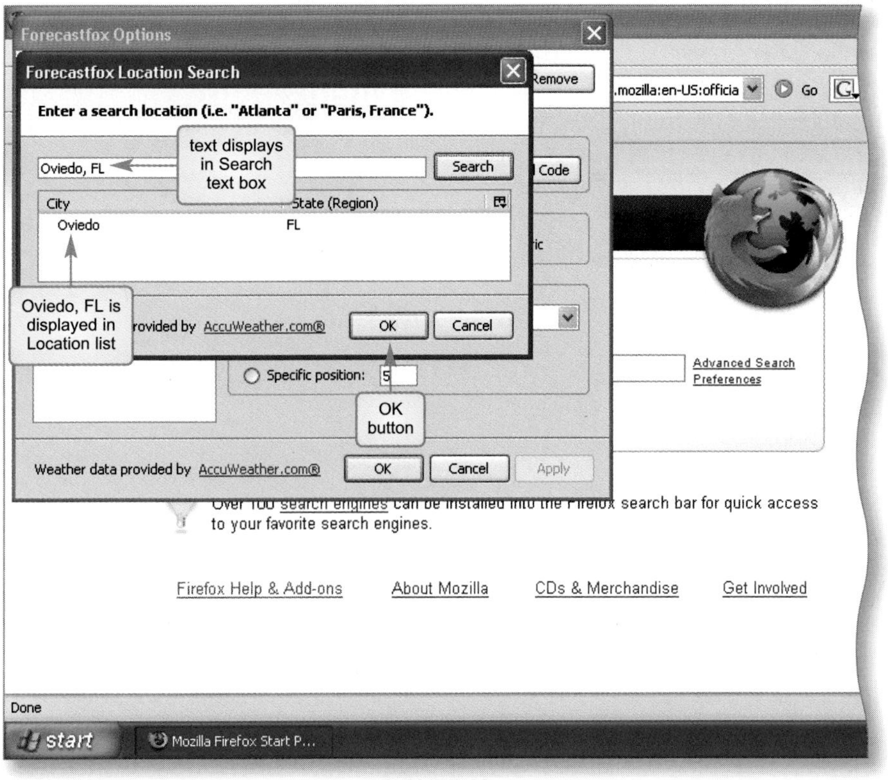

FIGURE 12

11

• **Click Oviedo, FL (or your city and state) in the Location list and then click the OK button.**

The Forecastfox Location Search dialog box closes and the 32762 code is displayed in the Code text box in the Forecast Location area in the Forecastfox Options dialog box (Figure 13). The code in the Code text box may be different on your computer if you chose a different city and state earlier.

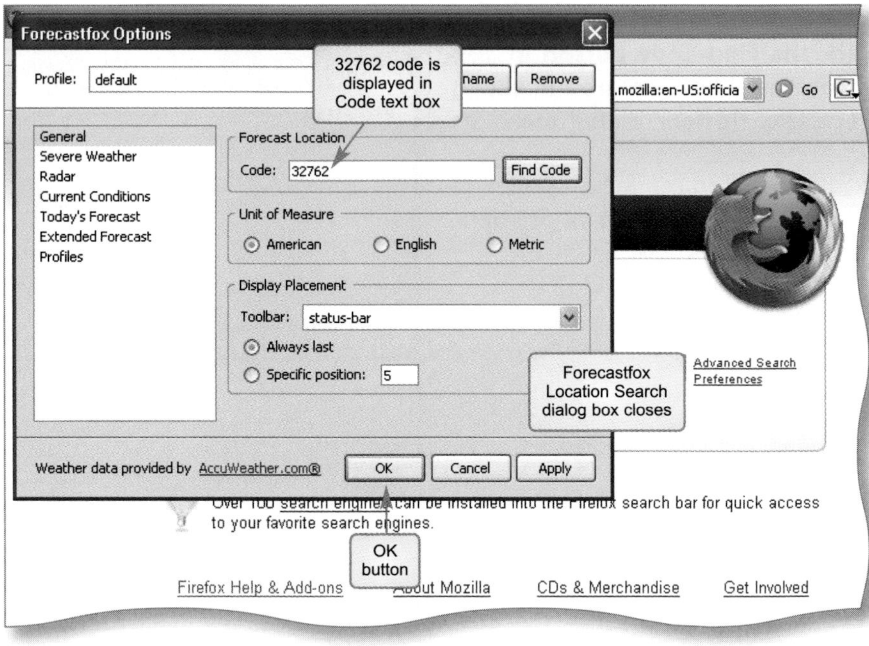

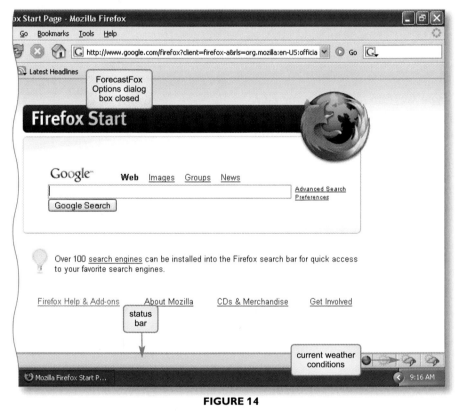

FIGURE 13

12

• **Click the OK button in the Forecastfox Options dialog box.**

The Forecastfox Options dialog box closes and the icons representing the current weather conditions are displayed on the right side of the status bar (Figure 14). Holding your mouse over one of the weather icons on the status bar will display additional weather information for the selected location. The weather conditions may be different on your computer (Figure 14).

FIGURE 14

Other Ways

1. Select Extensions on Tools menu, click Get More Extensions, choose extension to install

Uninstalling an Extension

If you no longer want to use an extension in Firefox, you should uninstall the extension. The following steps show how to uninstall the Forecastfox extension.

To Uninstall an Extension

1 Click Tools on the menu bar and then click Extensions.

2 If the Forecastfox extension is not selected, click the Forecastfox extension to select it.

3 Click the Uninstall button in the Extensions dialog box.

4 Click the OK button in the Uninstall Forecastfox dialog box.

5 Click the Close button in the Extensions dialog box.

6 Click the Close button in the Mozilla Firefox window.

7 Start Mozilla Firefox.

The Forecastfox extension is uninstalled and is no longer displayed on the status bar (Figure 15).

FIGURE 15

Installing a Theme

The Mozilla Update Web page contains links to many themes. A **theme** changes the appearance of the Mozilla Firefox Web browser. The following steps illustrate how to download and install the Qute theme from the Mozilla Update Web page. The steps on the following pages illustrate how to Install the Qute theme.

More About

Themes

Themes are sometimes updated to change the look and feel of the Firefox browser, as well as correct any bugs within an existing theme you have installed. To check whether an update exists for any theme you currently have installed, display the Themes dialog box, select the theme you wish to update, and click the Update button.

To Install a Theme

1

• **Click the Firefox Help & Add-ons link on the Mozilla Firefox Start Page window.**

The Firefox Central page is displayed in the Mozilla Firefox window (Figure 16).

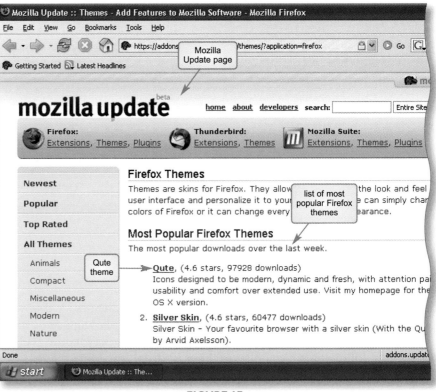

FIGURE 16

2

• **Click the themes link in the Enhancing Firefox area of the Firefox Central Web page. If the Security Warning dialog box is displayed, click the OK button to close the dialog box.**

The Mozilla Update Web page is displayed, containing a list of the most popular Firefox themes (Figure 17).

FIGURE 17

3

• **If necessary, scroll to display the Qute theme. If the Qute theme is not listed, select another theme.**

• **Click the Qute link.**

The Qute - Firefox Theme page is displayed, containing a quick description, a preview of the Qute theme, and the Install Now link (Figure 18).

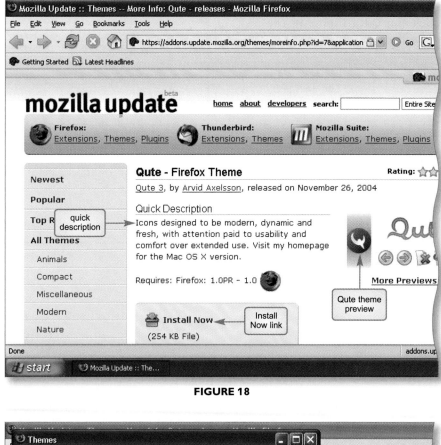

FIGURE 18

4

• **Click the Install Now link.**

• **When the Confirm dialog box is displayed, click the OK button.**

The Qute theme is downloaded and the Themes dialog box is displayed, containing the Theme list, a Preview pane, and the dimmed Uninstall, Update, and dimmed Use Theme buttons (Figure 19). The theme name (Qute) and author's name (Arvid Axelsson) are shown in the Theme list.

FIGURE 19

5

• **Click the Qute theme in the Theme list.**

The Qute theme is selected in the Theme list, the Uninstall and Use Theme buttons become active, and a preview of the Qute theme is displayed in the preview pane (Figure 20).

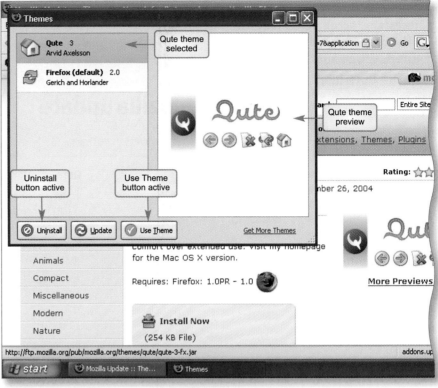

FIGURE 20

6

• **Click the Use Theme button in the Themes dialog box.**

The Use Theme button is dimmed and a message is displayed under the Qute name in the Theme list, indicating you must restart Firefox to use the theme (Figure 21).

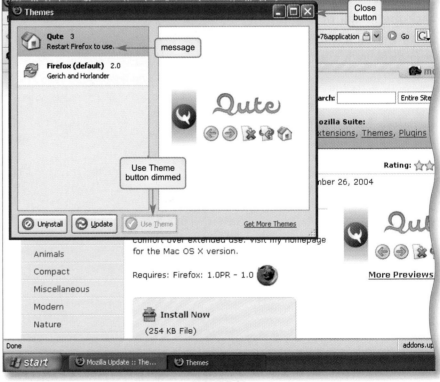

FIGURE 21

7

• Click the Close button in the Themes dialog box.

• Click the Close button in the Mozilla Update :: Themes -- More Info:Qute - releases - Mozilla Firefox window.

• Start Mozilla Firefox.

The Themes dialog box closes, the Mozilla Update :: Themes -- More Info:Qute - releases - Mozilla Firefox window closes, and Firefox starts. The Qute theme is now applied to the Mozilla Firefox window (Figure 22).

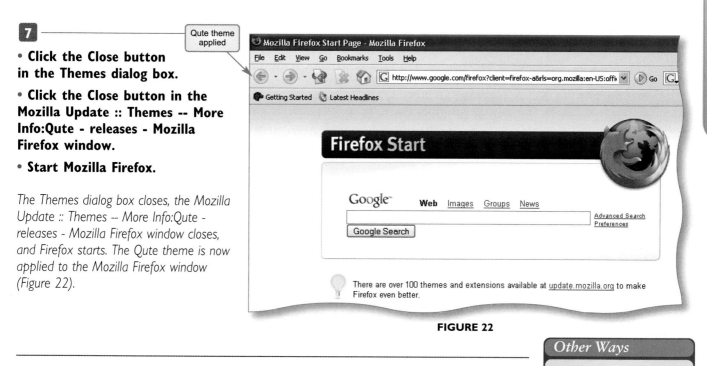
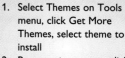

Qute theme applied

FIGURE 22

Uninstalling a Theme

If you no longer want to use a theme in Firefox, you should uninstall the theme. The following steps show how to uninstall the Qute theme.

To Uninstall a Theme

1 Click Tools on the menu bar and then click Themes.

2 With the Qute theme highlighted, click the Uninstall button in the Themes dialog box.

3 Click the OK button in the Uninstall Qute dialog box.

4 Click the Close button in the Themes dialog box.

5 Click the Close button in the Mozilla Firefox window.

6 Start Mozilla Firefox.

The Qute theme is uninstalled and the default Firefox theme is displayed (Figure 23).

default Firefox theme

FIGURE 23

Other Ways

1. Select Themes on Tools menu, click Get More Themes, select theme to install
2. Press ALT+T, press T, click Get More Themes, select theme

Q&A

Q: Do I need to update my plugins?

A: It is a good idea to check for updates periodically on the Web pages of companies that develop plugins you have installed. If a newer version of a plugin exists, it is usually a good idea to download the plugin. The Mozilla Update page contains links to the most up-to-date plugins.

Installing a Plugin

While extensions and themes are not required to display Web pages, sometimes you need a plugin to view certain Web pages. A **plugin** is a software program that extends the capabilities of a browser and is often used to enhance multimedia. Examples of plugins include the Macromedia Flash Player, Apple QuickTime, Real Networks RealPlayer, Adobe Acrobat Reader, and Sun Microsystems Java. The following steps show how to install the Macromedia Flash Player plugin and display the Biography.com Web site.

To Install a Plugin

1

• **Type** www.biography.com **on the Location bar and then click the Go button.**

The Biography.com Web page is displayed in the display area (Figure 24). A message below the Bookmarks toolbar indicates that additional plugins are required to display all media on this Web page. The Install Missing Plugins button is displayed to the right of the message.

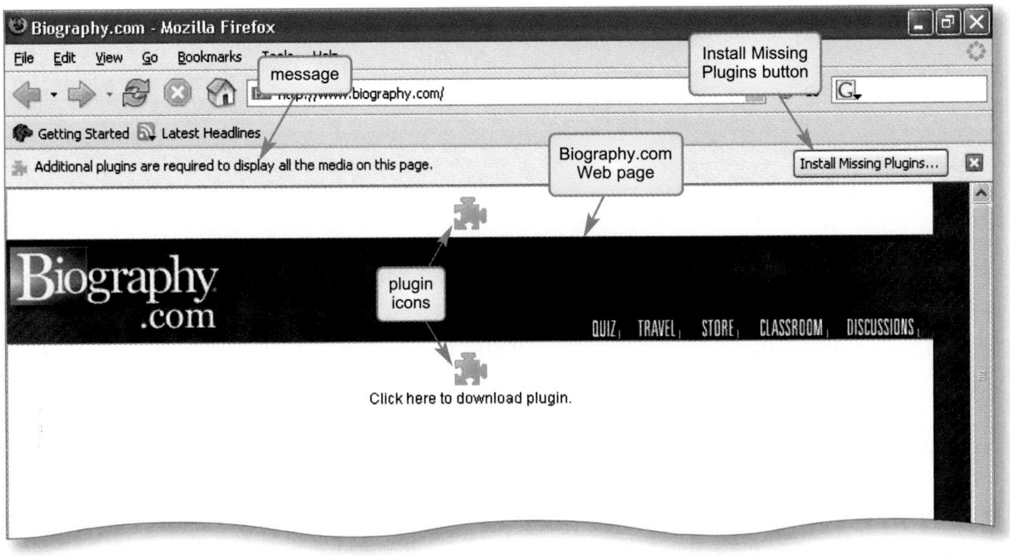

FIGURE 24

2

• **Click the Install Missing Plugins button.**

The Plugin Finder Service dialog box is displayed, containing the plugin list and three buttons (Figure 25). The Macromedia Flash Player 7.0 check box in the Plugin list contains a checkmark.

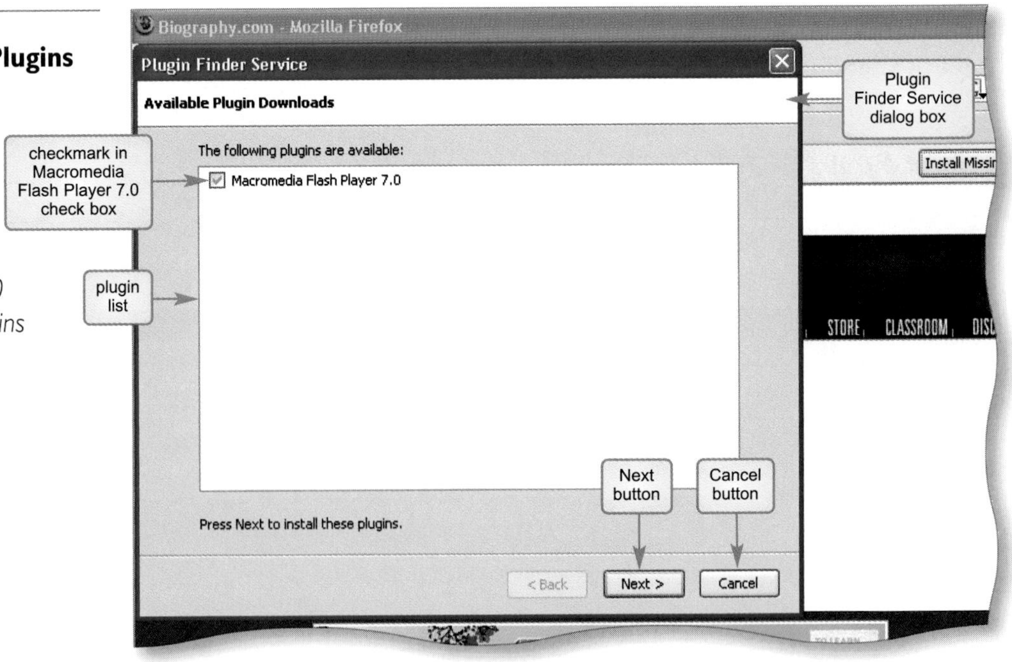

FIGURE 25

3

• **Click the Next button.**

The Plugin Finder Service dialog box contains the Plugin Licenses page, the license agreement, and two option buttons (Figure 26). The I do not agree (plugin will not be installed) option button is selected.

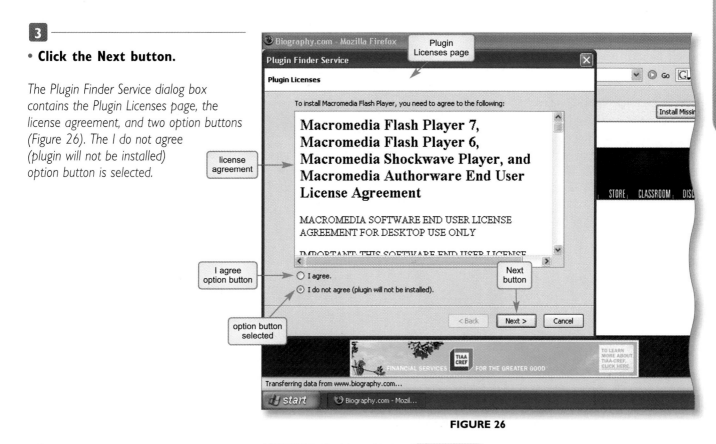

FIGURE 26

4

• **Click the I agree option button.**
• **Click the Next button.**

The Macromedia Flash Player plugin is downloaded and installed, and the Completing the Plugin Finder Service page is displayed in the Plugin Finder Service dialog box (Figure 27).

FIGURE 27

5

• **Click the Finish button.**

The Plugin Finder Service dialog box closes and the Biography.com Web page (using the Macromedia Flash Player plugin) displays the content that the browser was previously unable to display (Figure 28).

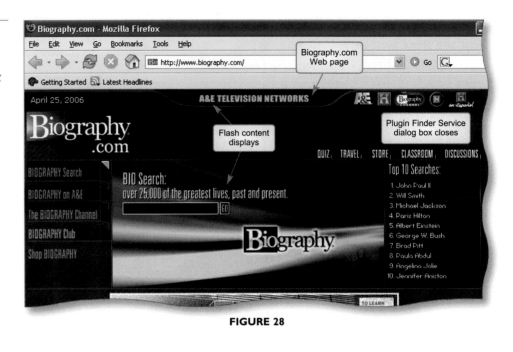

FIGURE 28

Quitting Firefox

After you have downloaded and installed your theme, extension, and plugin, close the Mozilla Firefox window by performing the following step.

To Close Firefox

1 **Click the Close button in the upper-right corner of the Mozilla Firefox title bar.**

The Mozilla Firefox window closes

Special Feature Summary

The Special Feature introduced the concept of open source software and the Open Source Definition. The special feature showed you how to install and uninstall the Forecastfox extension and install and uninstall the Qute theme. Finally, the special feature showed how to install the Macromedia Flash Player plugin to display the Biography.com Web page.

What You Should Know

Having completed this feature, you now should be able to perform the tasks below. The tasks are listed in the same order they were presented in the project.

1. Install an Extension (FX 201)
2. Uninstall an Extension (FX 207)
3. Install a Theme (FX 208)
4. Uninstall a Theme (FX 211)
5. Install a Plugin (FX 212)
6. Close Firefox (FX 214)

In the Lab

1 Installing the Bandwidth Tester Extension

Problem: Your Internet connection is running more slowly than normal, so you decide to test the bandwidth of the Internet connection using the Bandwidth Tester Extension in Mozilla Firefox.

Instructions: Perform the following tasks:

1. Start Mozilla Firefox.
2. Click the Firefox Help & Add-ons link to display the Mozilla page.
3. Locate and install the Bandwidth Tester extension. Restart Firefox after the installation is complete.
4. Select the Bandwidth Tester command on the Tools menu. Select your connection speed and then click the Run Test button.
5. When the test is complete, write down your results and submit them to your instructor.
6. Close the Bandwidth Tester dialog box.
7. Close Mozilla Firefox.

2 Installing the Silver Skin Theme

Problem: Your boss asks you to apply a new look and feel to his Mozilla Firefox browser. You need to go to the Mozilla Update Web site to download and install the Silver Skin theme on his computer.

Instructions: Perform the following tasks:

1. If necessary, start Mozilla Firefox.
2. Click the Firefox Help & Add-ons link to display the Mozilla page.
3. Locate and install the Silver Skin theme. Once the theme is downloaded, use the theme.
4. Close the Themes dialog box and then restart Firefox.
5. Press ALT+PRNT SCRN to save the image on the screen to the Clipboard.
6. Start WordPad.
7. Select Paste from the Edit menu.
8. Print the WordPad document, write your name on the printout, and submit it to your instructor. Close WordPad without saving any changes.

3 Installing the RealPlayer Plugin

Problem: Many Web sites use the RealPlayer plugin to display media. You decide to install the RealPlayer plugin to make such media viewable in the Mozilla Firefox browser.

Instructions: Perform the following tasks:

1. If necessary, start Mozilla Firefox.
2. Click the Firefox Help & Add-ons link to display the Mozilla page and then click the plugins link in the Enhancing Firefox area.
3. Click the RealPlayer link in the Get Common Plugins area.

(continued)

Installing the **RealPlayer Plugin** *(continued)*

4. Click the Download link to the right of the operating system in use on your computer.
5. Save the downloaded file and then open the file when the download is complete. Follow the on-screen instructions to install and configure the software.
6. Once the installation is complete and RealPlayer starts, print the current Web page by clicking the File menu, pointing to Print, and then clicking Print Current Web Page on the Print submenu. Write your name on the printout and submit the printout to your instructor.

Appendix A

Installing Mozilla Firefox

Installing Firefox

This appendix explains how to install the Mozilla Firefox Web browser from the CD-ROM that accompanies this textbook. Mozilla Firefox is also available for free from Mozilla's Web site (http://www.mozilla.org). To install this software on your computer system, you must be logged in to an account or computer system that gives you the authority to add new programs. The following steps show how to install Mozilla Firefox from the CD-ROM to the C:\Program Files\Mozilla Firefox folder on your hard drive (C:).

To Install Mozilla Firefox

1

• **Insert the CD-ROM into your CD-ROM drive. If the CT Resources Licensing Agreement dialog box displays, click the Yes button. When the Course Technology dialog box is displayed, click Software. When the Software files are displayed, click Mozilla Firefox 1.0.6.**

The Course Technology dialog box is displayed with Software and Mozilla Firefox 1.0.6 selected (Figure A-1).

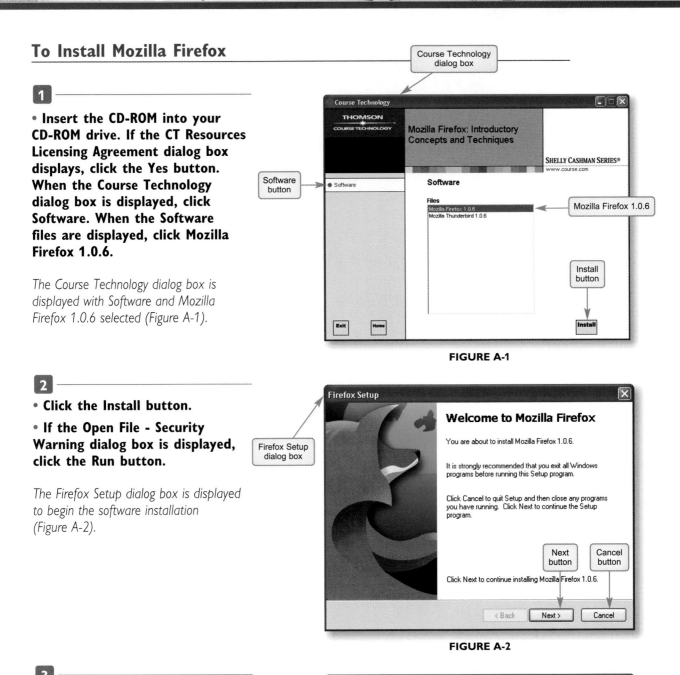

FIGURE A-1

2

• **Click the Install button.**

• **If the Open File - Security Warning dialog box is displayed, click the Run button.**

The Firefox Setup dialog box is displayed to begin the software installation (Figure A-2).

FIGURE A-2

3

• **Click the Next button.**

The Software License Agreement dialog box is displayed, containing the Software License agreement, two option buttons, and the Back button, dimmed Next button, and Cancel button (Figure A-3). The I do NOT Accept the terms of the License Agreement option button is selected.

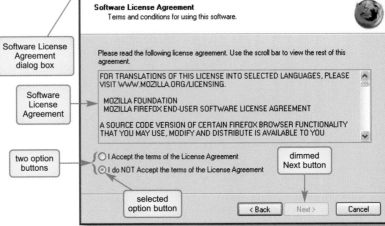

FIGURE A-3

4

• **Click the I Accept the terms of the License Agreement option button.**

The Next button is no longer dimmed, indicating you can proceed with the setup (Figure A-4).

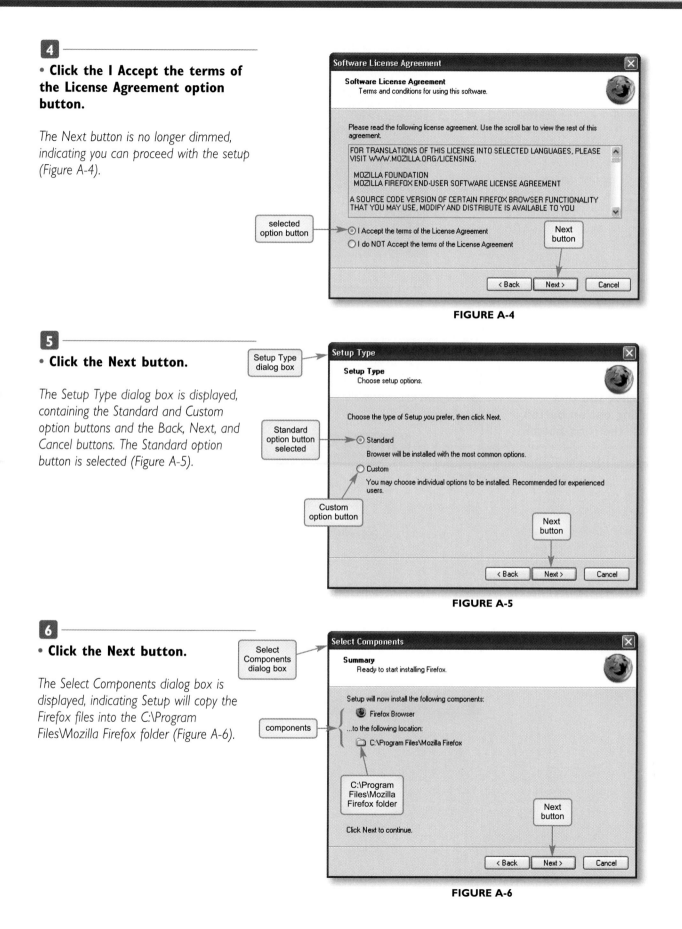

FIGURE A-4

5

• **Click the Next button.**

The Setup Type dialog box is displayed, containing the Standard and Custom option buttons and the Back, Next, and Cancel buttons. The Standard option button is selected (Figure A-5).

FIGURE A-5

6

• **Click the Next button.**

The Select Components dialog box is displayed, indicating Setup will copy the Firefox files into the C:\Program Files\Mozilla Firefox folder (Figure A-6).

FIGURE A-6

7

• **Click the Next button.**

The Installing dialog box is displayed while Setup performs the Mozilla Firefox installation and then the Install Complete dialog box is displayed when the installation is complete (Figure A-7). The Install Complete dialog box contains the Use Firefox Start as my Home Page check box and the Launch Mozilla Firefox 1.0.6 now check box. The Launch Mozilla Firefox 1.0.6 now check box contains a checkmark. The Finish button replaces the Next button at the bottom of the dialog box.

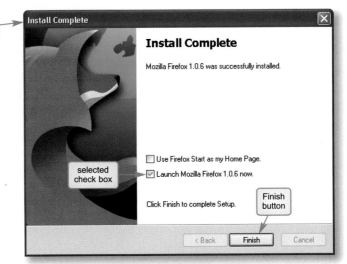

Install Complete dialog box

selected check box

Finish button

FIGURE A-7

8

• **Click the Finish button.**

• **If the Import Wizard dialog box is displayed, click the Don't import anything option button and then click the Next button.**

The Install Complete dialog box closes and the Mozilla Firefox Start Page - Mozilla Firefox window is displayed (Figure A-8). The Mozilla Firefox and Mozilla Firefox (Safe Mode) commands are copied to the Mozilla Firefox menu, and the Mozilla Firefox menu is added to the Start menu's All Programs submenu.

Mozilla Firefox Start Page - Mozilla Firefox window

FIGURE A-8

Appendix B

Installing Mozilla Thunderbird

Installing Thunderbird

This appendix illustrates how to install the Mozilla Thunderbird e-mail client from the CD-ROM that accompanies this textbook. Mozilla Thunderbird is also available for free from Mozilla's Web site (http://www.mozilla.org). To install this software on your computer system, you must be logged in to an account or computer system that gives you the authority to add new programs. The following steps show how to install Mozilla Thunderbird from the CD-ROM to the C:\Program Files\Mozilla Thunderbird folder on your hard drive (C:) and how to configure Thunderbird to access your e-mail account. To complete the installation, you need to know your e-mail address, the addresses of your incoming and outgoing mail servers, and whether your incoming server is a POP or IMAP server. Contact your instructor or Internet Service Provider to obtain this information if you do not have it.

To Install and Configure Mozilla Thunderbird

1

• **Insert the CD-ROM into your CD-ROM drive. If the CT Resources Licensing Agreement dialog box displays, click the Yes button. When the Course Technology dialog box is displayed, click Software. When the Software files are displayed, click Mozilla Thunderbird 1.0.6.**

The Course Technology dialog box is displayed with Software and Mozilla Thunderbird 1.0.6 selected (Figure B-1).

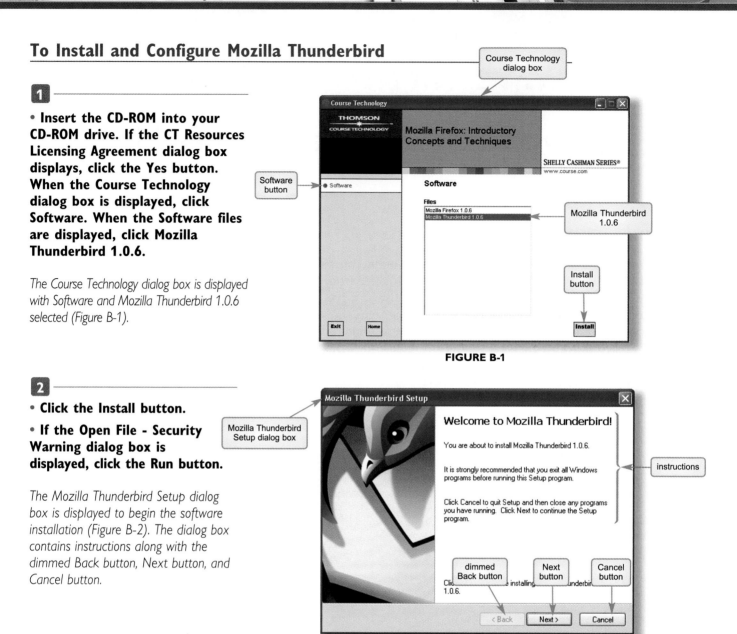

FIGURE B-1

2

• **Click the Install button.**

• **If the Open File - Security Warning dialog box is displayed, click the Run button.**

The Mozilla Thunderbird Setup dialog box is displayed to begin the software installation (Figure B-2). The dialog box contains instructions along with the dimmed Back button, Next button, and Cancel button.

FIGURE B-2

3

• **Click the Next button.**

The Software License Agreement dialog box is displayed, containing the Software License agreement, two option buttons, and the Back button, dimmed Next button, and Cancel button (Figure B-3). The I do NOT Accept the terms of the License Agreement option button is selected.

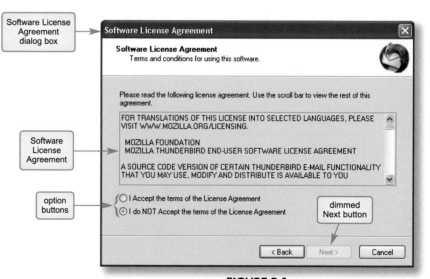

FIGURE B-3

4

• Click the I Accept the terms of the License Agreement option button.

The Next button is no longer dimmed, indicating you can proceed with the setup (Figure B-4).

selected option button

Next button

FIGURE B-4

5

• Click the Next button.

The Setup Type dialog box is displayed, containing the Standard and Custom option buttons and the Back, Next, and Cancel buttons. The Standard option button is selected (Figure B-5).

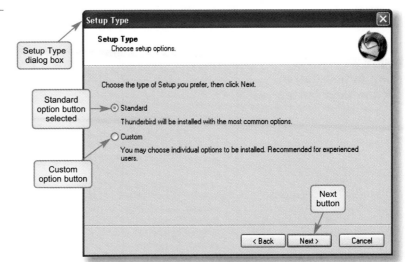

Setup Type dialog box

Standard option button selected

Custom option button

Next button

FIGURE B-5

6

• Click the Next button.

The Select Components dialog box is displayed, indicating Setup will copy the Thunderbird files into the C:\Program Files\Mozilla Thunderbird folder (Figure B-6).

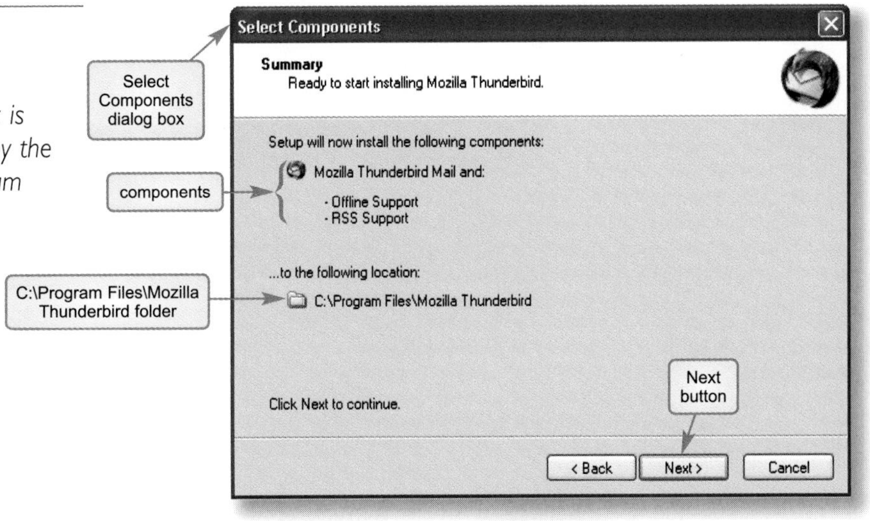

Select Components dialog box

components

C:\Program Files\Mozilla Thunderbird folder

Next button

FIGURE B-6

7

• **Click the Next button.**

The Installing dialog box is displayed while Setup performs the Mozilla Thunderbird installation and then the Install Complete dialog box is displayed when the installation is complete (Figure B-7). The Install Complete dialog box contains the Launch Mozilla Thunderbird 1.0.6 now check box, which is selected by default. The Finish button is selected at the bottom of the dialog box.

FIGURE B-7

8

• **Click the Finish button.**

• **If the Import Wizard dialog box is displayed, click the Don't import anything option button and then click the Next button.**

The Install Complete dialog box closes, and the Mail & Newsgroups window and Account Wizard dialog box are displayed, containing three option buttons and three buttons (Figure B-8). The License, Mozilla Thunderbird, Mozilla Thunderbird (Safe Mode), Profile Manager, and Readme commands are copied to the Mozilla Thunderbird menu, and the Mozilla Thunderbird menu is added to the Start menu's All Programs submenu.

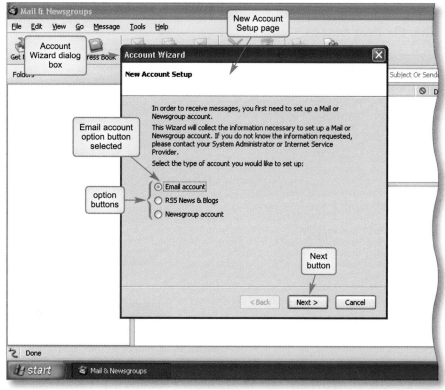

FIGURE B-8

9

• **Click the Next button.**

The Identity page is displayed in the Account Wizard dialog box and the Your Name and Email Address text boxes are displayed on the Identity page (Figure B-9). The Back, Next, and Cancel buttons are displayed at the bottom of the dialog box.

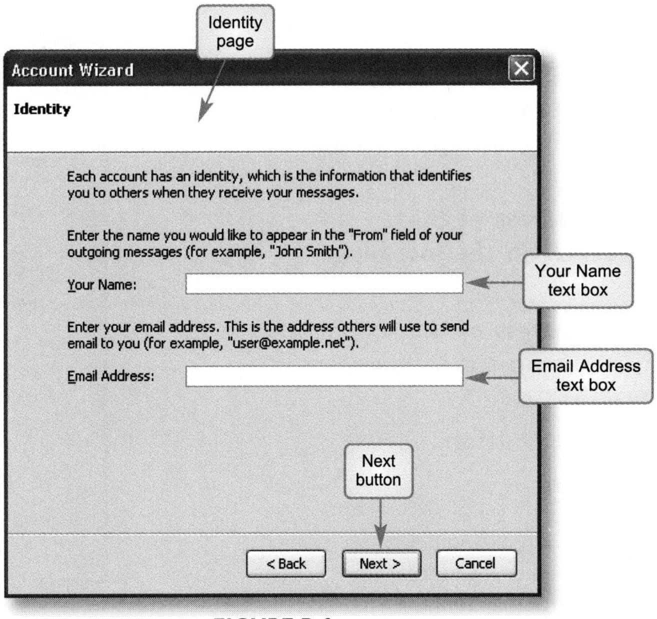

Identity
page

Account Wizard

Identity

Each account has an identity, which is the information that identifies you to others when they receive your messages.

Enter the name you would like to appear in the "From" field of your outgoing messages (for example, "John Smith").

Your Name:

Your Name
text box

Enter your email address. This is the address others will use to send email to you (for example, "user@example.net").

Email Address:

Email Address
text box

Next
button

< Back   Next >   Cancel

FIGURE B-9

10

• **Enter your name in the Your Name text box.**

• **Enter your e-mail address in the Email Address text box.**

• **Click the Next button.**

The Server Information page is displayed in the Account Wizard dialog box, and two option buttons, a check box, the Incoming Server text box, and the Outgoing Server text box are displayed on the Server Information page (Figure B-10).

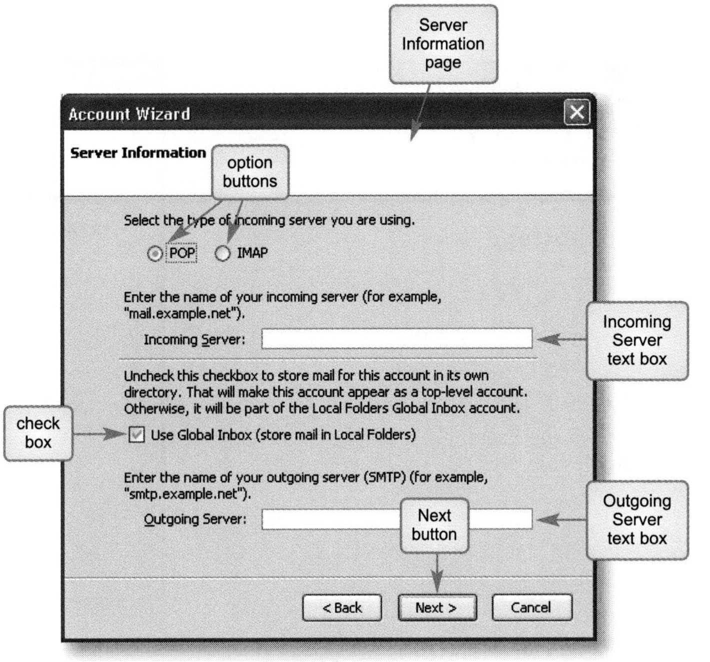

Server
Information
page

Account Wizard

Server Information

option
buttons

Select the type of incoming server you are using.

◉ POP   ○ IMAP

Enter the name of your incoming server (for example, "mail.example.net").

Incoming Server:

Incoming
Server
text box

Uncheck this checkbox to store mail for this account in its own directory. That will make this account appear as a top-level account. Otherwise, it will be part of the Local Folders Global Inbox account.

check
box

☑ Use Global Inbox (store mail in Local Folders)

Enter the name of your outgoing server (SMTP) (for example, "smtp.example.net").

Outgoing Server:

Next
button

Outgoing
Server
text box

< Back   Next >   Cancel

FIGURE B-10

11

• **Select the type of incoming server you are using (POP or IMAP) by clicking the appropriate option button.**

• **Enter the address of the incoming server in the Incoming Server text box.**

• **Enter the address of the outgoing server in the Outgoing Server text box.**

• **Click the Next button.**

The User Names page is displayed in the Account Wizard dialog box, and the Incoming User Name and Outgoing User Name text boxes contain the user name for your e-mail account (Figure B-11).

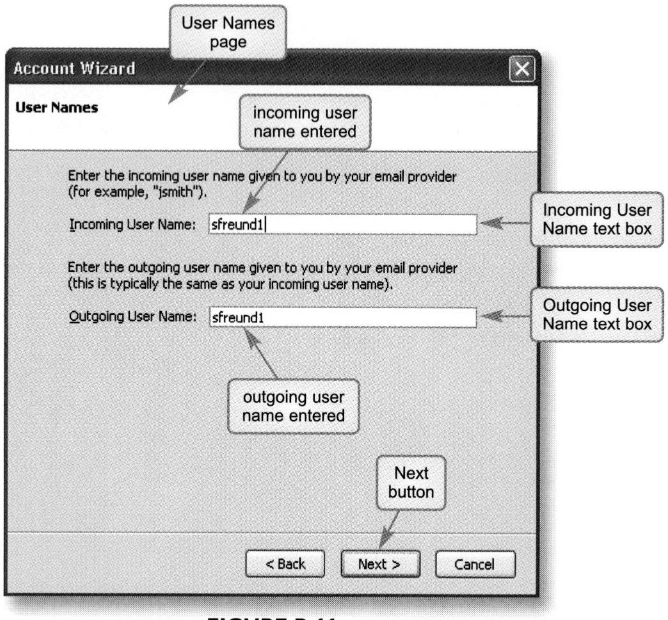

FIGURE B-11

12

• **If required by your Internet Service Provider, change your incoming user name and/or outgoing user name.**

• **Click the Next button.**

The Account Name page is displayed in the Account Wizard dialog box and the account name is entered in the Account Name text box (Figure B-12). Your e-mail address is displayed in the Account Name text box.

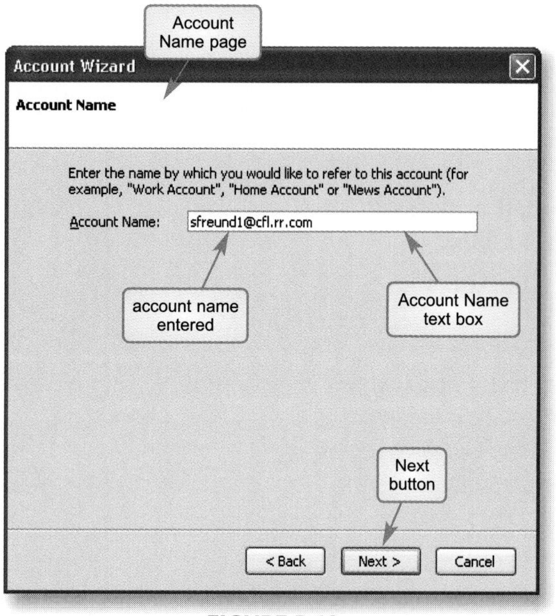

FIGURE B-12

13

• **Click the Next button.**

The Congratulations! page is displayed in the Account Wizard dialog box and contains e-mail account information, a check box, and three buttons (Figure B-13).

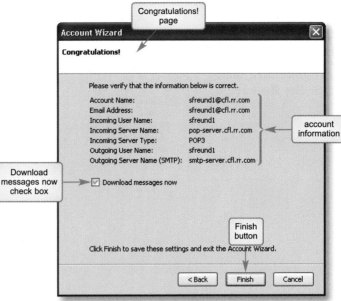

FIGURE B-13

14

• **Click the Finish button.**

The Account Wizard dialog box closes and the Inbox - Mozilla Thunderbird window is displayed (Figure B-14). The Enter your password: dialog box is displayed and contains a text box, a check box, and the OK and Cancel buttons.

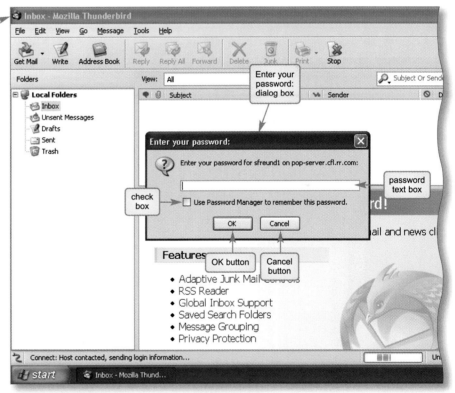

FIGURE B-14

15

- **Enter your password in the text box and then click the OK button.**
- **If the Mozilla Thunderbird dialog box displays, click the No button.**

The Enter your password: dialog box closes and Mozilla Thunderbird downloads the messages from the server to your e-mail account (Figure B-15).

FIGURE B-15

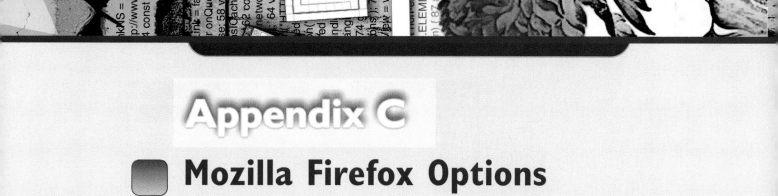

Appendix C

Mozilla Firefox Options

Options Dialog Box

When you first download Mozilla Firefox to browse the World Wide Web, learn about Web resources techniques, and communicate over the Internet, default settings control your interaction with Firefox. These settings remain in place until you change them. You can view and modify many of these settings by using the Options dialog box shown in Figure C-1 on the next page.

The Options dialog box contains five tabs (General, Privacy, Web Features, Downloads, and Advanced) that allow you to view and modify the Firefox default settings. Using these settings, you can change the home page that is displayed when you start Firefox; delete cookies and pages stored in the cache; control how Firefox displays Web sites; specify how Firefox handles downloads; control advanced settings such as software updates, security, and certificates; and much more.

To display the Options dialog box, click Tools on the menu bar and then click Options on the Tools menu. The remainder of this appendix explains the contents of the five tabs in the Options dialog box.

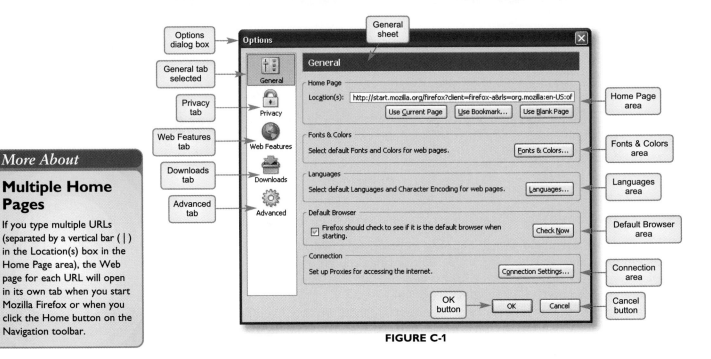

FIGURE C-1

More About

Multiple Home Pages

If you type multiple URLs (separated by a vertical bar (|) in the Location(s) box in the Home Page area), the Web page for each URL will open in its own tab when you start Mozilla Firefox or when you click the Home button on the Navigation toolbar.

The General Sheet

The **General sheet** illustrated in Figure C-1 contains the Home Page area, Fonts & Colors area, Languages area, Default Browser area, and Connection area. The **Home Page area** allows you to change the home page, which is the Web page that is displayed when you start Firefox. The home page should be the Web page that contains the information you use most frequently, such as a news page or the Web site of your school or business. The Location(s) box in the Home Page area contains the URL for the current home page. The three buttons below the Location(s) box allow you to: 1) use the Web page that is currently displayed in the Mozilla Firefox window as the home page (Use Current Page); 2) use a bookmark or bookmark folder (Use Bookmark) as the home page; or 3) display no Web page (Use Blank Page) when Firefox starts. If you use a bookmark folder as your home page, each bookmark in the bookmark folder will be displayed in its own tab when you start Mozilla Firefox or when you click the Home button on the Navigation toolbar.

The **Fonts & Colors area** contains the Fonts & Colors button. Clicking the Fonts & Colors button will display the Fonts & Colors dialog box. You use the **Fonts & Colors dialog box** to change the fonts, text colors, font sizes, background colors, and link colors. You also can choose whether Firefox will display links as underlined text or not.

The **Languages area** contains the Languages button. If you click the Languages button, the Languages and Character Encoding dialog box is displayed. Because some Web pages are available in multiple languages, the **Languages and Character Encoding dialog box** allows you to set your preferences for the languages Firefox will use to display such a Web page. You can also add and remove languages from the list of preferences. When a Web page does not specify the character encoding to use to display the page, the Character Encoding area of the Languages and Character Encoding dialog box allows you to specify the character encoding Firefox will use by default.

The **Default Browser area** in the General sheet contains a check box and the Check Now button. When a computer has multiple Web browsers installed, Windows uses the **default browser** to open all documents that require the use of a Web browser. When the check box in the Default Browser area contains a checkmark, each time you start Firefox, Firefox will perform a check to see if it is the default browser.

When the check box is not selected (unchecked), Firefox will not automatically perform this check. Clicking the check box will toggle its status between selected (checked) and not selected (unchecked). If you click the Check Now button, Firefox immediately checks to see whether it is the default browser.

The **Connection area** contains the Connection Settings button. When you click the Connection Settings button, Firefox displays the Connection Settings dialog box. You use the **Connection Settings dialog box** to specify how Firefox will access the Internet. This dialog box is useful when you have the option of, or are required to, use a proxy. A **proxy** is located between your computer and the Internet and is sometimes used by companies and Internet service providers to improve performance and/or security.

The Privacy Sheet

As you browse the Web, you may want to save information about the Web pages you view. The **Privacy sheet** (Figure C-2) allows you to control settings concerning privacy. The Privacy sheet contains the History area, Saved Form Information area, Saved Passwords area, Download Manager History area, Cookies area, and Cache area. To expand an area, click the small plus sign in a box to the left of the heading. To collapse an expanded area, click the minus sign in a box to the left of the heading. In the Privacy sheet, only one area may be expanded at a time. When you expand an area, any previously expanded areas collapse.

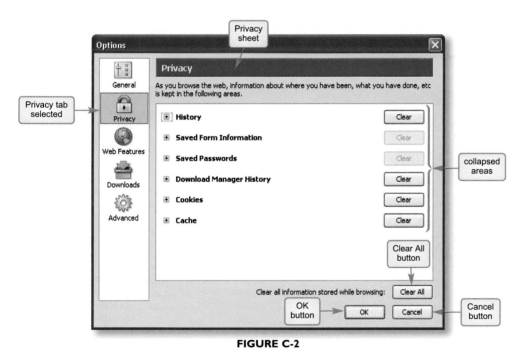

FIGURE C-2

The **History area** shown in Figure C-3 on the next page contains a text box and Clear button. The number in the text box indicates the number of days Firefox "remembers" the Web pages you have visited. By default, Firefox keeps this list of the Web pages you have visited for nine days. Decreasing the number in this text box increases your privacy, but may be a hassle if you want to quickly access a Web page you viewed many days ago. Increasing the number in this text box decreases your privacy, but makes it easier for you to get to Web pages you viewed many days ago. If you click the Clear button in the History area, Firefox immediately removes all the pages you have visited from the list.

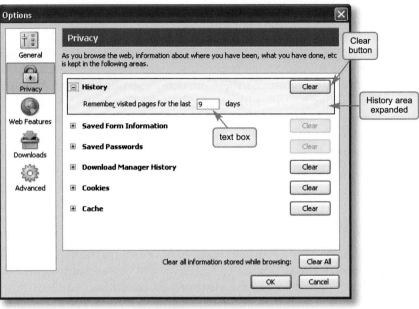

FIGURE C-3

The **Saved Form Information area** in Figure C-4 contains a check box and a Clear button. When the check box contains a checkmark, Firefox will save the information in a form on a Web page. When you complete subsequent forms, Firefox will offer suggestions based on the information previously entered. Firefox will not automatically save this information when the check box does not contain a checkmark. Clicking the Clear button removes saved information.

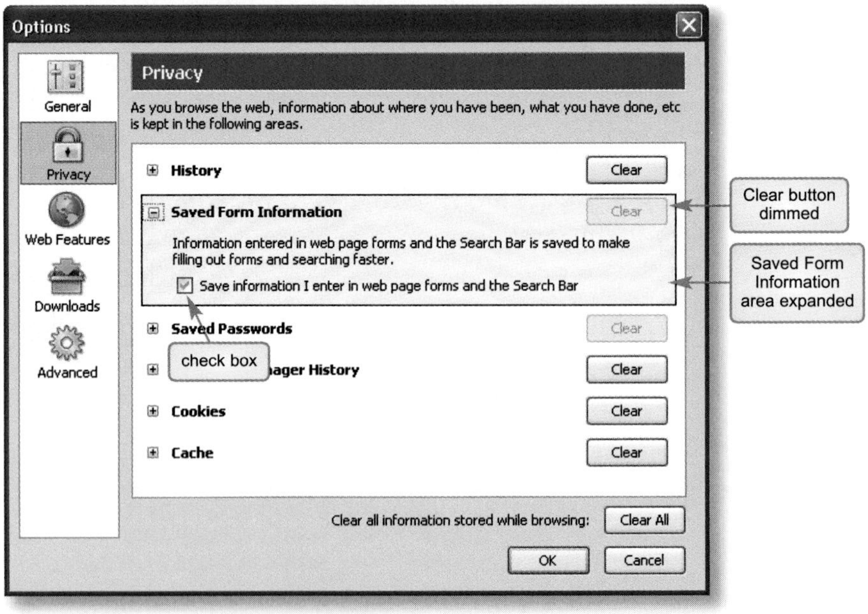

FIGURE C-4

The **Saved Passwords area** in the Privacy sheet in Figure C-5 is for users who regularly login to Web sites using a password. By default, Firefox remembers passwords you use to log on to password-protected Web sites. When you log on to these Web sites again, you do not need to re-enter your password. The Saved Passwords area displays a check box, dimmed Clear button, View Saved Passwords button, and Set Master Password button. When the check box contains a checkmark, Firefox remembers the passwords you use on these Web sites. When this check box does not contain a checkmark, Firefox will not remember your passwords. To view and manage the passwords, click the **View Saved Passwords button**. Clicking the **Set Master Password button** displays a dialog box that you use to set a password for sensitive information. If a master password is already set, this button will be replaced with the **Change Master Password button**. If you click the Clear button in the Saved Passwords area, Firefox clears any passwords it has saved.

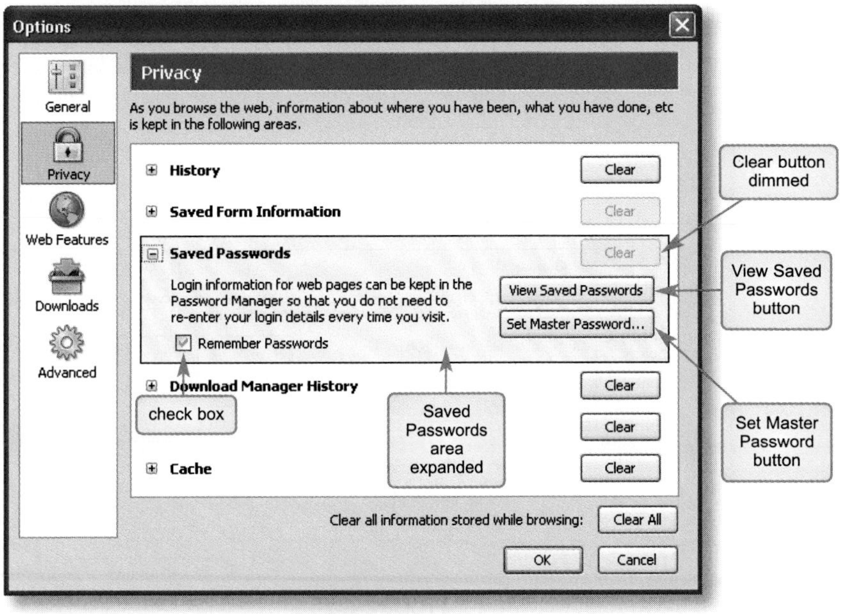

FIGURE C-5

You can use the **Download Manager History area** in Figure C-6 to specify settings to keep track of recently downloaded files. The Download Manager History area contains a text box and Clear button. You access the Download Manager by clicking the Downloads command on the Tools menu or by pressing CTRL+J. The **Download Manager** keeps a record of, and provides links to, recently downloaded files. The setting you specify in the Download Manager History area text box determines when, if ever, Firefox clears the Download Manager history. Clicking the Clear button immediately clears the Download Manager history.

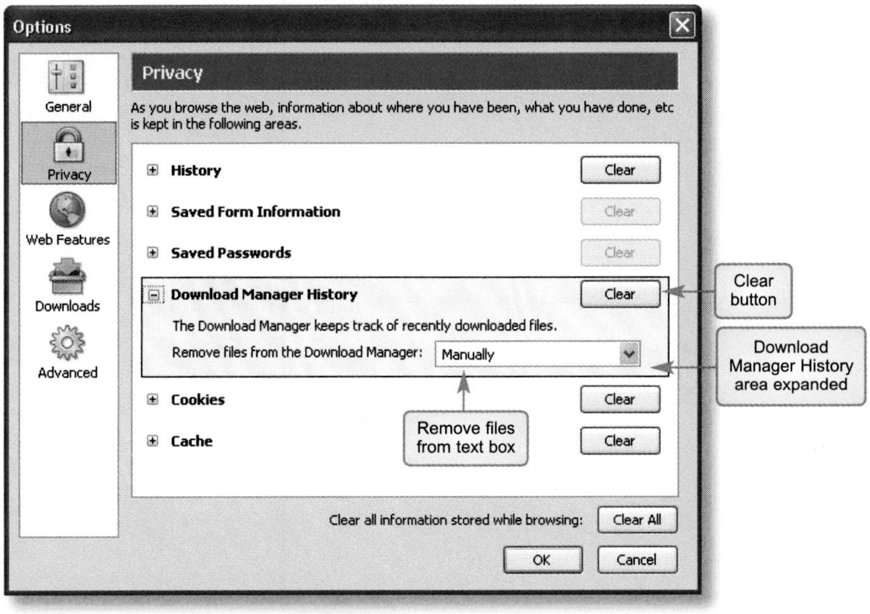

FIGURE C-6

The **Cookies area**, shown in Figure C-7, controls how Firefox handles cookies and contains two check boxes, a list box, and three buttons. A **cookie** is a file created by a Web site that stores information on your computer, such as your preferences when viewing that site. Because storing cookies on your computer raises privacy concerns, you can use the Cookies area to specify whether Web sites are able to store cookies on your computer and how long cookies remain on your computer. You can also view the cookies stored on your computer and clear them.

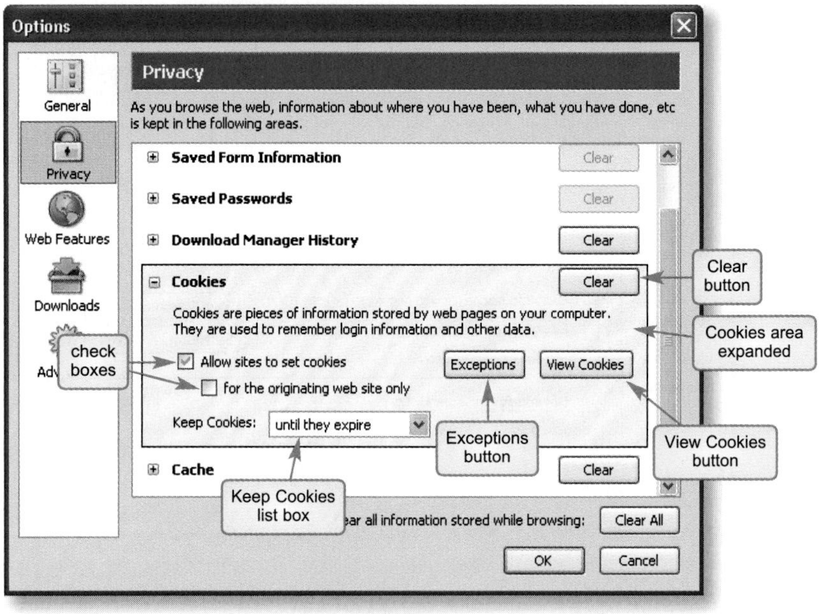

FIGURE C-7

The **Cache area** in Figure C-8 contains a text box and the Clear button. The Web pages you visit (in one session on the Internet) are stored in the **cache**. The number contained in the text box allows you to specify how much disk space, in kilobytes, Firefox reserves for the cache. Increasing the number in this text box will improve performance when revisiting Web pages. Decreasing the number in this text box reduces the number of Web pages Firefox can store in the cache. You also can click the Clear button to erase all the Web pages currently saved in the cache.

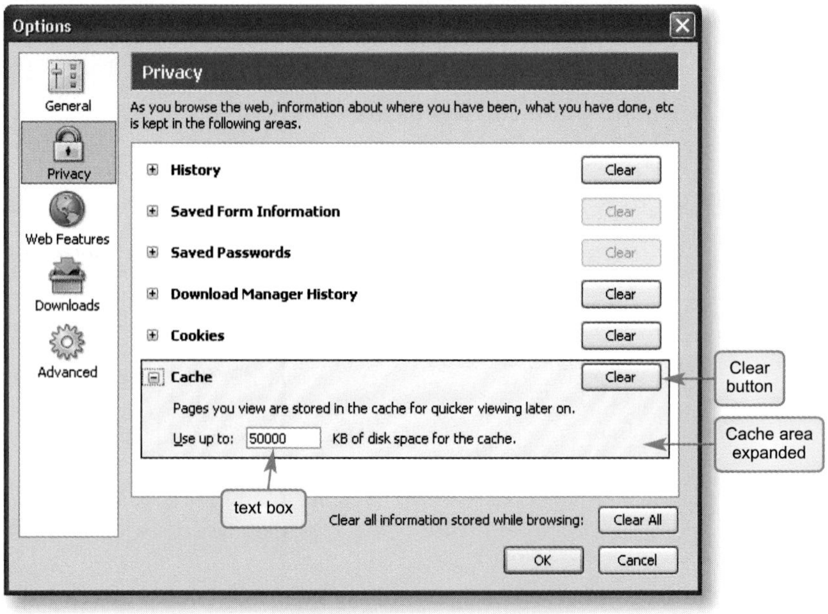

FIGURE C-8

In addition to the Clear button that is displayed within each area of the Privacy sheet, the Privacy sheet also has a Clear All button. The **Clear All button** clears the history, saved form information, saved passwords, downloads manager history, cookies, and cache simultaneously.

The Web Features Sheet

The Web Features sheet in Figure C-9 contains six check boxes and four buttons. You use the Web Features sheet to determine how popup windows are treated, whether Web sites can install software, whether images are loaded with Web sites, and whether Java and JavaScript are enabled.

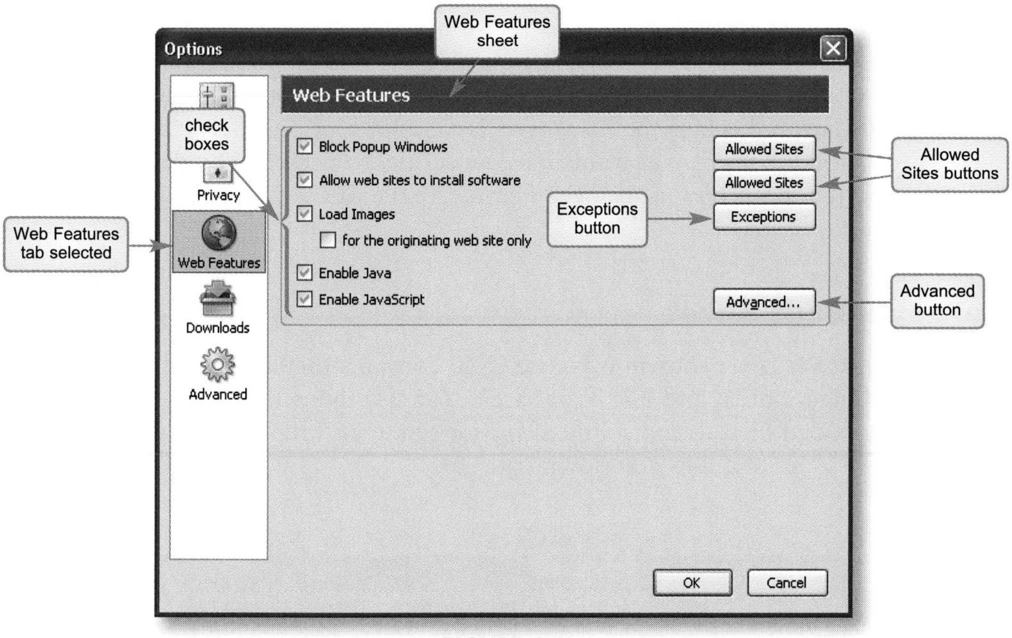

FIGURE C-9

By default, Firefox blocks popup windows on Web sites. **Popup windows** are windows that automatically appear, commonly containing advertisements. If you remove the checkmark in the Block Popup Windows check box, Firefox displays all popup windows. Because some popup windows are legitimate, you also can click the Allowed Sites button to the right of the Block Popup Windows check box to display the Allowed Sites dialog box. The Allowed Sites dialog box allows you to specify the sites where you wish to allow popup windows.

In some instances, Web sites may install software to your computer to improve your Web browsing experience. By default, Firefox allows Web sites to install software, although Firefox first seeks your permission by displaying a dialog box. To prevent any Web site from installing software, remove the checkmark from the **Allow web sites to install software** check box. Clicking the Allowed Sites button to the right of the Allow web sites to install software check box displays a dialog box to allow you to specify the Web sites you want to install software.

The third and fourth check boxes in the Web Features sheet allow you to indicate whether Web pages will contain images. If the **Load Images** check box does not contain a checkmark, images will not load when you visit a Web page; this saves time because images are generally large files that take a few seconds to be displayed. If the Load Images check box contains a checkmark, you have the option of loading images from the originating Web site. If the **for the originating web site only** check box contains a checkmark, Firefox will not load images on a Web site that are stored on a different Web site. For example, if you display the University of Central Florida Web page and the for the originating web site only check box contains a checkmark, only images stored on the University of Central Florida Web servers will load. The **Exceptions button** displays a dialog box that allows you to make exceptions for specific Web sites.

The **Enable Java** check box allows you to display applets developed using the Java programming language. A **Java applet** is a small program designed to run in a Web browser. You must install the Java plugin for Java applets to run. See your instructor for more information about how to install the Java plug-in. When the Enable Java check box does not contain a checkmark, Java applets will not run in the Firefox browser. By default, the Enable Java check box contains a checkmark.

The **Enable JavaScript** check box allows you to determine whether Web pages can use the JavaScript scripting language. Today, many Web sites rely on JavaScript to function properly. If the Enable JavaScript check box does not contain a checkmark, Web pages will not be able to make use of the JavaScript scripting language. Clicking the Advanced button displays the Advanced JavaScript Options dialog box, allowing you to specify the functions you want to allow scripts to perform. By default, the Enable JavaScript check box in the Web Features pane of the Options dialog box contains a checkmark.

The Downloads Sheet

The **Downloads** sheet shown in Figure C-10 contains the Download Folder area, Download Manager area, and File Types area. You use these areas to specify where to store downloaded files, to control the behavior of the Download Manager, and to determine how to handle files you download.

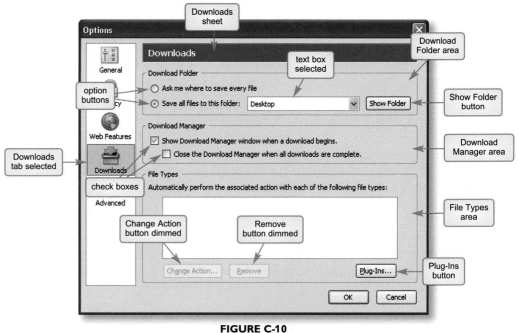

FIGURE C-10

The **Download Folder area** contains two option buttons, a list box, and the Show Folder button. Clicking the **Ask me where to save every file** option button in the Download Folder area sets Firefox to ask you where to store each file before you download it. If you check the **Save all files to this folder** option button, Firefox saves all files to the location you specify in the Save all files to this folder text box.

Clicking the **Show Folder button** sets Firefox to display the contents of the folder specified in the Save all files to this folder dropdown list so that you can choose whether to save the file there or in another location.

The **Download Manager area** contains two check boxes. If the first check box contains a checkmark, the Download Manager will be displayed as soon as you initiate a download. If this check box contains a checkmark, you also have the option of checking the second check box, to close the Download Manager when all downloads are complete. If the first check box does not contain a checkmark, you will not be able to check the second check box.

The File Types area displays a list of the types of files that have been downloaded and three buttons. When a file type in the list is selected, clicking the Change Action button allows you to specify whether to use a program to open files of that type, or to automatically save the file to disk. The Remove button is used to remove file types from the list. The Plug-Ins button displays the Plug-Ins dialog box, which you use to determine for which file types plug-ins are available.

The Advanced Sheet

The **Advanced sheet** illustrated in Figure C-11 contains the expanded Accessibility area, expanded Browsing area, collapsed Tabbed Browsing area, collapsed Software Update area, collapsed Security area, collapsed Certificates area, and collapsed Validation area. If an area you wish to view is collapsed, click the plus sign in the box to the left of the heading to expand the area.

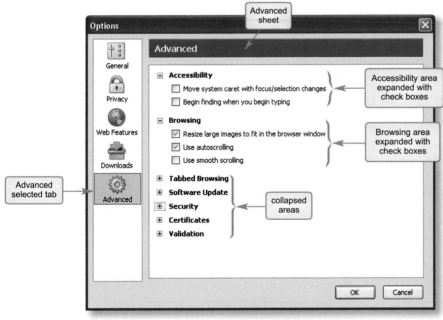

FIGURE C-11

The **Accessibility area** in Figure C-11 provides two check boxes to aid users who require additional software or features. By default, the two check boxes in the Accessibility area do not contain checkmarks.

The **Browsing area** in Figure C-11 contains three check boxes. When the **Resize large images to fit in the browser window** check box is checked, Firefox automatically reduces the size of large images to fit in the display area of the browser. When the **Use autoscrolling** check box contains a checkmark, you can hold down the middle mouse button (or scroll wheel) while moving the mouse up or down. If the **Use smooth scrolling** check box contains a checkmark, Firefox scrolls the page slower when you use the PAGE UP or PAGE DOWN keys to navigate through long Web pages.

The **Tabbed Browsing area** in Figure C-12 contains three option buttons and four check boxes. You use the three option buttons near the top of the Tabbed Browsing area to specify how Web pages are accessed from other Windows programs. Firefox can open links from other programs in a new window, in a new tab in the most recent window, or in the most recent tab or window. Use the four check boxes toward the bottom of the Tabbed Browsing area to hide or unhide the Tab bar when only one Web site is open; to select new tabs opened from links; to select new tabs opened from bookmarks or the history list; and to warn you when you are about to close multiple tabs simultaneously.

Updates are periodically released for Firefox, as well as for any extensions or themes you may have installed. For this reason, it is important that you keep your software updated to receive the latest features and guard against the latest security threats. The **Software Update area** in Figure C-12 contains two check boxes and the Check Now button. By default, Firefox periodically checks for updates to the Firefox browser, as well as to any installed extensions and themes. If you do not want Firefox to check for Firefox updates, remove the checkmark from the Firefox check box. If you do not want to receive update information for your browser extensions and themes, remove the checkmark from the My Extensions and Themes check box. Click the Check Now button to immediately check for Firefox updates, as well as for updates to extensions and themes.

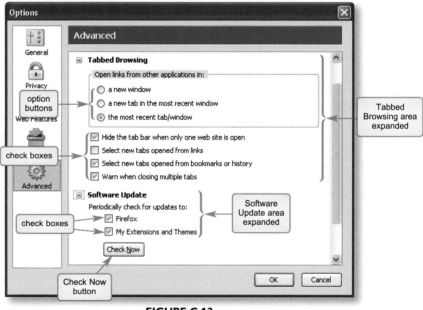

FIGURE C-12

Figure C-13 illustrates the **Security area**, which provides a place where you can specify how to send and receive secured information. Firefox supports Secure Sockets Layer Level 2, Secure Sockets Layer Level 3, and Transport Layer Security. **Secure Sockets Layer Level 2 (SSL2)**, the standard protocol for secured Web transmission, is supported by all secure Web sites. Some secure Web sites, however, also support **Secure Sockets Layer Level 3 (SSL3)**, a protocol more secure than SSL2. Some Web sites may support **Transport Layer Security (TLS)**, which is a security standard similar to SSL3. By default, Firefox enables information to be sent and received through SSL2, SSL3, and TLS. To disable secure communication using SSL2, remove the checkmark in the Use SSL 2.0 check box. To disable secure communication using SSL3, remove the checkmark in the Use SSL 3.0 check box. Finally, to disable secure communication using TLS, remove the checkmark in the Use TLS 1.0 check box.

The **Certificates area** in Figure C-13 contains the Client Certificate Selection area, the Manage Certificates area, and the Manage Security Devices area. **Certificates** help encrypt and decrypt data sent through connections with secure sites. The **Client Certificate Selection area** contains two option buttons to allow you to specify how to choose a security certificate to present to Web sites requiring one. You can choose to have Firefox select a certificate automatically, or to ask you each time a certificate is required. The **Manage Certificates area** contains the Manage Certificates button, which you click to display the Certificate Manager dialog box. You use the **Certificate Manager dialog box** to view, backup, import, and delete certificates currently installed on the computer. The **Manage Security Devices area** contains the Manage Security Devices button, which displays the Device Manager dialog box. You use the Device Manager dialog box to manage devices that are external to Firefox and that encrypt and decrypt connections, as well as store certificates and passwords.

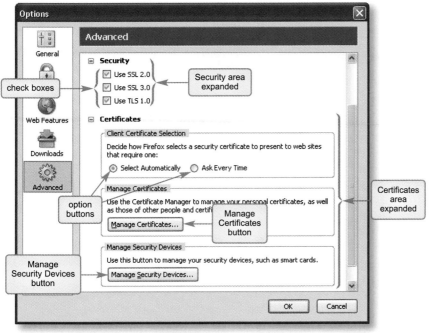

FIGURE C-13

The **Validation area** illustrated in Figure C-14 contains the CRL area and OCSP area. The **CRL area** contains the Manage CRLs button. The Manage CRLs dialog box is displayed when you click the Manage CRLs button. A **CRL (Certificate Revocation List)** protects against invalid certificates. The Manage CRLs dialog box allows you to add a CRL to Firefox, and to view information about existing CRLs. The **OCSP area** contains three option buttons and two text boxes. Use **OCSP (Online Certificate Status Protocol)** to validate certificates each time they are accessed. You use the three option buttons in the OCSP area to designate if and how to use OCSP for certificate verification.

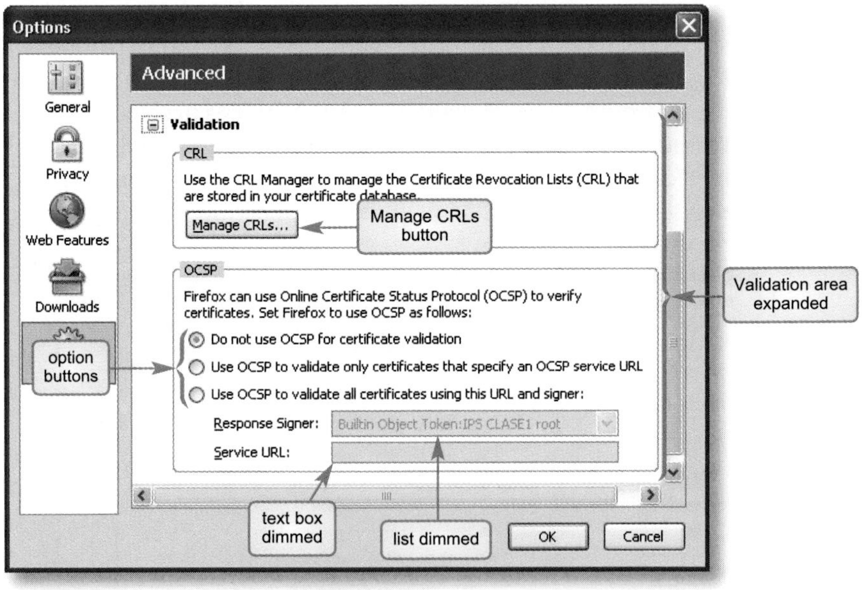

FIGURE C-14

Index

MOZILLA
Firefox
Quick Reference Summary

COMMAND	KEYBOARD SHORTCUT	MOUSE SHORTCUT
Add Bookmark	CTRL+D	
Back	BACKSPACE ALT+LEFT ARROW CTRL+LEFT ARROW CTRL+[	SHIFT+Scroll
Bookmarks	CTRL+B CTRL+I	
Caret Browsing	F7	
Close Tab	CTRL+W CTRL+F4	Middle-click on Tab
Close Window	CTRL+SHIFT+W ALT+F4	
Complete .com Address	CTRL+ENTER	
Complete .net Address	SHIFT+ENTER	
Complete .org Address	CTRL+SHIFT+ENTER	
Copy	CTRL+C	
Cut	CTRL+X	
Decrease Text Size	CTRL+-	CTRL+Scroll up
Delete	DELETE	
Delete Selected Autocomplete Entry	SHIFT+DEL	
Downloads	CTRL+J CTRL+Y	
Find Again	F3 CTRL+G	
Find As You Type Link	`	
Find As You Type Text	/	
Find Previous	SHIFT+F3	
Find in This Page	CTRL+F	
Forward	SHIFT+BACKSPACE ALT+RIGHT ARROW CTRL+RIGHT ARROW CTRL+]	SHIFT+Scroll up
Full Screen	F11	
History	CTRL+H CTRL+SHIFT+H	

Mozilla Firefox Quick Reference Summary *(continued)*

COMMAND	KEYBOARD SHORTCUT	MOUSE SHORTCUT
Home	ALT+HOME	
Increase Text Size	CTRL++	CTRL+Scroll down
Move to Next Frame	F6	
Move to Previous Frame	SHIFT+F6	
Go to Bottom of Page	END	
Go to Top of Page	HOME	
New Message	CTRL+M	
New Tab	CTRL+T	Double-click on Tab Bar
Next Tab	CTRL+TAB CTRL+PAGE DOWN	
New Window	CTRL+N	
Open File	CTRL+O	
Open Address in New Tab	ALT+ENTER	
Page Info	CTRL+I	
Page Source	CTRL+U	
Paste	CTRL+V	
Previous Tab	CTRL+SHIFT+TAB CTRL+PAGE UP	
Print	CTRL+P	
Redo	CTRL+Y CTRL+SHIFT+Z	
Reload	F5 CTRL+R	
Reload (override cache)	CTRL+F5 CTRL+SHIFT+R	SHIFT+Reload button
Restore Text Size	CTRL+0	
Save Page As	CTRL+S	ALT+Left-click
Select All	CTRL+A	
Select Location Bar	ALT+D F6 CTRL+L	
Select Next Search Engine in Search Bar	CTRL+DOWN ARROW	
Select Tab (1 to 9)	CTRL+ALT+(1 to 9)	
Stop	ESC	
Undo	CTRL+Z	
Web Search	CTRL+K CTRL+E CTRL+J	